MONSTER HIKE

Other books by Avrel Seale

Non-fiction

Dude: A Generation X Memoir

*Staggering: Life and Death on the Texas Frontier
at Staggers Point*

*The Hull, the Sail, and the Rudder: A Search for the
Boundaries of the Body, Mind, and Soul*

*The Tree: A Spiritual Proposition,
and Selected Essays*

True Freedom and the Wisdom of Virtue

Fiction

The Grand Merengue

The Secret of Suranesh

MONSTER HIKE

A 100-Mile Inquiry Into the Sasquatch Mystery

AVREL SEALE

ANOMALIST BOOKS

San Antonio • Charlottesville

An Original Publication of ANOMALIST BOOKS
Monster Hike: A 100-Mile Inquiry
Into the Sasquatch Mystery
Copyright © 2017 by Avrel Seale
ISBN: 978-1-938398-87-2

Book design by Avrel Seale

For information about the publisher, go to
AnomalistBooks.com,
or write to: Anomalist Books, 5150 Broadway #108,
San Antonio, TX 78209

For Ansen. Thanks.

*And for John Willison Green, 1927-2016,
who sought the truth for 59 years*

Contents

"The moment we begin to fear the opinions of others and hesitate to tell the truth that is in us, and from motives of policy are silent when we should speak, the divine floods of light and life no longer flow into our souls."

—*Elizabeth Cady Stanton*

Prologue

THE SNS, OR SYMPATHETIC NERVOUS SYSTEM, is activated in all mammals, including humans, by fear. The body enters fight-or-flight mode when the sympathetic nervous system releases catecholamines, better known as adrenaline, to mobilize organs and energy stores to flee a frightening situation. This, as well as I can understand it, is the process by which one's legs start to shake uncontrollably.

I am alone in a primitive camp six miles from my truck. It is seven p.m., less than thirty minutes since I retired to my hammock in the middle of the Sam Houston National Forest. Because it is late October, it is as dark at this hour as the night will get, which is to say completely so.

My hammock convulses for thirty seconds at a time, vibrating. I cannot stop my legs from shaking. From a distance, the olive-green hammock, enclosed across its top by a black bug net, resembles a cocoon, perhaps one containing a giant caterpillar straining to exit. But I am not straining to leave the cocoon; I am straining to stay within it. To be calm. To be still. To attract no attention.

I lift my cell phone out of the little mesh bag that hangs from the ridgeline above my hammock and, after fumbling it onto my bare chest, text my wife: "I don't know about this, honey. I think this might have been a mistake."

Five hundred yards away, a deer screams repeatedly, as if in agony, then goes silent. There are no shots or other signs of hunters. Three minutes later, another is apparently killed with only five seconds of pain.

Now, through the dark, a helicopter flies in slowly at treetop level, as if searching. I see its red tail light to my east and hear its rotors thundering through the black forest. It creeps about the charcoal sky, first louder, then softer, then departs. Some minutes later, shots ring out through the forest to my east. The chopper returns, then departs again.

Is there movement around my camp? It sounds like it. The snapping of sticks, the indeterminate crunch of leaf litter. Is it acorns falling? A small animal? A large animal? In one hand I clutch my spotlight, and with each sound, I flood the forest with it, pressing it against the inside of the bug net. The light is cold and harsh, turning the woods into a confusing pastiche of white glare and retina burn-in and black shadows that dance together as if in a mosh pit.

In my other hand, I clutch my sheathed knife to my chest like a child clutches a teddy bear.

My eyes are as wide as they will open. My ears strain toward the darkness. My legs will not stop shaking. I pray for sleep.

1
Fantastic Beasts and Where to Find Them

There are more things in heaven and earth, Horatio,
Than are dreamt of in your philosophy.

—*Hamlet, Act I, Scene 5*

WHEN WE ARE YOUNG, our parents tell us that Santa Claus is real, and that monsters are not. I was about ten when I discovered that first teaching was false. I was about fifty when I concluded the second one was too.

Of course, it all depends on your definition. But if a "monster" could be defined as something covered with hair, that walks on two feet, is as tall as your bedroom ceiling, is orders of magnitude more powerful than any man, easily kills wild animals with its bare hands and devours them raw, and can see at night, then I have bad news for you.

With my right hand to God, I do believe they exist, and if that makes me a fool to some people, or to most people, or to virtually everyone, then so be it. Such is the fate of anyone who strolls away from the safety of consensus knowledge and toward the tree line of the unknown.

This is not an April Fools' joke gone on too long. This is not an Andy Kaufman performance-art experiment I am subjecting my family and friends and coworkers to. This is real, as real as anything.

If maintaining your current world-view at all costs is your default setting, or if holding a cynical pose — hand on a cocked hip, eyes rolling — is important to your sense of self, then you may be dismissed at this time, and I wish you all the best.

If, on the other hand, you consider yourself open-minded, someone willing to be convinced, someone willing to look at the evidence before deciding, then come with me down this forest trail, and I will show you something that will blow your mind.

There are probably thirty distinct reasons I came to believe such beings exist. We'll get to most of those.

But I had always been interested in creatures like this, even those I knew were fictional. When I was young, the Planet of the Apes movies and TV shows were omnipresent. The main characters of those movies — aside from Charlton Heston and whichever attendant starlet strode mute at his side in a leather bikini amidst the ruins of that post-apocalyptic world — were apes, but they did not look exactly like apes and certainly did not act like apes, despite the estimable efforts of makeup artists, actors, and stuntmen. They ambulated on two legs, mostly upright. They spoke. They rode horseback. They were basically hybrids mixing human forms and faculties and simian hairiness and

4

strength. They were chimera — half human, half ape. And there was something about them that fascinated me at once. Many were the Sundays I sat in church and quietly drew the apes in the margins of the bulletins: Cornelius beside the Doxology, Dr. Zaius next to the sermon title, General Aldo on the back next to the announcements and prayer requests.

I greedily collected and assembled plastic models of the apes. I rode my bike to the fabric store down the street, spent my allowance on fake fur, and hand-sewed it to rubber monkey masks in an attempt to recreate the state-of-the-art makeup and prosthetics of those movies. The homemade costumes were worn not just at Halloween but around the calendar.

But back to those many reasons I believe, first among them, I suppose, is that at least 10,000 other people have said they have seen one and have gone to the trouble of filing a report describing what they saw. That number alone should make anyone pause and wonder: could it really be? For the most part these 10,000 people had nothing to gain from filing such a report, and many of them had much to lose — respect within their communities, even their livelihoods. And yet they reported them anyway, and a close reading reveals that they largely agreed on a wide range of subtle anatomical and behavioral traits.

For the few skeptics who nevertheless might be aware of these thousands of reports, it is popular to try to explain them away as a sort of mass hysteria, something akin to the Salem witch trials, this one however a manifestation of an American pop-culture phenomenon of the mid-twentieth century. The psychological term is "priming." If someone has just seen a documentary on, say, dachshunds, they are now primed to see dachshunds and so will begin seeing them everywhere. We've all experienced this phenomenon at times — a song we learn and then start hearing in the grocery store and the waiting room and all over, an obscure term that we learn one day, then hear again three times in the next two weeks in random places. If, as a society, we are primed to think about something trendy, the theory goes, then people will start seeing it whether it's there or not.

But there are two big hairy problems with this.

First, if these reports are simply a byproduct of twentieth-century pop-culture, why do they seem to extend back for virtually all of recorded history? In Medieval Europe artists depicted "woodwoses," upright hairy beasts with the faces of men, memorializing them in etchings and even stained-glass windows. Though they are probably not in Denmark today, might these creatures have inspired the villain of the first masterpiece of English literature, Grendel, of the epic poem *Beowulf?* Few remember that Carl Linnaeus, who in 1758 founded our binomial system of naming species, initially established two kinds of men: *Homo sapiens* and *Homo troglodytes*, the thinking man and the caveman, respectively. After his death, the latter category was discarded as absurd folklore. Whatever the case, it seems this is hardly our first rodeo with these guys.

Second, if these reports are simply noise generated by an American pop-culture phenomenon, why do we find descriptions that match these creatures coming from around the world? The Yeti of the Himalayas. The Yeren of China. The Almas of Russia. "The Gray Man" of Scotland. The Mande Burung of India. The Yowie of Australia. I was not a geography major, but I'm fairly certain these places are not in America. In fact, many of them are as far away as one can get from the United States and its culture, not only in miles but in remoteness. I'm pretty sure the Meghalaya people who report the Mande Burung in the remote hills of northeast

India and Bangladesh have not been heavily influenced by *Harry and the Hendersons.*

To explain away the global nature of this phenomenon, the mythic literary recurrences, and the long history of references, those who wonder about this stuff at all next resort to that staple of Jungian psychology, archetypes — timeless forms projected into culture from deep in our subconscious: "All people project these forms into their worlds because the wild man is an archetype, probably an ancient memory of what we ourselves used to be," goes the explanation. Now, I do believe in archetypes, but who is to say archetypes are not derived from real memories trickling down to us from eons-old run-ins with these creatures? Something need not be imaginary to be an archetype.

To the contrary, I believe something deep within us knows these things, even if we have never seen one, even if our rational minds don't believe in them. These monstrous forms that float through our dreams from earliest childhood — huge and powerful, grotesque and hairy and menacing — these are not idle threats ginned up by our subconscious for no reason, not mere figments or glitches in our psyches. I submit they are there for a reason. They might just be genetic memories. Their names change over time and geography, but these wild men / boogey men / bogey men / boogers / woolly boogers — they are real. Our deeper minds, below rationality, know they are real, and fear them just as instinctively as the newborn fawn knows and fears the wolf she has never encountered. Could these stock characters of our nightmares be like self-preservation software that comes preloaded on the hard drive of our brains?

After invoking archetypes, skeptics will nearly always play this card from the pop-psychology deck: "These sightings express our need to believe in something larger than ourselves," or, "This is our need to believe there is still mystery left in the world..." Ah— the ol' "need to believe"! Now, I was not a physics major either, but so far as I know, a need is not capable of leaving an eighteen-inch footprint in the dirt, impressed by hundreds of pounds of force, or of snapping branches twelve feet up, or of throwing 200-pound boulders through the air. The "need to believe" explanation requires that we ignore every scintilla of physical evidence ever collected or observed. It might soothe those who just can't cope with the whole notion, but it isn't very satisfying for those who actually want to figure this out.

Global though the phenomenon is, North America certainly seems to be their sweet spot, and the native people of North America have had so many names for them they would fill the two pages you are now looking at entirely, most of them translating from their indigenous languages as "mountain demons," or "forest devils," or "bosses of the woods." Certain American Indian nations have always known them to exist and view society's ridicule of believers as just one more way white Americans dismiss native culture and wisdom. For decades, and still, some seem to adhere to an unwritten gag order not to discuss the matter with outsiders lest that invite even more ridicule and discrimination than they already experience.

The Chehalis tribe of British Columbia called them "*sesquac*," and in the 1920s a longtime teacher on the Chehalis reservation east of Vancouver, J.W. Burns, began to write down the stories the Indians were telling him. Borrowing and transliterating their term, he coined the word "sasquatch." Burns wrote numerous articles relating stories the First Nations people had told him, which were published in Vancouver newspapers. When one of his articles was picked up in 1929 by *MacLean's*, a major Canadian magazine, the word "sasquatch" went mainstream. Titled "The Hairy Giants of British Columbia," the piece carried a preface by the publisher:

> This challenging article will no doubt arouse the derision of skeptics both in Canada and elsewhere. After many years of patient investigation, Mr. Burns, a responsible Government agent, shares the firm belief of his Indian charges that deep in the unexplored mountain wilds of British Columbia, there still lurk a few scattered survivors of the mysterious "Sasquatch" — primitive creatures of huge stature, covered from head to foot with coarse hair who have figured in Redskin legends for centuries. Mr. Burns recounts a number of seemingly well-authenticated stories of encounters with these uncanny "wild men" who carefully avoid all contact with civilization. Scientific expeditions had sought them in vain, and it is generally supposed that — if they ever existed — the giants have long since become extinct — but the Indians remain unconvinced.

In his zeal to bolster Burns' credibility, the publisher goes on perhaps too long: "They [the Indians] are a simple minded, unimaginative folk; the invention of so many different stories of encounters with the wild men would be quite beyond their powers."

Regardless of how imaginative or unimaginative the Chehalis might have been, the matter was hardly the sole province of America's indigenous nations. It's impossible to say when the first European settlers encountered them. A disputed claim has recently begun circulating that Leif Erikson encountered them in Newfoundland. There's a humorous take on a famous painting of pilgrims and Indians sharing the first Thanksgiving meal that includes a Photoshopped eight-foot sasquatch standing in the midst of the blessed event. And while one would expect encounters with wild giants, if they existed, to make it into the settlers' diaries, the same taboo that inhibits reporting them today surely existed back then too. Who knows if Captain John Smith might have spotted something in the tangled forests of Virginia or Massachusetts that he couldn't explain, that wasn't in the Bible (or so he thought), or that he just didn't want to deal with publicly? Nothing would put a damper on colonization quite like the assertion that giant monsters roamed the woods of the New World ("but please, by all means, move here anyway").

From the time of European contact to the middle of the twentieth century, most of these creatures were simply referred to as "wild men" or "wild women." Interestingly, while the Indians seemed to have accepted their reality as a population, indeed often as simply a separate kind of *human*, the white settlers had a curious tendency to assume that when they saw one, they were seeing a unique creature, such as "the Wild Woman of the Navidad" reported repeatedly in the coastal bend of Texas in the 1830s. Or the Fouke Monster of Arkansas of Boggy Creek fame. Or the Grassman of Ohio. Anglo culture seemed to give little if any thought to how a singular creature could have come into existence without being part of breeding population. Perhaps this was just a function of living in a world in which so many things had to be accepted as a mystery.

This tendency to regard them as singular, one-off monsters had the effect of eventually relegating all of these sightings to folklore. The Wild Man of (Fill-in-the-Blank) then had no more scientific standing than Babe the Big Blue Ox or anything else in folklore; they were just more colorful figments of country bumpkins' imaginations.

Then, in 1958, a new name was coined, this one for an individual who seemingly had left massive footprints in the dirt around road-building equipment one weekend in far northwestern California: Bigfoot. When the prints were cast in plaster and taken to a local newspaper editor, the headline that was put with the photo and then picked up by newspapers across the country read: "Bigfoot is a sasquatch." We see from this headline that "sasquatch" was a term already in wide enough circulation that a newspaper editor assumed readers knew what it was, and even more notable, that a "sasquatch" is treated as a kind of creature and not an individual. "Bigfoot" was the nickname for the individual who had left the prints, and "sasquatch" was the type of creature he was.

But in short order, people started using these terms interchangeably, and any notion that might have existed of this being a breeding population — a *species* — was lost. In popular usage, "Bigfoot" became a singular mythological creature — a stock character of American folklore: Babe the Big Blue Ox, Pecos Bill, the Easter Bunny. And those who assumed the singular meaning naturally regarded anyone who believed in the existence of "Bigfoot" as a nut job, as indeed they would be if they thought there was only one.

This was all reinforced by a pop-culture craze during the 1970s that saw bigfoot devolve from a legend with some indigenous gravitas to merely fodder for tabloid headlines and B horror movies. Who can forget the professional wrestler Andre the Giant, with pale blue contact lenses, portraying the beast opposite the Six Million Dollar Man on primetime TV, looking like Grizzly Adams with a gland problem and severe cataracts? Importantly, nearly all portrayals treated the subject as a singular figure roaming around the Pacific Northwest instead of as the result of sightings of various members of a species, a breeding population, something that, while still astonishing, would make infinitely more biological sense.

The truth is, we have always struggled with what to call them because we have never known what they are. We know they are close to us, but just how close? Are they just another kind of ape? Are they part-human, and if so how big a part? Or are they fully human, as some claim, just another race, albeit one whose appearance challenges us more than any other to accept them into our historically elastic notion of humanity?

Over the last fifty years the subject of these creatures' existence has been so thoroughly tied to the lunatic fringe that just the utterance of the words "bigfoot" and "sasquatch" elicits a laughter reflex in most people. (I say this with authority.) Because of this, I often have taken to calling them simply the Others.

Maybe there is even some mystical connection between us — the Others and me, because a seminal event in their story took place the very year I was born.

On October 20, 1967, two somewhat colorful characters were out on horseback in the mountainous forests of far northwestern California (not far distant from where "Bigfoot's" alleged prints had been found around the road-building equipment nine years earlier). The two had rented a 16mm camera and were shooting footage for a docudrama on the creature.

They had been doing this for two weeks when they rounded a corner and startled an enormous hair-covered creature that was squatting next to the large root ball of a fallen tree and drinking from Bluff Creek. The figure rose to stand on two legs and calmly but purposefully walked away. One of the men jumped off his horse, grabbed the movie camera out of one of his saddlebags, turned it on, and ran toward the creature. He tripped and fell to his knees, rose, and continued his pursuit. "Cover me!" he yelled to his partner, who raised his rifle to the ready in case the figure turned on the cameraman. At the shouting, the creature turned back and looked at his rolling camera. That frame, frame 352 of the Patterson-Gimlin Film, is the best photo ever taken of one of the Others. You have seen it. Everyone has seen it, and most think it is a man in a suit and that the whole matter was put to rest decades ago by one of several men who claimed to have been the actor.

But serious analysis of the subject in the film does not jibe with these claims of hoaxing; it points to its authenticity. For one thing, if you wanted to sell a monster to the world, wouldn't you make it the scariest version of that monster? Why, then, would these men give it pendulous breasts? What's more, on a zoomed, steadied, and slowed version, you can see muscles rippling under her hair. You can see a hernia bulging in her right thigh. Even more impossible to fake in 1967, photo-analysis shows that the creature's knees and elbows are in the wrong place for a human, even one in a costume. And the mechanics of its gait, especially the angle of its back-step, are nearly impossible to recreate. Add to that the conclusion by no less mainstream an organization than National Geographic that, based on photogrammetry — triangulation using surrounding landmarks and the same lens — the creature's height was seven feet, three inches, and you have so much evidence of authenticity that denying it becomes more cumbersome and complicated than accepting it.

Just because something is claimed as a hoax does not mean it is. And just as we should not blindly accept a sighting report as the gospel truth, neither should we accept the claim that something was a hoax without subjecting that claim to a similarly critical eye. Sometimes, the only hoax is the claim of a hoax.

As I say, to deny their reality you must hold that every single one of more than 10,000 sighting reports is a hoax, a case of mistaken identity, or a hallucination. Then you must factor in that these hoaxes, hallucinations, and misidentifications have been taking place across the northern hemisphere for hundreds — perhaps thousands — of years, and that American Indians are in on the joke and have been for centuries, or else that our continent's indigenous people are not capable of telling the difference between a large primate that walks on two legs and other common animals of the forest.

You also must accept that people in forty-nine states have concocted hoaxes that include photographs, cast footprints, and video that are sophisticated enough to agree on a large number of subtle physiological and behavioral traits and are sophisticated enough to fabricate DNA and hair samples that come back non-human but primate. (As a corollary, you must also believe that, for some reason, people in Hawaii are far less likely to have hallucinations than mainlanders and are also inherently more honest and therefore less likely to commit hoaxes.)

Most dismiss this whole subject with a chuckle and a shake of the head, the doings of bored hillbillies or transparent self-promoters, and it ends there. But for me, my curiosity about the fringes of our world has always been stronger than my need to cut the fringes off and throw them away.

Believe me, I know how crazy all this sounds. And as much as I would like to say I don't care what people think of me, I do. For twenty years I painstakingly calculated just how much to reveal of this interest of mine and to whom. Yes to some friends who telegraphed receptivity, no to others. Yes to some coworkers, but no to managers. Back when we all bought books in bookstores, I resented having to loiter in the "Paranormal" or "Metaphysical" section to find material on this subject, rubbing elbows with middle-aged women shopping for books on past-life regression and numerology. I'd snag the book quickly and carry it over to the Science aisle, where I thought it belonged anyway, to assess its potential. Riding the bus, I'd sit on the left so fellow passengers couldn't see the front cover of my latest purchase.

When I swallowed hard and broached the subject with someone, be they a virtual stranger or a friend I'd known for years, I could never predict their reaction. People I would have figured for hard-core skeptics fell right into easy conversation about it, asking question after question. Others, who claimed open-mindedness in virtually every other aspect of life, shut me down with a humiliating blank stare ("Are you being serious right now?") and a quick change of subject. Being trapped between a passion that is controversial and a deep psychological need to be liked and respected is an exhausting, never-ending exercise in vulnerability. It has given me a small taste of what a closeted life must be like. And yet none of us can force ourselves to lose interest in a topic that fascinates us. To really know me is to know this about me, and so for any acquaintance to progress to real friendship, the topic simply must be broached. Without really thinking about it, I had drawn a circle around myself — those who knew I studied the bigfoot mystery were inside it, those who didn't remained at arm's length.

It does sound crazy. As I was broaching the topic with one longtime friend, I said, "I know this sounds crazy—" at which point he nonchalantly interrupted and corrected me: "bat-shit crazy." So any serious discussion of the existence of sasquatches has to begin with an acknowledgement of the difficulties, which are chiefly these: How is it possible that modern science has named 400,000 beetles and yet has not recognized and named a species that by all reports is larger than ourselves, sometimes much larger, and that must be orders of magnitude closer to humans than anything else on the tree of life? How is it possible that we have not captured one, have not found a body, have not found part of a body?

As a species, we have utterly dominated the planet, infiltrating every nook and cranny of wilderness, heaven knows to a fault. The odds against us not having obtained proof of such a spectacular creature seem simply too great. It seems too fantastic, crazy-improbable. Therefore, it must all simply be a matter of hoaxes, misidentifications, and hallucinations. The default stance of the general public seems to be: This can't be, therefore, it isn't. I'll answer all of these questions in due course, but first, how did I get here? What is a nice, white-collar, city-dwelling boy like me doing in a place like this?

In my early thirties, for no particular reason I can remember, the subject bubbled up in my consciousness, and, fancying myself a budding fiction writer, I realized that rich themes in this mystery really had never been mined by literature. Rushing to fill that void, I wrote a novella and named it simply *Sasquatch*. I never published it, and neither did anyone else. The premise was too outrageous for a piece of plausible fiction. It was all about a huge government cover-up of these creatures, a giant collusion between federal agencies and big lumber, which had Northwestern senators in their pocket. The president was the protagonist, and the cast included hard-bitten career men in the CIA and FBI, a spiritually enlightened American Indian, a beautiful female scientist, blah, blah, blah. Ridiculous.

Little could I have known then how incredibly close to the mark that outlandish premise actually was. But I'm getting ahead.

As I say, the book went nowhere, but there was one lasting effect of my having written it, which was that the research I did during the writing really got my attention. Once I began looking into the subject in a sustained way, it quickly became clear that something was going on here that was much more than just pop-culture shtick. What really moved me from curiosity to belief was a book titled *Big Footprints* by Grover Krantz, an anthropologist at Washington State University who was virtually the only academic researcher at the time willing to investigate the mystery. The centerpiece of his research was footprints, which he found displayed a level of anatomical sophistication that would have required a vast team of PhDs to hoax. Moreover, on closer inspection of tracks left in especially conducive mud, he found dermal ridges, like those that make up human fingerprints, something virtually impossible to hoax.

Beyond being fascinated by his findings, I was deeply moved by the enormous courage Dr. Krantz showed, standing staunch against attacks and ridicule from throughout the academic world and insisting again and again that this was a legitimate field of inquiry.

And I began to realize that the themes pervading the sasquatch mystery cut right to the heart of the human condition and, what's more, in their own quirky way echoed all the great themes of humanity's experience with spirituality: faith and disbelief, evidence versus proof, the ridicule of skeptics and cynics, the introduction of hoaxes and frauds, lazy skepticism versus earnest investigation, taboos, and a circle of willful ignorance. Are we brave enough to admit the existence of something that we don't understand? Will our egos allow us to admit the existence of something that might be more powerful than us?

This topic functioned as a powerful Rosetta Stone for matters of faith and belief. Granted, nothing in theology has ever sounded funnier than the following sentence. But as of this moment in history, we can substitute sasquatches with God and see how many theological problems suddenly spin themselves out in analogy, and even come into focus: How much evidence does one need before they believe? Why isn't there a body? How can they be virtually everywhere and yet hardly ever seen and seemingly never captured?

Grover Krantz laid himself open to the endless ridicule of colleagues by asking questions — starting with "What made these footprints?" — and following the answers wherever they led. As I read his work I felt future historians might well regard him as a Galileo of our day, seeking truth amidst dogma and bias as strong as that of the Medieval church. His flinty indifference to fellow academics, caviling against him from the safety of their narrow, well-worn specialties and catered symposia, was inspiring.

Other books would follow Krantz's to my nightstand, like *Where Bigfoot Walks*, a fascinating read by naturalist Robert Pyle, who performed an exhaustive analysis of the phenomenon but would never render his verdict about their existence. Next came *Sasquatch: Legend Meets Science*, in which Dr. Jeff Meldrum became the heir-apparent to Grover Krantz as the only American academic willing to look into the mystery in a sustained way. (Canadian biologist John Bindernagel fills this niche for our polite neighbors to the north.)

All the while, more evidence was being amassed and curated online every day. Around 2010, an anonymous duo in Minnesota began curating the Facebook page "Facebook Find Bigfoot." In posting analyses of more than eighty of the most credible purported videos of sasquatches, they generated a body of work that, while not academic, provided a treasure trove of evidence that allowed enthusiasts like me to hone their own abilities to tell probable fakes from probable creatures.

Day by day, year by year, my knowledge grew, quietly, behind closed doors, in stolen moments online, reading, watching documentaries, emailing researchers with questions or ideas.

For many years, I have thought about dusting off the manuscript of *Sasquatch* and making another run at it. I'm a better writer now, and more importantly, I know much more about the subject and so could spin a more compelling tale. But something has kept me from it, and I think ultimately it is this — that any fictional treatment of this subject at this point in history only feeds the perception that the subject itself is fictional.

If the biggest mistaken assumption most people hold is that bigfoot is a single creature instead of a species, the next biggest is that this is a phenomenon of the Pacific Northwest, and that virtually all sightings have occurred in a three-state area including California, Oregon, and Washington. It typically shocks people to discover that, while they clearly like some places better than others, they are capable of living almost anywhere we can, and what's more, they do! I myself had researched the topic for perhaps five years before realizing this startling fact.

If you overlay a sighting map on a map of annual rainfall totals, you see an unmissable match. The vast majority of sightings occur in areas with forty inches of rainfall or more a year. And the sighting record is just as dense if not more so east of the Great Plains as it is to the west.

The Cascades of the Pacific Northwest are among the most storied, but from there sightings extend up through British Columbia to Alaska, virtually to the Arctic Circle. Along the west coast, they have been seen many times in the Sierras including just above Los Angeles in the San Bernardinos. They extend from the Canadian Rockies down throughout the American Rockies all the way into the forested regions of Arizona and New Mexico. Across Canada and the northern tier, with especially active areas in Ontario, Michigan, Wisconsin, throughout New England, upstate New York, and western Pennsylvania and southeastern Ohio and across the Ohio River into Kentucky, and all the way down the Appalachian Trail to Georgia and even farther south with large numbers of sightings in Florida, where they are known as Skunk Apes. Then west throughout every part of the South, the upper South in Tennessee, Arkansas into Oklahoma with the Ouachita range being an especially hot zone, and along the Gulf Coast from Florida's panhandle, through Alabama, Mississippi, the swamps and forests of Louisiana, and throughout East Texas, which is continuously "hot."

Beyond this vector of forty inches of annual rainfall, they appear able to push out hundreds of miles farther by way of river corridors. This makes perfect sense when you consider that lower rainfall totals are compensated for by topography that gathers what rain does fall into concentrated areas. Moving through these riparian temperate jungles extends their range over virtually the entire continent. Contrary to what I once believed about their natural range, this phenomenon has apparently brought them occasionally to my very doorstep in the Central Texas Hill Country west of San Antonio and Austin, an area that makes up for what it lacks in rainfall with two other features sasquatches have a known ken for — a forbidding terrain with plentiful caves, and some of the continent's highest concentrations of whitetail deer (it's what's for dinner). There have even been multiple reports from the Canadian River system of the nearly treeless Texas Panhandle.

In short, it's harder to find a place where they could *not* be than to find a place where they might be. In your state, look at: 1. areas of heaviest rainfall 2. in protected spaces like national forests, national parks, state parks, and wildlife management areas, and 3. within those areas, look to old-growth forest before new growth. Hardwood stands and mixed forests of hardwood and conifers sustain more abundant wildlife, on which they rely. Within those areas, look at rivers, lakes, ponds. If they are flesh-and-blood creatures, the one thing they cannot long live without is freshwater.

If you really want to cut to the chase, just look at a Google satellite map of your state. Blur your eyes and find the part that is the darkest shade of green. That's where the bigfoots are. I'm well aware of how crazy that sounds. Unfortunately, the truth doesn't care how crazy it sounds, it just keeps on being true.

Over a lifetime, and with an intensifying fascination that had lasted more than a decade, I had built up a significant amount of knowledge about this mystery. But it was all from books and photos and videos. I had never had any direct experience with it.

That was about to change.

2
Milestones and Mile Markers

"At fifty, everyone has the face he deserves."
—George Orwell

ANY SELF-RESPECTING MIDDLE-CLASS American man wishing to celebrate his fiftieth birthday would recruit five of his college buddies to join him for a hard-partying fishing charter out of Cabo San Lucas. One of them would have become a good cook in the twenty-seven years since graduation, and each night he would prepare the day's catch with a deft blend of spices and citrus — with a steak for the one with the seafood allergy — as the others played cards nearby, chewing cigars and reconstructing hilarious tales of debauchery and sexual conquest at State U. The last day would feature day-drinking through nine holes of golf, a massage, and a short flight home.

Me? I celebrated my fiftieth birthday by driving to a dirt parking lot outside of Richards, Texas, population 296, strapping forty pounds of camping gear to my back, and setting out to walk a hundred miles.

I had begun thinking about this trip perhaps three years earlier, and it was certainly not a bigfoot thing when it started. I suppose that was always in the back of my mind, something like, "... as long as I'm out there, I might as well take a camera and a tape measure." But it wasn't the main point.

As I left my mid-forties behind and considered the prospect of a half-century of life, I had wanted to set some sort of challenge for myself, put some sort of punctuation mark in the middle of this sentence of life — the middle because, you know, most of us live to be a hundred.

I have found that in order to not fall into depression, I need what leadership guru Jim Collins called a BHAG (bee-hag) — a big, hairy, audacious goal — and I used my fiftieth birthday as an excuse, a peg on which to hang a BHAG.

The need for a midlife BHAG is more acute because late-middle age, if you will forgive the expression, sucks. Slowly — if you're lucky slowly — the aches and pains creep upon you and settle into your joints and muscles and nerves one cell at a time. Sometimes this process is so slow and subtle you do not notice these pains at all until they join forces in the aggregate and burst out clapping and laughing like guests at a surprise party.

With late middle age comes a cascade of random aches, any one of which could be nothing or the beginning of a chronic or even terminal condition. Wake up one morning and your foot hurts for no reason you can think of. Might go away in five minutes, might hurt the rest of your life — you have no way of knowing. Is this pain my elbow just a tweak, or is it the first sign of muscular dystrophy that will eventually confine me to a wheelchair? Is this especially bad headache from a subpar breakfast, or will I look back on this as the day I felt the effects of my brain tumor for the very first time? When I forget what I came to the refrigerator for, is it a garden variety mental slip, or the first day of a twenty-year surrender to Alzheimer's.

My close-up vision had changed almost overnight, and now I constantly ripped my glasses off my face to see my phone, read a package, or do any other close work.

Every year or two, the dentist would comment on tiny chunks of teeth that had simply chipped away from the top edges of my bottom incisors in the course of living, never to return. "I could refer you to a good orthodontist for braces," he said, "or you could just live with it." I found his second option refreshing in a culture that insisted on perfection, and usually at a price that could put someone through college.

Age crept upon me like a wolf in the night. Good Lord, the creaking and the snapping of the first steps of morning! Walking from the bedroom to the bathroom sounded like a Buddy Rich drum solo.

My physique, never that much to write home about, had slowly morphed into a pear with four toothpicks protruding from its sides and bottom. This was thanks in no small part to the inexplicable habit of consuming an entire sleeve of Saltines every night in front of the television, if not also a generous bowl of Blue Bell Tin Roof ice cream. I know, I know, we reap what we sow. The unfair part was that I had not become any more gluttonous than I was when I was an alarmingly thin twenty-four-year-old, six-foot two and 140 pounds. And also no fair, my arms and legs had winnowed down to sticks despite no change in my physical activity. "Yeah," my chiropractor had once advised me, "when you get past forty, you've got to start pushing weights." BOOORRR-iiiing!

I went gray in my early thirties, prompting well-meaning questions from strangers in public about my "grandchildren." And, of course, in short order that white hair beat a hasty retreat from its original frontline position, so that if I stood before a mirror with any sort of strong back-lighting I could see the egg-like dome of my scalp with alarming clarity.

To add insult to injury, in an untimely flood of testosterone, hair spread and sprouted in every place but where I wanted it. I began to look as if I had gone to the barber, gotten my head shaved, and left before she had a chance to clean off my shoulders and back. My own body was now improvising blows to my ego like a great jazz artist, and soon enough that body hair began turning white as well, so that by forty-five I might as well have been descended from some strange, pear-shaped upright primate and a polar bear.

But at forty-nine I had a great life by any reasonable measure, better than I probably deserved. Happily married. Three healthy boys — fourteen, twelve, and nine — who were the lights of our lives. A steady job, being paid to write in a clean, well-lighted place, and having the benefits of working for a large state university. My nights and weekends were dominated by Boy Scout meetings, teaching Sunday school, attending band concerts, piano recitals, birthday parties, swim meets — a happy and exhausting treadmill of child development I wouldn't trade for the world.

For many people, this was enough, more than enough. But not for me. Blessed as I had been, there was and is a sort of uncomfortable sameness to stable suburban existence, kids or no kids. Work, home, Target ... work, home, Lowe's ... work, home, Target ... work, home, Lowe's ... Was it just this for the next thirty-five years, until being propped up by a space heater in a nursing home, eating Werther's caramels and slowly digesting one large-print Michener novel after another until all my vital organs gave out.

I hungered to go off-script. I needed at least one thing that was not safe and predictable and on a schedule. I thirsted for that thing we felt as kids if we were lucky, that elusive sensation known as adventure, or as much of it as I could afford with a one-week vacation balance.

Many people reaching for a mid-life challenge choose a marathon. And good for them. That indeed would have been a major accomplishment, but I had no affinity for running. I had seen marathon training up-close before, and not only did it seem like misery, but the whole affair was over by three p.m. A marathon would be a great accomplishment and an ordeal, to be sure, but was it an adventure? Was something completely unexpected going to happen in mile 17?

Another go-to middle-class adventure was skydiving, which, aside from being terrifying, seemed a bit of a cliché. And it was over in far less time than a marathon, no matter how well or poorly it went. And skydiving was adventurous on the surface, but at the same time, did you want *anything* unexpected to occur after leaping out of an airplane?

I craved something more than either of those could deliver. I craved some outing in which there was at least the *possibility* of the unexpected.

A hike.

A through-hike — that seemed like something that was both audacious and achievable. America's marquee through-hikes were the Appalachian Trail and the Pacific Crest Trail, each popularized by best-selling books that had been made into films: Bill Bryson's *A Walk in the Woods* and Cheryl Strayed's *Wild*.

But I was not a best-selling author who could take nine months away from home to do experiential journalism. And I was not an unemployed, single, childless twenty-six-year-old trying to salvage my life from heroin and sex addiction. I was married with three children at home and approximately three weeks a year of vacation time, two of which were spoken for. To do a *section* of the Appalachian Trail or the PCT would have been well and good, but I wanted to do *all* of something, even if it was more modest than those colossal twin pillars of American outdoorsmanship.

As it turned out, there was a trail I could do all of, and do in about a week. What's more it would not require a flight to the East or West coasts; the trailhead was only a three-hour drive from my home in Austin. It was called the Lone Star Hiking Trail, and it traversed the entire breadth of the Sam Houston National Forest, about an hour north of Houston, in a circuitous path laid out not for getting from point A to point B but for maximum distance. It had bragging rights as "the longest footpath in Texas" (although that "footpath" included a fair number of roads).

What's more, I had dipped my toe into this pool on several other occasions. In fact, I had spent a total of four nights on this trail on four different trips over the previous five years. I knew enough of it to know what I was getting into and had hiked enough of it to be able to extrapolate that if I set my mind to it, I really could do it all.

I started floating the idea past friends and colleagues. One co-worker, who had an annual tradition of hiking with friends in the mountain West, asked with a mixture of pity and barely masked revulsion why I would voluntarily choose to hike in *East Texas*. "If you're going to take off work and do something big like that, you might want to think about something more scenic." She was trying to be helpful, but could *nothing* in East Texas be scenic?

One of my best friends, who had never been one for this type of activity, said of hiking a hundred miles and camping every night, "That sounds like something that would happen on a vacation if everything went terribly wrong."

While some like him questioned the ambitiousness of the goal, others needled me from the opposite side. For example, my father-in-law reminded me multiple times that Meriwether Lewis reportedly traveled twenty-five miles a day. It was probably an innocent observation, but the implication I took was, what's with me taking twice as long?

Forests intrigued me for many reasons, but I think the main one was that I grew up in a land without them. I hungered for them the way Arabs relished oases or snowbound Midwesterners coveted tropical beaches. I grew up in deep South Texas, just ten miles from the Rio Grande, where nothing but palm trees grows above about twenty feet, and those are only used for landscaping. And I had settled in Austin. It has far more and larger trees than South Texas to be sure, but Central Texas is dominated by relatively short live oaks and junipers, the tallest trees being pecans and baldcypresses that grow along rivers and creeks. Geology dictates biology, and the clay and limestone under Austin brook no large evergreens.

A forest, a true wilderness, was something I had barely ever experienced before the age of forty. Prior to that I had been an enthusiastic outdoorsman so far as that can go in Texas if one does not own a large ranch or have access to a deer lease. The word "Texas" may have been derived from the Caddo word for friendship, but you wouldn't know it from the number of fences and KEEP OUT signs and the hegemony of private property. The state motto should be whatever the Latin translation is of POSTED. Because the republic had no money at its birth, it paid its soldiers and its debts with the only thing it did have, land. The massive state was carved up to a fare-thee-well and just about every acre of it awarded in lieu of cash to folks like my ancestors, who moved here seven years before the Alamo fell; of course, their enormous tracts of gorgeous post oak savannah had passed to lineages other than mine and eventually were sold out of the family altogether.

Ever since those days, the government has been clawing back parcels of it a few acres at a time to create Texas' fifty-four state parks and its four national forests. But for its enormous size, second only to Alaska, it still has pitifully little public land of recreational value. Two notable exceptions are the state's national parks, Big Bend and Guadalupe Mountains, but they are eight to ten hours by car, which in any other part of America would be three states away.

All this is to say that my outdoors life — the camping, hiking, and fishing I had enjoyed and merrily forced upon my three young sons — had been limited to state parks, which are pleasant but awash in regulations. Visitors may not leave the trail or they risk damaging fragile ecological zones. One must camp only in designated sites, numbered and monitored closely. And within those sites, one must put one's tent only on the tent pad, the leveled dirt square surrounded by a concrete curb or railroad ties. Quiet hours are from ten p.m. to six a.m. No gathering of dead wood. Even camp fires are permitted only on the seemingly rare occasions when the state is not in drought. State parks are outdoors, yes, but are thoroughly anti-adventure.

When I decided to go a little farther afield, specifically to the eastern, forested part of the state, I was astounded to learn that a person could just walk off into the woods, just leave the trail, and camp anywhere he wanted. He or she could just build a campfire anywhere! He could pitch a tent or tie his hammock to trees. He could stay out there for a couple of weeks if he wanted to. And it was free!

So, once again to the ledger: State parks — make a reservation, pay a fee, be shoe-horned into a campsite twenty feet from families on either side that may or may not observe the quiet hours regulation, and don't step off the designated trails if you want to hike. National forest — show up without a reservation, pay nothing, go wherever you want, do whatever you feel. You see the calculus. For a boy who had grown up in the Tamaulipan Scrub, far from a true wood, and who had spent the first twenty years of adulthood plying his campcraft in the ultra-confining state park system, *the national forest was nothing less than a revelation*. Both the tyranny of private property and the shackles of the nanny-state were off!

I vividly remember the first time we left the truck behind and backcountry camped. It was actually in a "national preserve," the famed Big Thicket National Preserve north of Beaumont, Texas. I took my older two boys, then ten and eight, a tent for them and a hammock for me, and took off up Turkey Creek. We walked for a little over an hour, probably two and half miles, then just veered off the trail and into a beautiful section of towering pines where the understory was cleared out revealing a springy floor composed of an endless sea of pine needles. In a couple of hundred yards we stopped and, in a brief burst of manifest destiny, claimed this land for the Seale family, if just for one night. When the tent and hammock were up, we gathered downed branches and started a smoky pine fire that the boys merrily fed pine needles into for the next four hours before turning in.

Out here, with literally no one else for miles in any direction, we could sing and scream and dance around and no one would ever hear or see us, and we did. It was the freest I had ever felt. It was so special. Here were a few humans, together but alone, just existing on the untouched canvas of God's creation. It was so fundamentally right. Primordial, yes — in fact maybe the oldest thing in our genetic memory; our blood and tissue somehow remembered this place where none of us had ever personally been. But against a backdrop of plastic and Styrofoam and childhood obesity and ubiquitous video screens, the primitive forest camp also felt progressive, even subversive, like a blow against the excesses of a lazy, wasteful, and corrupt civilization.

From the first five minutes, this was in my blood. I knew I would come back again and again for as long as I was able to move under my own power. At least once a year, probably twice. Mentally and spiritually I would go back there for a few minutes every day. And it ruined me for state park camping for all time.

That night as the fire died and I lay in my hammock, completely open to the forest without so much as a mosquito net or tarp, I felt the flipside of this freedom. I felt a visceral fear, a fear that reached down to my physical core. There was no rational reason for this fear. There were no bears out here; they'd all been killed by the 1950s. There weren't any mountain lions so far as I knew. The most threatening animals I was aware of out here were hogs.

Mainly to gin up a sense of adventure with the boys, I had taken some paracord and strung a tripline about six inches above the ground in a perimeter around an outer ring of trees, then tied it to a tin pitcher that would fall and clang, in theory waking us, if the line were tripped.

But there didn't have to be an established list of threatening wildlife for this to be scary. At the most fundamental level of our being, a forest at night is a scary place.

I think it is that not only do you not know what's out there, but you *can't* know what's out there. Not only is it dark, which is just fundamentally against our nature as diurnal creatures, but because of the trees, any approaching threat can remain hidden from your view for so long that it could be practically on top of you before you would see it. Unlike having the high ground in battle, in which the downhill aggressor is at greater risk, here, the approacher has all the advantages. The surrounding world is veiled to you by different degrees at different distances. In a 360-degree view, you might be able to see 70 percent of the forest at a 20-foot radius, 40 percent at 100 feet. You might be able to see 10 percent of what's out there 100 yards off, and 1 percent of that 360-degree view at 1,000 yards. This diminishing vista on all sides does something to the psyche, and when coupled with darkness, it conjures up a limbic fear in us that must date as far back as mammals themselves, some 200 million years.

Daylight came, as it tends to. We made breakfast, experimented with the forest's echo by shouting silly phrases as loud as we could, broke camp, and made the easy ninety-minute walk back to the car, and the four-hour drive west to home.

I made good on my pledge to self to do that, to backcountry camp with the boys, as often as I could. We returned to that very same spot in the Big Thicket, but over the course of the next several years, my eyes fell on a target closer to home. And during that period I came to regard Sam Houston National Forest as my "home forest." It was the closest national forest to Austin, and I adopted it as our base of backcountry operations.

On a mild October weekend in 2015 I took the boys over to that timberland to do a "wilderness survival campout." One step beyond backcountry camping, we took no sleeping bags and no tents or hammocks. Only a sheet to lie on and tools with which to fashion our shelter. We went in on the Lone Star Trail from I-45, just south of Huntsville, walking west into the woods. We had been strolling along less than an hour when we passed a man twenty years my senior with an impressive backpack. He looked like a through-hiker to me, and so we paused to chat. He explained that he had recently retired and was doing the whole Lone Star Trail. He was going west to east and so was in about mile 34 of the nearly 100-mile trek.

"That's great!" I cheered, and told him I'd considered doing the same thing myself one day. Thinking how tired he must have been, I released him from the clutches of conversation, and he moved on briskly toward the trailhead we had come in from.

I didn't want to wait until retirement though. I had nothing but respect for this gentleman, but in my mind, for whatever unkind reason, he became fixed in memory as "That Old Fart," as in, "Well, if That Old Fart can strap on a huge backpack and hike a hundred miles, I ought to be able to." Or, "Hey, if That Old Fart could get through this creek bed at mile 34, I had better be able to do the same." Seeing That Old Fart happily traipsing along through the forest, retired, relaxed, happy, alone, and self-sufficient, cemented the notion that I could actually do this if I set my mind to it. I was going.

This was my BHAG — my big, hairy, audacious goal. And the more I learned about this forest and the things that apparently lived there, the bigger and the hairier it got.

3
Knock Knock. Who's There?

I have been one acquainted with the night.
I have walked out in rain — and back in rain.
I have outwalked the furthest city light.

—Robert Frost, "West-Running Brook"

I WANTED TO TRY MY HAND at backcountry camping with my boys, but I thought it best to try it out first with my oldest, then nine. I set our sights on Bastrop State Park, which had a pretty extensive backcountry section adjacent to the developed park and was just an hour east of our home in Austin. It was the Sunday afternoon before Labor Day. As we pulled closer to the park, we saw smoke billowing in the distance. At first I thought it was just a house fire, but as we got closer, I learned that the forest itself was blazing. We were turned away from the park entrance by state troopers and headed back home. On the TV over the following twenty-four hours, we watched that inferno grow into the worst wildfire in Texas history. Bastrop's backcountry section, now a massive burn area, would not be open again to campers for several years, and it will take a generation or more for that forest to look anything like it once did.

We were disappointed but would not be denied, and I started looking farther afield for an opportunity to pitch our tent wherever we wanted. Two weeks later, we were rolling again east but this time to a much bigger wood, Sam Houston National Forest. We were ready for the bigtime.

It had taken us longer than I expected to get over there, and it was only about thirty minutes until dark when we wheeled into the Double Lake Recreation Area inside the national forest. We would hike until dark, then click on the little headlamps that clipped to the bills of our baseball caps and pitch our tent.

We had just gotten our backpacks on and were applying mosquito repellant when the park host stopped us to explain that there was no camping allowed out on the trail because of the extreme drought and a burn ban that was in effect.

Then we heard it.

It sounded like a very loud, whooping howl, echoing across the dry lake bed from a half mile or so to the east. I looked at Andrew and smiled. I didn't want to lead the witness, so I asked the host innocently but incredulously, "What's that?!"

"Prob'ly a coyote," he responded.

I had heard plenty of coyotes, and, to be sure, they make a wide variety of unearthly sounds. But this was not among those sounds. Neither did I think it was an owl, the only other conventional candidate; one can easily tell the difference between a soft sound made at close range and a very loud sound made at a great distance, and this was the latter. I didn't argue with him, but simply looked down at Andrew and raised my eyebrows. Andrew returned a smile, a mix of authentic wonder and amusement. We both knew what the other was thinking.

I can't say with 100 percent certainty that what we heard that evening in the failing light of an East Texas forest was a sasquatch, but I can and do say that it might have been. Andrew and I were on the same wavelength because we had spent a fair amount of time over the previous couple of months discussing the sasquatch mystery, prompted by the premier season of a TV series devoted to the subject, *Finding Bigfoot*, and my discovery of a surprisingly large number of alleged photos and videos of the creatures online that had rekindled my long-held interest in the subject.

Of course, I thought it was unlikely that we'd have any sort of encounter, but I knew from research that this was a place where sasquatches *could* be. San Jacinto County alone had seven encounters on record since 1996, the latest occurring in this national forest in 2008. Add the sightings from the five surrounding counties (Montgomery, Liberty, Polk, Trinity, and Walker), and the number climbed to an even fifty. And those were just the sightings on one website, and, of course, only counted those that had been reported, which common sense tells you had to have been a small fraction of the total.

In the days afterward, I emailed the two research groups I knew of — the Texas Bigfoot Research Conservancy and the national Bigfoot Field Research Organization — asking if they knew of anyone doing research in the area that night, perhaps using a technique known as "call blasting," playing recordings of reputed bigfoot howls over an amplifier in hopes of getting a response. The last thing enthusiasts needed was to be reporting each other's calls like Keystone Cops. I never got an answer from either group.

Denied access to the trail, we stayed in the campground that night. I distinctly remember feeling butterflies in the pit of my stomach as darkness fell. Maybe it was the eerie call of owls, or just the inkiness of the forest gloom, blotting out whatever moonlight there might have been. Or the closeness of the woods. Far from being cozier, as you might think it would feel, there was something menacing in that closeness. There was something unsettling about that place.

We again had been denied a backcountry campout, and, by the way, for a reason I didn't entirely buy, even way back then: "It's too dry in the forest and trees might fall on you"? Umm... oh-kay.

But we had come all that way, and we still wanted something to show for the effort. We wanted to get a hike in. So we rose in the dark the next morning, got our shoes and backpacks on, zipped the tent, scarfed a protein bar, and tunneled into the thicket south along this thing called the Lone Star Trail. About a hundred yards past the trailhead, I heard something large move in front of us, stepping off the trail and into the yaupon understory. We froze and then heard nothing. A deer, I thought, but in retrospect, when a deer is flushed, it usually goes more than ten feet before stopping. To this day, I have no idea what it was, only suspicions.

The hike itself marked the first time I felt the unsettling thrill of true isolation. One mile from the truck. Two miles from the truck. Three miles from the truck. As the markers went by, and as we continued not to encounter any other people, I felt in my stomach a sense of growing risk. If I broke my ankle, if I had chest pains, if a tree really did fall on me — it would be a bad situation. As we walked, I rehearsed scenarios with Andrew. Which way would he go on the trail if something happened to me? Who would he find? What would he say? How would he tell them where I was?

Interestingly, one of the to-do's I had given myself on this trip was to tell our oldest son the truth about Santa. He was getting wise and asking a lot of questions in front of his younger brothers, and my wife and I had decided it was time to bring him "into the club" lest he spoil the fun for everybody. So I told him the ugly truth — it had been Mom and me all along. Like all parents, we had done it because we wanted it to be fun for our kids. And then I added something else, which, given our surroundings, was poignant. I told him that I would never again lie to him about anything, period. Never again pretend something was real if it wasn't. (And by implication, I would never tell him that something was *not* real if I thought it was.)

As we went along, we whooped like we imagined bigfoots did, marveling at the echo, and picked up sticks and knocked on the passing tree trunks like the guys in *Finding Bigfoot*. We saw and heard nothing more cryptic than green and brown anoles skittering through the leaf litter, all the way out and back. But it did feel like an adventure, and my hardy fourth grader certainly had some new material for his next theme paper.

That was a day-hike, but at last we succeeded in breaking into backcountry camping, on the aforementioned trip to Big Thicket National Preserve, as well as other trips here to "Sam."

Time has a way of rounding the edges off of experience like water rounds off stones. And after nearly five years I had just about convinced myself that what we heard that evening from the Double Lake parking lot probably *was* a coyote, or maybe just a really powerful barred owl.

Then mystery upped the ante.

January 3rd of 2016 was a Sunday. The next day would have been my first day back at work after the holiday break, but I had convinced an old high school buddy we should do a quick backcountry trip, and Monday was the day he had open. I targeted the closest section of a national forest to Austin, the westernmost edge of Sam Houston near the town of Richards.

This trip was more about the camping than the hiking, so we had set no mileage goal for ourselves, opting simply to walk in until we saw a good spot, camp the night, then walk back out.

We had been on the trail less than an hour when Wade spotted something weird. It was a small green plastic box, perhaps the size of a deck of cards, suspended nine feet off the ground by a thin white rope flung over a horizontal branch and tied off near the base of the tree. Curious primates that we were, we untied it and lowered it. Inside was a substance that looked like peanut butter. We discussed the possibilities. It was clearly wildlife bait of some sort. Of course, with sasquatch on the brain, everything was bigfoot-related. But the way it was hung, nearly ten feet up, it had to either be for birds or for the Others. We raised it back to its original position and started on down the trail.

In another mile or so we came upon a pond. It would do nicely, and we proceeded around the far side of the pond and about fifty more yards away from the trail. We extracted the camp stove from my pack and proceeded to heat a couple of cans of Spaghetti-O's with meatballs. We built a very small fire, more just to say we had done it than to benefit from any light or heat it would put off. It was dark early in the dead of winter, and so we were early to our hammocks. The night was cold and clear. We can pick up the story from a report I submitted the day after we returned:

YEAR: 2016
SEASON: Winter
MONTH: January
DATE: 4
STATE: Texas
COUNTY: Montgomery
NEAREST TOWN: Richards
NEAREST ROAD: Texas State Highway 149

OBSERVED: On Monday, January 4, 2016, at 6 a.m., I was backcountry camping with a friend in the Sam Houston National Forest. We had made camp near an unnamed pond west of the hiking trail.

The night was clear, 35 degrees, and perfectly still. My friend and I were hammock camping and, because of the cold, were both under low-staked tarps that prevented us from seeing out. Our hammocks were about fifteen yards apart.

At 6 a.m. it was still completely dark. I had been awake for about fifteen minutes but remained in my sleeping bag inside my hammock. At that point I heard a sharp clack perhaps 75 yards on the other side of my friend. Two seconds later I heard a double-knock much farther away, perhaps a half-mile to the north or northwest.

The first pop was crisp and close. To my ears it had to be either rock on rock or wood on wood. As there is nothing in that area but sandy soil and trees, my conclusion was that this was a well-struck tree knock followed by a distant response. To the best of our knowledge there were no other people in the vicinity. We had arrived at the trailhead to begin our one-night backpacking trip at 2 p.m. the previous afternoon, and we had only seen one other party of hikers, who passed our camp at 4:30 Sunday afternoon and continued eastward on the trail; we saw no one else during the entire trip, which ended when we arrived back at the parking lot at 11:30 a.m. Monday morning.

Had it been windy I could have written the sounds off to cracking limbs, but there was not the slightest breeze, and the two sounds appeared to me to be a clear call and response, perhaps: "Humans over here" ... "Roger that."

After the sounds, I froze and listened hard for several minutes for any other noise such as footfalls, stick breaks or other evidence of visitors but heard none. Within five minutes I asked my friend if he had heard it and he had not, having his ears covered by his cap and his head inside his sleeping bag at the time. Within fifteen minutes we both were asleep again. We awoke for good at about 7:20 a.m. and vacated the area at 10 a.m. We heard distant coyotes, dogs, ducks, and owls, but no other such sounds during our stay.

The absence of footfalls or other noises initially made me think it must not have been a sasquatch, but on reflection, the visitor could easily have frozen in his spot when he discovered our camp and then moved slowly away, perhaps using fallen logs, fifteen minutes later once we were back to sleep. Considering the stillness of the night, the crisp, unambiguous clack, and the quick double-knock response, I can think of no other cause for these sounds.

OTHER WITNESSES: No other witnesses

OTHER STORIES: Many sightings in Sam Houston National Forest as in all of East Texas

TIME AND CONDITIONS: 6 a.m., clear skies, predawn, moon low in the east

ENVIRONMENT: Loblolly pine forest with a small pond nearby and a web-like network of seasonal drainages

The follow-up investigation report by a BFRO investigator states:

> I spoke with the witness on the afternoon of 6/15/16 about his encounter. While there is no way to tell for sure whether or not the tree knocks were from a bigfoot, there are other parts to this story that make me believe it likely was.
>
> This report was from an area just a mile or so from the site of the BFRO Texas Expedition October 2015. One whole team of participants on that Expedition had a Class A sighting very near to where this event occurred. In short, there has been a lot of reported activity in this part of the forest. Lastly, unlike some areas, wood knocks are very common in East Texas forests. Heard and reported all the time, signs point to wood knocks as being a communication tool used by bigfoots — perhaps because the forests of SE Texas are relatively flat and the wood knock sound travels farther.
>
> The witness intends to continue hiking in the same forest and promises to update us on any further observations.

The investigator told me he thought the green box we saw hanging from the tree was probably set where it was to position a sasquatch in front of a camera trap. Wade and I hadn't thought to look for one of those, and we are probably immortalized on someone's computer right now, lowering and investigating the peanut butter box.

A few months passed, and unlike the fading of conviction I experienced after the howl at Double Lake, I remained fairly convinced that I had had a real encounter, and a close one. I was browsing bigfoot sighting databases on my lunch break when I found an intriguing report on a different site, one maintained by a bigfoot research group with the rather opaque name of North American Wood Ape Conservancy. I squinted at the screen. The report was from the same county, on the very same day, and just one hour earlier:

> **Witness Observation**
> At approximately 0500 on January 4, 2016, I was traveling to work on FM 1375 heading east towards I-45. As I was approaching the river bridge I saw a reflection of eyes from the bridge and thought it was deer eyes. As I got closer the eyes were approximately 7-8 feet high. Then I noticed the body of this "thing." It was huge. I have spent many a year in the woods and I have never seen anything like this. When I first saw it I thought it was a person or maybe a bear standing on its hind legs. But by its size alone it was clear it was not a person.

The witness had to swerve into the oncoming lane to avoid the figure. As he drove by, the subject and the witness locked eyes. The man did not tell anyone what he saw as he continued on to work. About an hour later, his wife called him and told him that she had seen something "really strange" on her way to work as she crossed the very same bridge spanning Lake Conroe.

As she drove out onto the bridge, she saw up ahead a very large figure that she at first thought was a person jogging across the bridge, clearly seeing arms and legs. She described the subject as very large, black in color, and seven to eight feet in height; it was facing east with its back to her as she drove toward it and then passed it. She never saw it from the front and never saw reflective eyes. The subject was actually out on the bridge, and it was her impression that it was walking east across the bridge. She was in a small car and had to look up at the subject, coming to within ten to fifteen feet of it as she passed it. Like her husband, she too was stunned.

The significance of this story is this: Baker's Bridge was nine miles east of my position, and I heard *two* of them to my *west* at the precise moment of the second sighting. This meant there were at least three sasquatches within a nine-mile-wide area in the westernmost third of Sam Houston National Forest that morning. Rarely have there been simultaneous independent reports that clearly establish multiple creatures in a fixed area like this did.

Most who grant the existence of sasquatches assume that, because nearly all reports describe a solitary individual, they are essentially solitary animals. But researchers believe, and primatology would predict, that they move in small family groups, and that for every animal that is seen, there are probably two or three others hiding nearby. The growing sighting and video record, and my own experience with knocks, bears this out. Living in small groups as opposed to large ones would be one clear evolutionary adaptation allowing easier avoidance of humans. One intriguing area of research would be around what the upper limit of groups might be. In 2008, researchers uncovered a colony of 125,000 lowland gorillas in a Congo swamp, immediately doubling the number of these gorillas thought to exist. There is not enough remote cover to support anything on this order for the sasquatch, but it is intriguing to contemplate a group of even a few dozen of them living in a virtually unreachable hanging valley or high basin in Alaska or northern Canada. A grandmother in Oregon claimed to see nine of them outside her window — one female and eight males — mating for hours at a time. I'm going to go out on a limb here and guess that she skipped her soap operas that day. Anyway, that's as many as I've ever heard of being seen at once. All the same, you read enough stories citing four here, seven there, and you get the distinct feeling there are a whole lot more of these things than anyone probably imagines.

The name FM 1375 rang a bell for me, and then I remembered another report from years earlier.

The morning of September 11, 2001, is one every American alive at the time remembers — where they were and what they were doing when terrorists attacked the World Trade Center and Pentagon using civilian airliners. There is one American, however, who remembers that morning with equal intensity for a completely different reason.

At 4:30 that morning he was on his way from his home in College Station to his job in Conroe. The most direct route of this rather long commute took him over Lake Conroe on the same bridge. His sighting reports tells the story:

> Due to the drive and the time I needed to be at work I often left long before the sun was rising. I had just crossed that bridge headed east when I decided to pull to the side of the road. I am a heavy

coffee drinker and for obvious reasons the rural nature of the spot made it an easy stopping point. ... Where I had stopped, years of fishermen had worn a path down from the roadbed to the lake's edge. I had just started to step onto that path when I noticed a VERY heavy musky odor. ...

I had taken maybe two or three more steps when the hairs on my neck literally stood on end and to this day I swear I heard a "woofing" noise, not like a dog does but kinda like that and as if something was telling me I was not where I needed to be. I stopped, and that is when to my immediate right something stood up and grabbed the branches of a small tree right next to my head and began to shake.

I had left my lights on in the truck, and though they were not shining in my direction the reflection was enough to get a general idea. It stood well over a foot taller than me and was still below me on the slope of the embankment. I am 5'8" so I would think it was about 7 feet tall. It had dark-colored hair, a rather large head, and I could not see the nose or eyes due to shadows. It had long arms I think and large hands. ... The stench was amazing. Enough to make my eyes water. It began to make a squealing bark kinda noise and in two or three strides was past me and headed for the road. I don't know why it didn't turn and head back into the forest, but it didn't. I turned to watch and as it started across the road a light-colored truck came around the bend in the road headed west. I don't know if the driver saw what I did but I can remember the red lights of the brakes shining so he/she must have seen something. The creature moved up the hill on the other side of the road and went into the pine trees there.

> I got back into my truck and got the heck out of
> dodge, so to speak. I have only told one other
> person about this cause to be honest I don't want
> to look like some idiot seeing a ghost in the middle
> of the woods in Texas.

The whole observation lasted between five and ten seconds. The follow-up investigator noted that the reddish-brown creature had arms that were uniformly the size of a big Folgers Coffee can all the way down.

The witness also mentioned that he shook for two days after this event, and he has since given up deer hunting.

Though it sounded terrifying, for whatever reason I could not help wanting to experience the Others in some way. I was drawn to it like a moth to a flame. Book learning and online videos and other witness accounts were interesting. But for me there simply could be no substitute for direct experience.

I once bought a telescope with a four-inch mirror, pretty good for front-yard viewing of the moon and planets. I had not owned it long when I tried to interest a friend, who was already at my house, in going out to the yard and looking through it at Saturn. He declined the invitation, saying he preferred to observe the universe through books and TV. I was astonished. Sure, you could watch *Nova* and see a more impressive view of Saturn than you could in looking through my little $200 telescope. But wasn't there something thrilling about the experience of seeing magnificent ringed Saturn with so few elements between you and it? You could make out more detail in a Hubble coffee table book, or on TV certainly, but what of direct experience? Did we always need to experience the world through culturally or politically approved filters? Through media?

As compelling as the stories of 10,000 sasquatch witnesses were, they could never supply that final link in the chain of belief. I was fairly sure I had heard them, not once but twice, and I wanted to take the next step in this strange relationship. I had read enough and seen enough videos and photos to last a lifetime. If they were out there, I wanted to *know*, in my bones, to my core, and the only way I could really know was to investigate it directly. I had to go and try to see the Others for myself.

But what were the odds I was going to just walk into a forest and see one of these things? After all, some people had held a lifelong interest in the bigfoot mystery and had gone out dozens of times in search of evidence and never found a shred. René Dahinden was a famous investigator and author of several books on the subject. In his 2001 obituary, friend Christopher Murphy remembered Dahinden in his twilight experiencing a pang of doubt. "One day he said to me: 'You know, I've spent over forty years — and I didn't find it. I guess that's got to say something.' "

But what was *my* history, and what was this area's history? Here was the ledger: I had spent a total of four nights in Sam Houston National Forest on four different occasions, and *twice* I had heard them! I was not a math major, but I believe that's a fifty percent success rate. That's a .500 batting average for someone with no real experience doing this. And my first experience came within *five minutes* of getting out of my vehicle on my first trip there. Based on that record, I must say I was feeling pretty good about my chances of seeing or hearing *something* during eight days and seven nights.

I'd get it done for the both of us, Mr. Dahinden.

4

Adventure Pants

"By failing to prepare, you are preparing to fail."
—Benjamin Franklin

IN ITS ENTIRETY, THE PREPARATION for my hike took years, and it included numerous other much shorter backcountry trips during which I was all the while figuring out what was really necessary and what was not.

There was the backcountry trip to Big Bend National Park, when my sons proved too young for the demands of the exhaustingly steep and rocky trail and the darkness of a winter night that came too soon.

And, as I've said, there were other backcountry trips to East Texas, to Big Thicket National Preserve, a patchwork of nine wilderness units north of Beaumont where we had hiked in and camped twice.

In addition to other virtues that distinguish backpacking from car camping, such as the greatly increased athleticism it requires and the access it gives you to secluded and pristine scenes of nature experienced by few others, it has another less-considered benefit: it forces you to really take the measure of your material needs.

Human nature dictates that we surround ourselves with comfort, and so to take something with us that will address every contingency. Better take a poncho in case it rains. Shorts in case it's hotter than expected, and every conceivable combination of layers to maximize comfort in any climate. Binoculars in case some rare bird alights a hundred yards off. Food, of course, usually way more than needed lest we risk a single moment of hunger or unfulfilled hankering of any kind. Sunscreen, and chapstick, and aspirin, and something with caffeine for the morning to avoid a headache. And so on.

This impulse has no real consequence so long as you are car-camping, parked fifty feet from your tent pad. The more the merrier. But in the backcountry, every *single* thing you choose to bring — be it for comfort or safety — must be weighed against, well, its weight. Because it quickly adds up to a crushing load. A war is waged in the mind of the backcountry novice between two competing fears: the fear of encountering some need in the wilderness, including needs that can mean life or death like enough water, and the fear of loading oneself down so much that the whole journey turns to misery. The most serious backcountry hikers have it down to such a science that they even cut the handles off their toothbrushes to shave a quarter ounce off their load. It's a highly enlightening exercise made even more so when carried out in the context of the most materialistic and materially laden society the world has ever known.

For several years I had been dialing in my gear: the ninety-liter backpack that I had bought five years earlier would do nicely. I knew what it held. It had been a tough and reliable companion.

Four years earlier, I had converted from tent camping to hammock camping and was now an enthusiastic evangelist for sleeping off the ground. The hammock was my biggest luxury. I had parted with $225 for it two years earlier. But when I amortized that over the number of nights I had stayed in it, I was now well below $10 a night, and, as one friend put it to me, that's a lot cheaper than a hotel. It took a little getting used to, but once I had mastered it, I was loath to return to terra firma. One of its chief beauties, besides the way it supported my back, was that it could be tied above any type of surface and be just as comfortable. Sharp rocks, ant bed, cactus, even a creek, nothing below mattered so long as you were tied to trees stout enough to remain vertical.

One critical addition to the setup had been a tarp, which had saved my hide on many a stormy night. By the time everything was assembled, it was essentially a tent suspended in the trees.

Being half-bald and of northern European extraction, I had become increasingly dependent upon and enthusiastic about hats. And while it's true that I would be in shade a good percentage of every day in a forest, I also knew I would have road walks during which, especially around the noon hour, I could count on full sun. A wide-brim hat was the proper call so as to shield the ears and neck as well as the crown and face. But it couldn't be too wide without the top of my pack constantly harassing the back of the brim. And as I would be wearing it at least fifty hours, comfort was a non-negotiable.

Three months before go-day, I was in an outfitter store near my office when I spied a novel piece of headwear I had never previously considered — the pith helmet. I tried it on in the store mirror and let out an immediate chuckle. It was silly looking — its perfectly round and downward-curving brim with a leather strap coming over the front brim. I appeared to be sporting a UFO, and I immediately recognized it as the key component of the gentleman-explorer cliché and the head covering of choice for colonial tyrants everywhere. But it was light — I'd give it that. And it was cool, sitting a little off the scalp and woven out of the pith of palm leaves such that air escaped through hundreds of tiny holes in every surface, the better to spend long hours oppressing native peoples in their own humid homelands like India and the Congo. I liked its rigidity as well. But it did look silly. I put it back.

Two days later I was riding home on the bus after work, a brand-new pith helmet cozily riding in my lap. The family was highly amused at my new look as I came through the door. Add it to the list.

For night-time headwear, I took a camo tuke my wife had given me that would provide plenty of warmth and had the bonus of two small but powerful lights that were sewn into the headband — dual use.

Surveying then from top to bottom, below the helmet I packed a hunter-orange neckerchief that would serve as a do-rag under the helmet, a headband to keep stinging sweat out of my eyes, and of course could serve as a small towel, washrag, flag, arm sling or any number of other useful things. I opted for my wireframe glasses, which, unlike my hipper plastic frames, stayed on my nose when I sweated. And on those, clip-on sunglasses from the drug store, which neither fit the glasses perfectly nor looked very cool, but which accomplished the task.

I took two shirts, both of technical fabric, and, in compliance with hunting season regulations, bright orange —

one short-sleeved, one long. I took one pair of pants, the kind my sons called "adventure pants." They were khaki colored, lightweight, and zipped off at the knee. They also contained what we in our family referred to as a "willie net," like a bathing suit, which in most cases obviated the need for underwear, though I packed two pair of those as well as a token nod to civilization. The adventure pants had a strong elastic waistband but were assisted further by a lightweight belt of olive webbing, which had a secret zipped compartment along the inside of the belt where one could stash money or an address and phone number that might help in identifying the body.

Socks were of great concern, and there were several schools of thought about how this critical piece of clothing could make or break a through-hike. Fellow Scouting dads encouraged the concurrent wearing of two pairs, one inside the other, so that the foot, if it needed to scoot, would rub inner socks on outer socks. So I packed three pairs, including a gray wool pair my wife had just bought me on a trip to Iceland. I regarded the Icelandic socks as a totem from her — her symbolically carrying me along and comforting me on the journey.

The importance of one's shoes was, of course, unequalled, and I made a nine-month study of which shoes would be both adequate for the task and maximally comfortable. Instead of a hiking boot with ankle support, I chose a low-rise hiking shoe. I knew from experience that most of what I would be traversing was sandy and leafy, not rocky and bumpy, and so I traded ankle support and rigidity of sole for lightness and comfort. They also needed to be waterproof, as I had suffered mightily on a previous outing without that feature.

On my belt I wore an iPhone, bought two days before the trip, in a plastic clip on my left hip, and on my right, a knife.

The knife was an important choice, as it would serve multiple functions known and unknown at the time of departure. I knew I would use it to cut branches if I needed to clear a spot for my hammock, and to dig "cat holes" in the sandy dirt when it came time to answer nature's call.

The decision of which knife loomed large, as I had become something of a collector and had far more than I needed from which to choose. The machete was too large for a trip this long. The eight-inch bowie knife with wooden handle — the *"that's a naif"* knife of Crocodile Dundee fame — would have been a manly choice but had been made of cheap steel and thus was now missing an inch-long chip along its blade because I had pried with it a year earlier. Two Buck knives were in contention, the classic folding 110, which didn't seem quite enough to dig with, and the fixed-blade 119 Special, almost right but leaving me wanting just a little more heft.

In the end, I found myself driving the thirty miles to Cabela's for yet another knife and coming home with something called a GI Tanto. The blade was six inches long, and, notwithstanding my vigilance in every other regard about taking the lightest of any class of item on this trip, it was the heaviest knife I'd ever owned. It was a "tactical" knife, weighted for throwing. It was all black, including the blade, which was made in the "drop-point" style and contained no curves but rather four straight edges that formed its profile, two long straight edges on top and bottom and two short straight edges creating the point. One of the reasons I liked it was that I could envision it being duct-taped to a pole or branch to form an extremely badass spear in case I came in contact with a hog with attitude or a rabid coyote or a water moccasin — or, you know, whatever. The GI Tanto rode in an unsentimental black-plastic sheath held together by rivets and screws. It looked like what I imagined a scuba-diving Navy SEAL would carry, but I'm sure it was a far cry.

It was getting to be a lot of stuff, but I was still debating whether to hold anything as I hiked. For many years I had favored a large staff, Gandalf style, that was given to me by a thoughtful elderly acquaintance. It had an outline of Texas branded onto the top of it, and he joked that it was a built-in map, just in case I ever got lost in the 268,597-square-mile state.

But in recent years I had been experimenting with trekking poles, which I had read took some of the weight of the pack off your back and hips, and also opened up your posture, lessening your fatigue. I had gotten a pair for free as a reward for buying my backpack, but they had since fallen apart. I had kept them, however, and decided to salvage the handles, putting them on thin bamboo sticks sold at the home improvement store as garden stakes. Each pole was capped at the bottom with a black plastic chair foot, also sold at the home store, to keep the base of the pole from splitting. The bamboo was great because not only was it lightweight but it could be cut to length, which for someone my height was a little longer than normal. With that decision made, I turned my attention to food.

Since I was going to camp all the way through, and thought better of trying to carry a week's worth of food with me, I hatched a plan to cache food along the way in large ziplock bags. Inside the bags I would have canned meat and other sealed meals.

I started with the king of canned meats, Spam. Not really being a regular consumer of this product, I wandered the aisles of the grocery store. Well, I thought, I'll be hungry for sure, so I just bought one of every kind. (Good thing there are no bigfoots in Hawaii.) In my local store, those varieties included regular, bacon, and turkey. I had only a passing familiarity with this product, so I thought it wise to inspect some out of the can before embarking on a trip during which I would rely on it so heavily. I had questions, such as did it come pre-sliced or would I have to cut it with the GI Tanto?

I knew from the moment the giant block of pink particle meat slid slimily from the rectangular can and thudded onto the cutting board that this would not be the form in which I consumed it day after day in the wild. Fewer than fifteen seconds had passed before my wife rose from her laptop, quickly retrieved two candles from the front room, and lit them between herself and me, attempting to set up an invisible force-field against the scent. It was a strong smell, I gave her that. But to me not a repulsive one.

All the same, it was not appetizing in this form to anyone but Gracie, our pit bull mix who now sat six inches away at full attention. No, it had to be cooked, and I was not that keen on cooking on this hike. Food needed to be fast and nearly effortless. But how to cook it without consigning my sweet wife to a week's exile? I decided to smoke it, which would 1. cook it 2. outside, and 3. mask its natural aroma with the smell of smoke. I cut all four cans into quarter-inch slices and laid them out on cooling racks that rode on cookie sheets. I stoked the smoker with live oak from the yard and fired it up. Nine hours later, I brought the Spam back inside, each slice was bone-dry and ten shades darker than it had started. I bagged them all up and put them in the freezer. Of course, I sampled a few of them on my way— Holy Mary, Joseph, and all the saints and angels that's a lot of salt! The cans still sat on the counter, and I decided to break with habit and look at their labels. Incredibly, I was eating from cans advertising "Low Sodium." As my sons would say, this was *no bueno*. I was going to be challenged enough to stay hydrated without desiccating myself from the inside out. I had visions of showing up at the end of the trail a mummy, then crumbling to the ground in a Spielbergian cloud of dust. I would have to change course.

I turned to canned tuna and chicken — neither of which is a stranger to sodium — but better than Spam. (I later would eat all the Spam in the safety of my own home and with water running nearby.)

Again, I wasn't going out there to cook; I was going out there to walk. If there were some sort of human kibble I could just take to give my body what it needed, that would have been perfect. Peanut butter was that kibble. I had once read a great book by a guy who rowed a boat around the eastern third of the United States, and virtually all he ate was peanut butter and Saltines — a man after my own heart attack. My carbohydrates would come from two main sources — ramen noodles and water crackers — sturdier and less salty than my beloved but flakier Saltines.

In one of the food bags, one I knew I would not have to lug far, I loaded a large can of Spaghetti-O's with meatballs, and also in that bag I put a treat to dream about on the trail — a reward for making it to the fifth cache — a jar of Nutella. Of course, all the peanut butter and Nutella needed a vehicle on which to ride — I couldn't just lick it off the GI Tanto. And bread was no use as it would be instantly crushed in my pack. So I settled on tortillas, cooking them in the kitchen then packaging them two to a baggie and freezing them until go-day.

It was interesting how trail necessities must include whatever our addictions are. In his fantastic 1906 tome *The Book of Camping and Woodcraft*, Horace Kephart included several lists of camping necessities, and high up on the list was tobacco and rolling papers. In his day it was simply inconceivable that anyone would set out into the wilds without a good supply of smokes.

I had thus far managed to avoid that particular addiction, but I did have my own. I decided to sate my caffeine dependency not with the customary coffee or tea, but with a daily bottle of 5-Hour Energy, the ubiquitous little red bottle found by every convenience store cash register.

I would also need to think long and hard about the aches and pains that doubtlessly lay ahead, the tremendous muscle soreness of the feet, hips, back, and shoulders. All of those were certainties, and there were a great many possibilities beyond them: diarrhea, nausea, allergic reactions, bee stings, snake bites, and on and on. For all those, my wife gathered an impressive collection of the pills we always kept on hand — ibuprofen, acetaminophen, Zyrtec, Benadryl. I guess I *could* have always gone with what old Horace Kephart recommended in his old-timey list of camping essentials, cocaine pills. At a minimum I suppose those would have obviated the need for caffeine. A morning bump and "move aside Meriwether Lewis!" I'd be done by midweek.

Two years earlier I had experimented with something else Horace taught me about, *pinole*. This was simply parched corn ground into a fine powder, and it went by many names. The Southern pioneers called it cold flour (a corruption of "coal flour," from the process of roasting corn in coals). Indians of the East Coast called it rockahominy. And the Spanish called it *pinole*. I had made some, and put a pinch of brown sugar in it for good measure. But although Kephart reported that Indians would go into the backcountry for weeks at a time with nothing but a long pouch full of this stuff, I found it had to be chased with tremendous amounts of water, and was not very filling by modern American standards.

But I had never tried that other staple of old-time travel, hardtack. Made with nothing but flour, salt, and water, it was also known as "sea biscuit" and was the go-to carbohydrate of pioneers, sailors, and Civil War soldiers. I found a recipe — if you can call something with three ingredients a "recipe" — and baked a batch about a week out from go-day. I rolled out the flour and cut it into unsightly strips of dough that, when baked, resembled jagged bookmarks, but were far tougher. Taking care to not chip a tooth, I cracked off a piece and let it soften in my mouth, then gave a few chews and swallowed it down. It wasn't bad, and I had a few more bites before bed.

I bagged up the rest and threw it on the pool table in the front room, which was becoming ground-zero for everything I was planning to take. I laid out each day's repast in a column. At the top, the gallon ziplock bag with its destination written in Sharpie: Stubblefield ... Huntsville/I-45 ... Double Lake. Then I laid out the food top to bottom down the table in the order I imagined eating it: 5-Hour Energy, tortilla baggie, peanut butter, oatmeal packet, water crackers, canned chicken or tuna, ramen, and so on. Over three weeks the pool table became a spreadsheet, laden with probably forty pounds of nonperishable groceries and baggies within baggies.

Laid in on top of those was the media and electronics bag with phone chargers, camera, selfie-stick, GoPro, audio recorder, extra batteries, and three power banks I bought to recharge it all. What good was getting back to nature if you couldn't capture every moment of it in an electronic medium?

Around the pool table, the floor of the front room was taken over by everything else: the backpack, the sleeping bag, the hammock bag, the tarp bag, the orange shirts, the adventure pants (with willie net), the pith helmet, the trekking poles, and so much else, a daunting mountain of stuff all of which somehow had to be carried on my back for more than a week.

LSHT Packing List

Backpack
Hammock, suspension
Tarp
Sleeping bag, ground cloth
Camp pillow
Thermarest pad
Trekking poles
Water bottles (2-3 Nalgenes), CamelBak
Knife
Phone / recharger
Chilly Pad
Mess kit
Kleenex purse packs (for TP)
Fishing line

Clothes
Hiking shoes
Flip-flops for camp
Pithy the Pith Helmet
Fleece
Rain gear (Frogg Toggs)
Socks - 3 pairs - wear two pairs at a time to prevent blisters, or special hiking socks
Lightweight long pants, belt
Tuke w/headlamp (fresh batt.)
Undies (2)
Long sleeves
Short sleeves
Bear spray
Backpacking stove, fuel, lighter (multiple)
Water filter
Pitcher

Paracord (for dry line, trip lines, misc.)
Camp suds (laundry soap), ziplock bags
Leatherman (multi-tool for can opener, pliers)
Spotlight (fresh batts)
Duct tape
Camera (Pro Shot (batt), ex SD card)
GoPro, battery, SD card
Audio recorder
Tape measure
Notebook, pen
Meds - Pain reliever, Zyrtec, anti-diarrheal
Moleskin
Trail notes & trail book
Clean clothes bag for ride home

At this point, my impressions of the trail, apart from the short trips I had already made there, were most heavily influenced by two people. The first was Karen Borski Somers, the author of the authoritative book on the Lone Star Hiking Trail, named, appropriately, *The Lone Star Hiking Trail*. For more than a year, her slim green volume was my constant companion, traveling in my messenger bag, the passenger seat of the truck, resting on the night stand, the back of the toilet. It went with me everywhere — on the bus to work and home, to the waiting room at Jiffy Lube, to my son's swim practice. Chock full of helpful information, detailed maps, and a pleasant, descriptive narrative, I read it so many times that by the time I left, I seemed to have memorized long passages of it. That being the case, I scarcely needed to take it with me on the trip, but I did anyway.

The second influential person was a YouTube DIY juggernaut with more than 40,000 subscribers, Kenneth Kramm. Mr. Kramm is a gentleman of retirement age with a short gray beard and gentle smiling eyes behind aviator glasses. In his introductory video, Kramm says, "Occasionally, I am described as the Mr. Rogers of bushcraft because a bear puppet sometimes joins my adventures." In Kramm's well-executed videos, he gamely guides us through nature's wonders, mostly in Texas, demonstrating along the way how to build a Swedish log stove or a chair without nails or cordage, the glories of hammock camping, mountain biking on woodland trails, starting a fire with char-cloth or a bow drill, fixing meals al fresco, and so on, video after video, all thoroughly adult activities involving knives and fire, but all the while carrying on an oddly juxtaposed childlike conversation with his sidekick, "Bear." It's as if he's not sure if his target demographic is men forty and older or girls five and younger. (Ken, it's the former.)

The material preparation was only one phase. Of course, there was the conditioning that was worrisome as well. Could I really do this? This was orders of magnitude harder than anything I had ever asked of my body before. I was accustomed to three-to-five milers, Cub Scouts stuff. A year and a half earlier, Wade and I had even done a bold twenty-five-mile loop around Lake Georgetown near our homes. The Goodwater Loop, as it's known, was much longer than anything I had attempted before. It was two days and one night. On the way home from that hike Wade and I pulled into a Whataburger. We had been still for about thirty minutes on the drive back to town, and both of us felt like concrete had been poured into our hips, knees, and ankles. It took him ninety seconds to get from my truck to the front door, and I had parked three spaces away. He moved like Tim Conway as Mr. Tudball. I shot a video and posted it immediately.

It felt like twenty-five miles was about all this fortysomething hominid's body had in it. And somehow it was going to do four of those back to back?

My wife was rightly worried that I was not training enough in the months before the hike. I suppose I had a long history of just up and doing things without really preparing for them. During our courtship when she set out to run a marathon for the first time, she enrolled in a class, went every Saturday morning for instruction, made friends with her classmates and built a support network, gradually increased her mileage every week, and even took ice baths after the longer distances to help her muscles recover.

By contrast, when we decided to split a half-marathon between us, I started preparing the day of the race, which included eating breakfast and finding the best running shoes I had in my closet. As I crossed the finish line after six-plus miles of pounding the asphalt in some ill-suited tennies, I shouted to her over the din of pulsating music, *"Should I be able to feel my feet?!"*

I guess I took Nike's exhortation to "Just do it" a little too literally. But hey, I finished. I'm sure she extrapolated from this pattern of behavior — quite reasonably — that I was biting off more than I could chew, the big difference being there would be no EMS crew standing by if the lack of preparation finally came home to roost on *this* race route.

So I loaded my backpack with weights and did a handful of practice hikes around the neighborhood and on the hike-and-bike trail near our house. I got a lot of stares, I don't mind telling you, from folks who probably thought I had lost the Appalachian Trail in a major way.

You wouldn't think that an act as basic as walking could be made complicated, but we're humans, and we can overthink absolutely anything. Sure enough, it turns out there's more to walking than putting one foot in front of the other. Ol' Horace Kephart wrote extensively about the different modes of ambulation adopted by, on the one hand, "townspeople," and on the other, "the woodsman and the Indian." And you might be able to guess which group did it better, that is to say more efficiently, covering more ground with less effort. Kephart said that while the townsperson struck the ground heel-first, the Indian and the woodsman tended to step with a more pointed toe so that the whole sole landed at once. He said the result was greater stability and less energy expended on correcting balance.

In my practice hikes I tried to incorporate this motion but every time wound up looking like a strutting ostrich with a huge backpack, and after a dozen or so steps — the nanosecond I stopped concentrating on it — defaulted back to whatever way I had been walking since the age of one.

Another variable was the length of the step. Even though I, at six-two, had long legs, I had a natural tendency toward quick short steps, the steps Andre Agassi took around the tennis court between points. But this was no way to hike. Kephart said that by incorporating the hips a hiker could add one, two, even three inches to every step, and over the course of a day, those inches can really add up.

During all of my practice walks, only one fellow pedestrian paused to ask if I was training for a hike. "Sure am," I replied, slowing and turning backward to face him.

"Where you going?" he asked.

"Sam Houston National Forest," I panted, "a hundred miles."

"Oh, wow!" he said. "That sounds awesome!"

Finally! I thought. A little enthusiasm. Take that, coworker who doesn't believe East Texas could possibly warrant taking a week of vacation for! I came within two seconds of asking, "Wanna go?" I really, *really* did not want to go by myself. But as he was a total stranger, and the hike was one week away, I refrained.

I had asked three friends sequentially if they would go along, and one by one they had had to turn me down. One, who for months had planned to come with me, even sitting through several planning lunches, had misread his vacation balance and now couldn't spare the five days out of the office. Another was self-employed and single, and I was sure he would be able to come. But he was flipping a house and was being held hostage by contractors and the city permit office. The third wished he could but other out-of-town family obligations had put dibs on his vacation balance as well.

I did not want to go alone.

I went to Facebook and scrolled through all 644 of my friends, family, and acquaintances to see if there were any good candidates I hadn't yet thought of. In deference to my wife, of course, women, no matter how hale and hardy some might have been (and many were *far* hardier than me), were not eligible. The men one by one fell off the list — bad back, bum ankle, new baby, new job/no vacation balance, didn't like camping, too busy, couldn't get a kitchen pass. The things that took them out of the running — or should I say "the walking" — for me congealed into one monolithic "thing," an amalgamation of everything that was wrong with society. We fancied ourselves a free people, I stewed, but how free were we really when I could not think of one eligible companion who could find five days and two contiguous weekends to go and do something life changing that cost almost nothing? Land of the free indeed.

For a few days I entertained the notion of punting the whole thing to spring in the hope of recruiting a wingman then. But in the last analysis, I felt in my gut that if I waited to find someone who 1. had the vacation time, 2. was healthy, 3. whose wife would allow it, 4. had no blow-ups at work the week before, 5. had no family emergencies either from a. children or b. aging parents — that if I waited for all that to align, I would never go at all.

More likely, it was just my impatience. But in my own mind I had already waited three years, and if I had to wait another five months, I would drive my wife insane with talk of The Hike and spend another thousand dollars on crap I didn't need. No, it was time to go, fit or not, accompanied or not.

But there was one last piece of equipment I could not decide whether to take — a gun.

5

The Torn-Up Camp and the Benevolent Conspiracy

"The reason people don't buy conspiracy theories is they think 'conspiracy' means everybody's on the same program. That's not how it works. Everybody's got a different program. They just all want the same guy dead."

—*James Lee Burke,* Sunset Limited

THE VIDEO BEGINS WITH THE SHAKY camera following a bright spot from a flashlight through the dark. The cameraman speaks haltingly in a gentle East Texas accent: "OK ... we just came across this camp in the middle of the woods." The camera pans back and forth as the flashlight illuminates cans, cups ... "and as you can see there's ... trash everywhere," he continues. He speaks deliberately and slowly, processing and narrating at the same time. "And the tent's collapsed. There's absolutely no cars around." The flashlight illuminates a tent not just collapsed, but crumpled, ripped, as if the poles are deliberately snapped.

"Hello, the tent!" he calls out. "Oh hell! … It's a brand-new tent. … It's torn apart. Travis, bring the big flashlight. Hello, the tent! … There's nobody in it."

Off camera, Travis, the cameraman's grown son, says, "The fire's still going. Looks like the tent caught on fire." They continue inspecting the site.

Four minutes in, the flashlight turns on the tree line behind the camp. "Look at the woods! The woods are torn to pieces," the cameraman exclaims. "Oh hell, there's something in there... The woods are literally torn to pieces. Hey look, look at the X." Two small trees are in an X formation. "That's just been done. It's just all tore to pieces, look! Shhhit!"

"It wasn't like that last time," Travis adds.

"Look at that!" the cameraman continues. "It's just torn … to... pieces, all through here."

Travis concurs. "It almost looks like a hurricane came through here."

For twenty minutes they go on to discuss the broken logs, broken trees, the fact that it was done that night, that something took a big pee. Still smoldering logs are all around the site including on top of the tent. "We're going to have to report this." Then the camera operator starts to more consciously narrate to the audience, as if starting fresh: "We came down here to do sounds and go up into the woods, and we found this camp out here in the middle of nowhere." Charcoal is strewn about. Tracks are everywhere, many of them barefoot. But they can't make heads or tails of what happened. In time they conclude logs were thrown on top of the tent. "And we have a tore-up forest, literally torn to pieces."

This online video was my introduction to an extraordinary individual named Bob Garrett. And whether that campsite was actually destroyed by Others, as is the implication, or whether it was just a couple of drunk rednecks raising hell, getting into a huge fight, and then driving off and leaving most of their gear behind, this video was my first exposure to the idea that this was something the Others *could* do if they wanted. Either it was one scary piece of cinema verite, or it was one scary piece of citizen journalism, but either way, it got my attention, and it began a long, gradual shift in my thinking about the Others.

Until then, for me, the world had been divided into those who believed in sasquatches and those who didn't. Now, the believers were subdivided again, into those who believed the Others were gentle giants and those who just believed they were giants — some gentle, some not.

I didn't know what the reality was behind the video. It's clear enough what those who posted it wanted us to believe, and it was summed up neatly by one of the video's commenters: "Some heads definitely got popped off that night. Sad."

Whether some heads got popped off that summer night in 2013, or whether it was campers in a terrible fight (there was an empty liquor bottle among the litter) or whether it was all a setup, the video's significance was, as I say, that it introduced into my thinking a possibility — that sasquatches were not always what I had assumed they were — an uncannily furtive primate, an ever-receding target, something that *always* avoided man.

I knew that, in accordance with great ape and human behavior, when they felt their territory or young were being threatened they would harass and intimidate intruders. This often included throwing rocks or sticks from a hidden position, paralleling hikers to "escort" them out of an area, screaming, grunting, oofing, snapping branches or pushing over whole trees.

Scary enough. But what if a few of them, or even many, were not bluffing? Dangerous as hell. Tearing up camps, "popping off heads." In fact, I started getting the sinking feeling that there was a self-selecting quality to the bulk of bigfoot accounts in circulation: *The stories about sasquatches moving* away *from humans were all from those who had lived to tell them.*

But what of the others? What of all the people who had gone missing in national forests, national parks, state parks, state wildlife management areas, river bottoms, mountain passes, swamp lands? Sure, most are probably the victims of more mundane causes: getting lost, hypothermia or dehydration, hunting or hiking accidents, bear or cougar attacks (in the right parts of the country). But *all* of them? David Paulides has explored this notion with his book series *Missing 411*, in which he documents hundreds of cases of people who have gone missing in national parks and national forests, many with extremely unsatisfying explanations from the authorities according to the author.

What's more, by 2016 it had become common knowledge among sasquatch researchers and enthusiasts that the most aggressive sasquatches seemed to live, just my luck, in East Texas. For a long time, I could not figure out why this would be. Then one day I was reading Dan Flores' excellent book *Coyote America*, in which he writes: "Coyotes may also attack cats for the same reason they attack small dogs: they perceive domestic cats and dogs as intraguild predators operating in their territories." A light came on. If sasquatches kill humans, perhaps it is not to eat them but because of an instinct to protect their own prey, to remove intraguild predation from their territory? In nature, to survive, you have to not only kill your food, you have to kill the things that are killing your food, and that's us.

Some female witnesses report bigfoots as indifferent to their presence. But many men, and especially hunters, describe the creatures as incredibly pissed off. Why the difference? If I could channel the sasquatches for a moment, it might sound something like this, best voiced as the comedian Lewis Black and accompanied by a flailing index finger: "*Son* of a *bitch*! You *friggin'* people live *everywhere* and can eat *anything* you want at any time of day or night. Us? All we have is this forest, and all we have to eat are the deer and the hogs. So what do you do?! You drive all the way out here, come into *our* house, and start killing and dragging off the only thing we have to feed ourselves and our children! *Get ... out!*"

If East Texas sasquatches are more bloodthirsty, maybe it's simply because there are more hunters out there, hunters unknowingly competing with what easily would be the apex predator but for the existence of gunpowder. Do the Others know a hunter from a non-hunter? Do they know what a gun is? Some say they do. They might not know why gunpowder works or the mechanics of bullets and rifle barrels, but they probably know that when men hold those long black sticks up to their faces, deer get taken out of the forest.

When I would broach the subject of the Others with a friend or acquaintance, the first question from them would almost always the same: Why haven't we found a body? People in general seem to be able to countenance the fact that we haven't captured one alive, but they cannot get past the fact that we have no bones.

Occam's Razor, a basic principle in logic, holds that the simplest explanation (the one that requires the fewest assumptions) is generally the best one. Unfortunately, in this case, the simplest explanation for why there are no bodies makes me sound even crazier than I already do. And that explanation is simply to reject the premise. Why haven't we found bodies? Well, we *have*. And the reason most people don't know that is ... I guess I'll just say it ... that the government is covering it up. See? Told you I would sound crazier.

I suppose this belief officially relegates me to the lowest of all human life forms, the conspiracy theorist. It is a theory based on a conspiracy. But just because a theory involves a conspiracy does not make it false. Allow me to put on my tin foil hat and explain.

Government conspiracies exist. Without even really trying, we can think of the "Tuskegee Study of Untreated Syphilis in the Negro Male," in which hundreds of black men were denied treatment for syphilis over a period of forty years, during which time penicillin had been proven effective, all the while the government denying it was happening. There was the Gulf of Tonkin incident, which is a case of the government completely fabricating a confrontation to justify a war action, covering up the fabrication for decades, then finally admitting it. Incidentally, that conspiracy led us into a war that cost 1.35 million lives, 58,209 of them American. There was the Iran/Contra conspiracy, in which agents of the U.S. government illegally sold arms to Iran, an enemy nation, and used the proceeds to fund rebels in Nicaragua, an act which also was illegal under the Boland Amendment. Anyone who thinks the government is not capable of covering something up is just not adequately familiar with history.

What's more, if they wanted to cover up the existence of the Others, would it not serve their purpose if the whole subject came to be seen by the general public as kooky and the province of fringe lunatics? Who knows how much of a hand government has had over the years in sowing the seeds of doubt, hiring freelance hoaxers to muddy the waters.

Nor would I be surprised to learn that government operatives had convinced those who have found them to walk back their stories with bribes or offers they can't refuse. Government has the means, and it has multiple motives, of which more in a moment.

To claim elements within our government are covering them up is mostly just a matter of inductive reasoning: If so many thousands of people have reported seeing sasquatches, then they probably exist. But they would not be in dispute if there were not some cover-up of evidence. Therefore, there must be a cover-up, and the only entity that *could* effectively cover it up is the government.

Now, we're in a tough spot, because a government conspiracy is extremely hard to prove. It is hard to prove because it is the government itself we most often turn to for authentication — as the arbiter of truth. In this case, the parties involved might include the Department of Agriculture, which oversees the Forest Service and 154 national forests encompassing 193 million acres of public land, the Department of the Interior, which oversees the National Parks, and the Smithsonian Institution, which has been accused of cover-ups for years. (Interestingly, the Smithsonian Institution reports to no cabinet-level agency but is its own agency, overseen by a board of regents that includes the vice president, the chief justice of the Supreme Court, and fifteen others.)

These are the agencies that are most authoritative about our nation's forestlands and wild places and natural history. But if you went to these agencies for answers, and they were conspirators, then you are exactly nowhere. You would expect them to refute the allegations, which of course they do on the rare occasions they deign to respond at all. Search on "forest service" and "sasquatch" and you get an oh-so-hilarious press release from the USDA's communication office dated April 1. For its part, the Smithsonian, through its eponymous TV channel, cashes in on sasquatch interest with the sensationally titled *The Missing Evidence: Bigfoot*, then methodically lays out arguments to explain it away: a Yale psychologist calmly explains pareidolia, in which the brain is compelled to recognize faces and bodies wherever possible, and also the phenomenon of priming, seeing things because they are on our minds. "If the popular milieu is getting us to think of bigfoot or Jaws, or whatever it is, that's going to make it all the more likely to actually perceive that concept in any context where the information is ambiguous." Oh how I wish these talking heads would spend one night with me in Sam Houston National Forest. Would they consider their own urine-soaked pants to be "ambiguous information"?

Sure, there are many academic and scientific establishments that are not under the aegis of the federal government. But consider how deeply the federal government is entwined with the academic establishment and the leverage it has over the scientific research community in the form of billions of dollars in annual research funding. The federal government comes as close as it is possible to having complete control over the scientific enterprise and in declaring what is and is not real in our world.

But while a government conspiracy is extremely hard to prove, it is, of course, *impossible* to disprove. You can't prove a negative. And in and among our sprawling crazy quilt of federal, state, and local government — with hundreds of agencies, hundreds of thousands of civil servants, elected and appointed, and millions of military personnel — we can never say with certainty there is no corpse in cold storage, there is no genome being studied, there is no plan to deal with the conundrum of another hominid roaming our continent. Conspiracy — nearly impossible to prove, and completely non-falsifiable.

With all of that said, I am deeply skeptical of theories that describe conspiracies that are long-running, vast, uniform, and complex, because I don't believe humans in general are disciplined enough to keep such secrets for very long. When I say "conspiracy" I am not suggesting Illuminati, Templars, Bilderberg, and the like. I am suggesting a *patchy* conspiracy — a district manager here, a sheriff's office there, maybe an agency-level executive but more probably a loose confederation of mid-level career people with occasional brass brought into the loop if things get too hot. Nearly 40 million Americans work in government jobs at the federal, state, and local level. I am one of them. If 1,000 of those 40 million know about the existence of sasquatches, does that mean "the government knows"? I suppose the answer depends on which 1,000 and how well they are connected, if at all.

In 2012, I posted a single essay about bigfoots on my blog. Three years later I received this comment on it: "Great article. I work in Austin for TPWD [Texas Parks and Wildlife Department]. These creatures do exist although most wildlife biologists don't necessarily agree based on the fact so much ridicule has been cast on this subject that no one cares to study it. These are real animals. Thanks!"

Why haven't we found a body? Well, who is "we"? There are many accounts of bodies being found. In one case, a creature was reportedly hit on a highway. Local police, not knowing how to report something that is not supposed to exist, cordoned off the area and called a higher authority, the state, who, facing the same dilemma, in turn called the National Guard. The subject was allegedly hauled away in an unmarked van, never to be reported or officially acknowledged.

Another account tells of a live subject who, dazed and injured, wandered out of a Nevada forest fire and, finding himself surrounded by firefighters and EMS, simply "surrendered." He sat before them and reportedly even allowed himself to be cared for for three hours before he was eventually taken away in a utility vehicle without official report.

Yet another account holds that multiple sasquatches were killed on Mount St. Helens during the eruption of 1980. They were allegedly airlifted out by Chinook military helicopters, hairy arms and legs hanging lifelessly through heavy nets below the choppers. The pile of bodies rested briefly under a tarp flanked by armed guards before they were trucked away on covered flatbed trailers.

These accounts are, by definition, hearsay, and subject to serial campfire embellishments. But it doesn't require a widespread conspiracy theory to imagine that when government officials suddenly face an unprecedented and sure-to-be-sensational situation, they would opt simply to make it quietly go away, "unmarked van" style, rather than risk being swept up in a media circus with which they forever would be associated.

Some tell of bigfoot killings, in which the shooter remained anonymous out of fear of being prosecuted for murder or manslaughter. Other accounts tell of eight-foot skeletons discovered in a Kentucky cave, only to disappear into private hands. And while many people are motivated to find and document them, others apparently are just as motivated to keep their existence apocryphal for a range of reasons — fear of ridicule, fear of career damage, fear of regulation, fear of prosecution, fear of inciting hunting mobs or mob tourism, and the reflexive denial of government officials who assume common citizens couldn't handle the truth.

I learned the identity of Bob Garrett, the cameraman of the Torn-Up Camp video, through a podcast I began habitually listening to in 2016 called *Sasquatch Chronicles*. The podcast's creator and host, Wes Germer, an investigator living in Washington state, interviewed a wide variety of witnesses about their encounters. Garrett, a resident of Montgomery, at the southwest corner of the Sam Houston National Forest, who had spent the better part of two decades "squatching in that forest" ("squatching" being a term of art for bigfoot investigation), was a regular on the show, and, in a folksy East Texas drawl and a humble, down-to-earth demeanor, matter-of-factly told the most astonishing encounter stories you will ever hear.

Garrett's many hours of testimony on the show can be boiled down to this: His first encounter was as a teenager in East Texas. Years ago he moved near Durango, Colorado, where he spent five years prospecting for gold, and while there saw them on multiple occasions, even living near one, who Garrett says may have carried him out of the wilderness when he was delirious with a fever.

Garrett led bigfooting expeditions in Sam Houston for several years. He believes sasquatches are in there from one end of the national forest to the other. He's seen them so many times he has created maps showing their travel corridors and "can practically predict where they're gonna come out" of the thicket. "This is an all-the-time place," he says. He describes a highway-like network of crisscrossed trails on which they travel that start just beyond the wall of yaupon that borders just about every human trail. Beyond the easy reach of roads and human trails, he says there are meadows in which they will rest during the day near spring-fed ponds. In the heat of the summer, they take to the region's muddy little rivers for relief.

Not only has Garrett seen them innumerable times, but he has captured them on infrared cameras, and says, "Their heat signature's fantastic. You know it's a squatch. They're huge."

"I have mapped it through trial and error. You can hear them coming down this corridor, their screams, their tree knocks, breaking limbs, [they] pick up and throw dead trees. They knock trees down and eat larvae out of them," he says. And the claims get wilder from there.

"Not far from that area you will suddenly hear a helicopter go up. It has a huge flood light, and they fly that corridor. Many times it goes over us. I believe they have ground sensors. They know that the population is getting bigger, moving up from the south. They're keeping an eye on the population out there. I've been out there for twenty-five years. I've gotten myself in trouble actually surveillancing [sic] them, because I believe that they do cover this up."

What's more, he also believes the Others are extremely dangerous. Of course, this brings us back to the Torn-Up Camp, and there have been other incidents, he says. Three in the same area. "It's hard to believe people would leave a $300 cabin tent. We find things like that." In the Overflow campground near Stubblefield Lake, right on the San Jacinto West Fork river channel, he's seen evidence of people throwing their whole tents in the backs of their vehicles and dragging them along behind them in an attempt to get away.

"[Sasquatches] go *right* through that camp and right into the Lone Star Trail, which is right across the street," he says.

"We have been out there when a woman and her child were screaming. Everybody went that direction, and the woman was screaming 'A monster! A monster is trying to take my daughter!' Apparently she described a squatch... It opened the tent and tried to take the kid."

"We run into them out there, and we run into them in an area near Coldspring," he says. I filed that away.

Garrett declares forthrightly he believes sasquatches have killed people in this wood. He says that two people are missing and presumed dead from the Torn-Up Camp episode. He says the only reason he knows that two are missing from the camp is that he and his son were interrogated by law enforcement after posting the video, and that fact came out in the questioning. The sole survivor has not come forward. The Torn-Up Camp story has taken on a life of its own beyond Garrett's claims. The lore now holds that the two dead victims were found stuck high up in trees, with the barrels of their long guns bent at right angles. To me this sounds like an embellishment to a story that hardly needed one; again, I don't know.

But this episode aside, "A lot of people go missing out there," he claims. On one road they found twenty human bones, a matter that is in the criminal courts, Garrett claims. "They find them [bones] all over the Sam Houston National Forest, from one end of it to the other, and they find them in what is known as bone yards." Most of the bones in these bone yards are of deer, hogs, and smaller animals, but mixed in with that, "sometimes you might unfortunately find a [human] femur," he says with a sigh of melancholy resignation.

When people go missing, "they [law enforcement or the Forest Service] keep it pretty quiet," says Garrett, "and you get a story like a hunter shot a hunter." He then goes into even more colorful detail, saying that it seems like sasquatches "always" drag their human victims to water. They drag them to islands, eat what they want, and then pin the remains underwater with logs and branches. When the water recedes during drought, the remains surface.

So, to review, Garrett believes there are sasquatches in Sam Houston National Forest, that some of them are lethally dangerous, and that government agencies know all this. And finally, he believes that since there is no practical way to tell the dangerous sasquatches from the benign, those agencies are actively hunting and killing them, whenever, wherever, and however they can — hoping to deplete the population or at least keep it from growing.

He believes those involved in this — possibly an off-the-books team within the Forest Service — have ground sensors and go after the Others when those sensors are tripped. They take to the sky in Blackhawk helicopters that fly with powerful searchlights trained on the corridors the Forest Service knows they travel. He believes these "kill teams" also work from sniper's nests mounted far up in trees.

Now and then, Garrett does try to sound a down-to-earth caveat: He realizes there are things in Sam Houston that can kill you besides sasquatches. He reports there has been a serial killer out there before who was actually living in the woods, dumping bodies. And gangs bring rivals out there to execute them, he says. As you might imagine, these caveats were little comfort to someone about to don a backpack and saunter out into this wilderness. The videos of Kenneth Kramm, YouTube's smiling DIYer so often in Sam Houston National Forest, contain none of these pro-tips. Nor did Karen

Borski Somers in her otherwise immensely helpful *Lone Star Hiking Trail* make any mention of cartel violence, serial killers, or, for that matter, marauding eight-foot monsters reaching into tents to extract children. Instead, she opts for: "Walking past the picturesque shores of Lake Conroe, slipping through the bottomlands of Caney Creek, camping in seclusion near Winters Bayou, kids, moms, dads, Scouts, naturalists, and the explorer and adventurer in all of us can take something from the Lone Star Hiking Trail."

So why? Why would government agents be waging a clandestine war of extermination on an animal so close to us that in the final analysis it might not even be a separate species? If these claims are true, there could be micro- and macro-level motives at work, and you could take your pick or mix and match them.

However far-fetched all this sounds, it makes a certain amount of practical sense: From the Forest Service perspective, no good can come from the Others becoming an established reality. For one thing, the woods would fill with curiosity seekers, like me, and, more troublesome, weekend warriors pursuing the ultimate trophy. More people means more work, more accidents, more rescues, more wear and tear on what few facilities there are — in general, more *headaches.* If you are a rank-and-file forest ranger who just wants to punch the clock and go home to your spouse and kids, and go fishing on the weekend, no good can come of this huge complication to the natural order.

After a lot of reflection, I came to regard this as a conspiracy, yes, but a benevolent conspiracy. Why? Because you couldn't keep people on board with this kind of secret over an extended period of time if they didn't believe that what they were doing was for the greater good. For a model of this institutional secrecy we have the CIA. It has 21,000 employees and an estimated 4,000 foreign spies, all sworn to secrecy around a large and shifting body of knowledge, with concentric levels of clearance and need-to-know oversight by civilian leaders. That all works because for the most part they are true believers in what they perceive as a noble and even heroic cause. Granted, it is not exactly the same because the CIA is not covering up the very existence of espionage — we all know that it exists — but still, if it's true, then the spirit of that clandestine service is probably much the same. Think about it. If forest professionals know bigfoots better than anyone else, and they believe they themselves are "doing the Lord's work" by killing them, that tells you something important about the Others' nature, or, at a minimum, about how dangerous they actually are.

Let's assume for the moment that certain Forest Service managers know they exist and believe them to be extremely dangerous. They are thinking about all those Boy Scouts in the Four Notch Section. They are thinking about the retired man happily walking by himself. They are worried about the young couple backcountry camping off the trail, the ladies' birding club up from Houston.

As it stands now, these concerned managers can do something to mitigate that danger; they can go out and kill them. It is not illegal to kill bigfoots now. In practice, there is no difference between them and hogs: there is no bag limit, there is no size limit, there is no technique for killing them that is off the table. Of course, all that is true only because in the eyes of the law sasquatches don't exist. If they were to exist, imagine the cascade of restrictions and regulations immediately imposed. In this scenario, then, *suppression of evidence becomes just as central to the mission as the act of killing them itself.*

Let's play this out. If tomorrow their existence were confirmed by the government, and their purported dangerous nature were confirmed as well, what then would be the government's posture relative to citizens going into wild places? Would there be signage at every parking lot? "WARNING: You are entering known sasquatch habitat. Do not proceed in groups of fewer than five or without heavy firearms." Or more likely, would they just close huge areas to recreation altogether?

I suppose grizzlies offer our only analog for how such risky encounters might be handled by agencies and outdoors lovers. But although grizzlies are strong, fast, and ferocious in tooth and claw, they have none of the sasquatch's apparent stealth, tactical intelligence, or teamwork.

Then, of course, what would it mean for one leg of the Forest Service stool, the timber industry, if large swaths of federal land were suddenly declared the habitat of this rare and spectacular species — one so charismatic that it has firmly ensconced itself in our public consciousness even as its very existence is denied by four out of five people?

Lastly, it is interesting to ponder that Forest Service employees are under no legal obligation to report the existence of new species, although such willful ignorance certainly would not be in the spirit of the millions of tax dollars appropriated to the service each year for wildlife research. People have claimed to see all manner of things in national forests, some even weirder than these, but rangers are not duty-bound to investigate their reality; they are only bound to uphold the Forest Service's mixed-use mission — to keep things humming for big lumber, oil and gas companies, deer hunters and fishermen, ATV and horseback riders, hikers.

Nevertheless, according to some accounts, government officials have been studying them — for a very long time.

6
Cebidatelidae texicanus

*"Strange tales have been told
in the wanderings of dying men ..."*

—*Charles Dickens*
The Drunkard's Death

THE LAST ITEM ON THE PACKING LIST was the one I labored over most. To "carry" or not to "carry," that was the question. To take a gun or not. For any of the folks I was accustomed to listening to, it was unthinkable to go forth unarmed into the national forest. In fact, none would go alone either. I called an investigator familiar with the area, asking him if there were any portions of the trail he would advise against me camping on. "Oh no," he said. "There's no part of that forest I feel unsafe in," he reassured, then added, "of course, I always carry at least a pistol." He never heard the irony in his own words.

I had decided from Bob Garrett's stories that a shotgun would offer the only meaningful protection in the event of an aggressive encounter. I did own a shotgun, a bolt-action Winchester 12-gauge I had bought off one of my former high school teachers twenty years earlier. But it was heavy. I could not envision carrying it a hundred miles even to save my life. I needed something lighter, and I didn't want to pay a king's ransom for a new gun I probably would never even fire. So I began lingering over newspaper circulars from sporting goods stores longer than normal, my eye scanning each spread for the lowest number that wasn't for a bb gun or air rifle. The weight being the paramount consideration, I narrowed my search quickly to youth sizes, single-shot break-open models. But every sporting-goods store within driving distance was sold out of the models I was after.

And so it was that two weekends in a row the boys followed Sunday school by trawling through pawn shops all over north Austin while Daddy shopped for a gun. It was an odd sensation that made me think perhaps I should follow this citywide tour of pawn shop gun counters by introducing them to liquor stores and tattoo parlors. The only gun I saw that was both within my price range and was the size and gauge I was looking for happened to be, of course, pink. Was I really that desperate? I pictured the scene as I trudged into a hunter camp filled with grizzled killers bedecked in camo, and me pulling Dora the Explorer's hot pink shotgun from my backpack. "Shotgun! ... *escopeta!* (blink ... blink...) Muy bien, Boots!" I left it at the store.

I then recalled that a friend of mine had given his eleven-year-old son a single-shot 20-gauge. He invited me to drive down and look at it. And as our families are close friends, the whole clan decided to tag along. When we got there, the shotgun came out to the coffee table for my inspection. It was a beautiful firearm, but, again, too heavy, I concluded.

"What do you want a gun for?" he asked, logically enough. Suddenly the room felt quieter than before, and I felt eyes on me. "Hogs," I said, ".... mainly, although there might be other stuff ... you know, snakes and ... stuff." He nodded.

But throughout the process I had deep doubts about the wisdom of carrying at all. I had owned guns and hunted with them. But I wasn't an enthusiast, and it had been since before the boys were born that I had handled one on any kind of regular basis. Age and wisdom whispered that I was far more likely to accidentally shoot myself out there than to successfully defend myself against something that had decided I was worth the effort of an attack.

And then there was a nagging feeling that we attract whatever it is we prepare for. If I went out there like I was going to war, might I just attract a war? And if I went out there unarmed and open-minded, might I instead attract peace? Was this just new-age mumbo jumbo, or was "the law of attraction" a real phenomenon? All of these questions — the weight consideration, the greater likelihood of an accident, the law of attraction — tilted my decision away from carrying.

The dye had been cast. I was going, and against all advice and common sense I was going unarmed and alone. In the final analysis, if my hammock was smashed beside Stubblefield Lake with me in it, or if my head was popped off near Kelly Pond, or if I was ambushed and eaten in the Big Woods Section, well, we all have to go sometime, and at least I would go out doing something interesting. I would go out vital and adventurous, instead of propped up in a nursing home rec room, choking on a Werther's Original as *Matlock* blared in the corner. Or in a hospital bed, crushed to death under a Michener novel.

In 2012, a blogger by the name of Linda Newton-Perry claimed to have received a letter from a woman who purported to be the great niece of a recently deceased government scientist, "Dr. H. A. Miller." The writer claimed that while going through his papers (he had had no children, and the job had fallen to her), she came upon a letter he had written toward the end of his life, a letter full of extraordinary claims.

The universe of bigfoot enthusiasts is filled with hearsay. In fact, by its very nature, it is virtually all hearsay. The internet is constantly boiling over with incredible claims, each one wilder than the last. Every other search engine hit on the words "sasquatch" or "bigfoot" is a lame, self-evident hoax. "Bigfoot Caught On Tape!!!" Click through and see a guy with duct tape on his own foot. Or a mom or dad playing an oh-so-hilarious prank on their kids during a camping trip. For any piece of evidence that's presented as real, there quickly spring up warring camps that troll each other mercilessly about the picture or video's fraudulence or authenticity.

But over a long time, one tends to develop a sixth sense about this stuff. You come to be able to tell a hoaxed print from a real one, and to tell a hoaxed video from an authentic clip, and a story that is pure bullshit from one that is likely.

I cannot make this document, now known to bigfootology as the Miller Document, more interesting than it is in its own words, so I will excerpt it at some length. We pick up the purported Dr. Miller's narrative in the 1950s:

> It was at this same time [the early 1950s] that several of our team members were called to

Bandera County, TX [northwest of San Antonio] where the forestry scientists/biologists assigned to Edwards Plateau reported the dead bodies of a strange type of human. The first reports I received were speculating that they were feral humans from the local Comanche Indian tribes. The bodies were supposedly found in or around one of the massive caves within the Edwards Plateau area.

When I arrived in Texas, I was surprised to find 3 bodies; one adult female and two female juveniles. I examined them as I typically would any human subject. But to my dismay — one of these creatures still seemed to be alive. I became quite upset with the local scientists — but they reassured me that they confirmed all 3 were deceased.

After further investigation, I found that these creatures were not human. They, in fact, had a remarkable rapid reparative process (hence the reason one of the creatures seemed dead — but in fact was regenerating to a degree). Unfortunately the restorative abilities of the creature were not enough to keep it alive. They were massive in size and distinctly a new primate species unknown to science at the time.

I spent years studying these creatures (which are scientifically known as *Cebidatelidae*), confirming that they were most certainly not human; they were definitely of Primate origin, but with traits seen in various species of primate — most of which were New World monkey.

Cebidatelidae found in the San Antonio, Texas, area very much "howl" like a howler monkey (quite frightening to hear at night). At one point early in my analysis, I found a great deal of similarity between these bigfoot creatures and the Howler Monkey — that was until 1962.....

In late 1962 early '63 I was notified of a large human-like creature by the Redding forest service folks in California. I arranged for transport of the body to my primary location in Colorado. It was reported to me that the body was found under a large tree that had been violently struck by lightning and blown to the ground, apparently killing this large creature.

During my investigation I found the animal to be very similar to those I had studied in the Bandera County area of Texas, with some marked differences. This northern version of *Cebidatelidae* seemed to have the same new world monkey attributes I notated in the Texas animals (known today as *Cebidatelidae texicanus* or *C. texicanus*).

Miller goes on to delineate six subspecies of the animal:

Cebidatelidae arktos
Cebidatelidae nerteros pacificus
Cebidatelidae somphos
Cebidatelidae americanus
Cebidatelidae texicanus
Cebidatelidae amazonia

He then elaborates...

C. texicanus have oversized lower jaws, including massive sternocleidomastoid musculature. This must have been due to their rugged diet and, moreover, their need to crush bones. Their lower dentum at first looked as a second row of molars. But after years of research and examining the dead bodies of these animals, I have found that the lower molars are simply oversized or fused resulting in massive, bone crushing tools.

Due to their jaw size and bone crushing dentum, it is also clear that all sub-family of this creature are omnivorous, predacious and opportunistic...
All of my experience with this primate has been post-mortem, save a few unique experiences in the wild. To my knowledge a live specimen has never been captured except for once in Northern Research station in California. However, the animal did not survive in captivity and died after only several days.

I, of course, examined the body. There were many rumors that this captured "Sasquatch" was somehow magical and could shape shift and that is why it couldn't be found. The truth is... the folks at Northern Research station were very devastated and embarrassed that this live specimen died so quickly after being in captivity. So no, they are not magical. They are highly intelligent primates.

.... the USFS and the DOI is recognizing now that the natural resource industry is not the economic center as it once was. So a final decision has been made to finalize the class 1 identification of the species. There is a 20 year plan to incorporate all wildlife protection areas throughout many areas of the United States to ensure federal land protection for *Cebidatelidae* starting with California, Colorado, Idaho, Oregon, Utah, and Washington.

I was upset by this decision because the first location the species was identified scientifically was Texas. I petitioned and as a result, the Government Canyon State Natural Area will be protected, opened to the public and expanded in Bexar County, TX. The long-term plan will be to open each of these designated "Natural Areas" to the public. Once all of the designated *Cebidatelidae* "Natural Areas" are open to the public, the DOI will announce the species as an endangered New World Primate. I am not sure if this will happen, and the Government Canyon State Natural Area will not be open to the public until 2005 and then expanded later in 2009, and then again in 2012. This will all happen long after I am dead I'm afraid.

Let the record show that Government Canyon State Natural Area indeed opened in 2005, with 8,624 acres. In 2009 the city of San Antonio transferred 3,000 more acres into the reserve, and in 2013 it was expanded to 12,085 acres (off by just one year from the Miller Document's 2012 prediction). And other "State Natural Areas" in Texas have been established in the same timeframe, including Hill Country State Natural Area in Bandera County (sound familiar?)

opened to the public in 1984, and others are planned in the area.

An encyclopedia entry on Hill Country S.N.A. states: "It is designated a *Natural Area*, rather than a *State Park*, and therefore the primary focus is maintenance and protection of the property's natural state. Accordingly, access and recreational activities may be restricted if the Texas Parks & Wildlife Department deems such action necessary to protect the environment." Hmm.

Whether the Miller Document is just an especially clever hoax, reverse-engineered to closely align with events that took place after the purported author's death, or whether it is rooted some way in fact, I just can't say. But I include it because it influenced my thinking and feelings on the subject in ways that soon will become clear.

When I first read the document, I took it in and reserved judgment in the moment. I have thought a lot about this piece of writing and have accepted it provisionally as an interesting source of potential knowledge. (How's that for qualifying?) I will say that if it is a hoax, it is extraordinarily well done. I will also say this. In the early days of David Letterman's career, his somewhat odd-looking head of hair would often attract accusations that he wore hair piece. To this he once replied (paraphrasing), "If I were going to wear a wig, do you really think I would pick *this*?" If you were going to create a bigfoot hoax, would you really make the setting of your story a place, not in the remote mountains of Washington or Oregon, but right outside of San Antonio, Texas?! The story's very nonconformity to what people would expect is one of the things that, to me, lends it some credence.

So was there was a Dr. H. Miller who lived in the time and place the letter claims? Indeed, graduating from Harvard Medical School in the early 1940s. But beyond this, researchers have failed to make any strong independent connections between the purported biography described in the document and the facts of this known man's life. On the other hand, one who had led such a life might be careful not to leave much of a paper trail, so that in and of itself is not proof of falsity. As they say, absence of evidence is not evidence of absence.

As I've said, it might be hoax. But it might not be.

About four days before go-day, I got a call from my oldest brother. Ansen was six years my senior and had lived in San Antonio since he'd moved away to college thirty-five years earlier. How was my trip preparation going? he asked. He was thinking he might drive over and stay near the forest, just in case something happened. He added, before I had the chance to ask him, that camping was not especially his thing, but that he could be a sort of emergency support for me. Somewhere in his thinking was a friend who had landed in the hospital for dehydration and exhaustion recently from a similar undertaking. Ansen had set up some meetings in Houston, so he could make the most of being over east.

Well, if he was sure it wasn't too much of an imposition, sure, that would be great. I encouraged him to come out for two nights that would not require hiking. On Night Two and Night Seven I would be in developed camps with bathrooms and everything. We settled on a plan. I would meet him in Stubblefield Lake Campground on Night Two.

I was frightened, truly scared — but everything in my being was driving me onward toward the woods. Nerves were building as zero hour approached. I told my coworker who occupied the cube opposite me that he could have my headphones if I didn't come back. He laughed, but I was only half joking. In an uncharacteristic show of affection, I hugged my supervisor before I left the campus that Friday. A look of genuine concern washed over her face as she smiled her goodbye.

By the eve of my departure I was in perpetual motion, walking in short, crisp, Andre Agassi steps between the garage, which was my camping equipment's permanent home, the front room, a chaotic disaster that had become the staging area, and the bedroom, home of clothes, toiletries, and my computer.

I had kept the trip relatively quiet until now, with only family and an inner circle of friends in the know, but I was ready to go public, mainly as a way of forcing myself to jump. I took a photo of all my gear spread out on and around the pool table in the front room and posted to Facebook about my trip for the first time: "Tomorrow, I leave for a 96-mile hiking trip, eight days across Sam Houston National Forest. Prayers gratefully accepted!" A few minutes later, I commented on the photo: "I don't know ... maybe I should leave the pool table."

Fewer than five people on Earth knew this had anything whatsoever to do with bigfoots, and I kept it that way.

As I had planned to leave at dawn the next morning, I told the boys both goodnight and goodbye, nervously blinking back hot tears and clutching them a little too long for their comfort. In the darkened study, I told my wife that my nerves were getting the best of me, though I spared her the details of why that was. It was too long of a story. It sounded too crazy. Most of all, I just didn't see the point in making her worry.

Calmly she said, "You've got this," and I felt better.

I slept fitfully.

7

Where the Wild Things Are

"And when he came to the place where the wild things are
they roared their terrible roars and gnashed
their terrible teeth..."
—Maurice Sendak,
Where the Wild Things Are

I WAS UP IN THE DARK OF PREDAWN, fumbling with the last of my gear in the front room. As butterflies took up residence in my stomach, it felt like I was being pulled toward something I did not really want to do, and yet I wanted it more than anything. Continually oscillating between hot and cold, I was in the throes of an emotional fever.

My wife offered more reassuring words and a cheerful smile as I struggled through the front doorway with my pack and poles, wearing my pith helmet and carrying multiple two-gallon ziplock bags of food in each hand.

Five minutes later the pickup was pulling through a Whataburger drive-through for two taquitos and a small coffee, and after a few minutes idling in the first light of day, I was rolling to the east through heavy fog.

It was ten days until the presidential election in which America would choose between heavily favored Hillary Clinton and professional celebrity Donald Trump, and I was giddy at the prospect of entering the woods and escaping the daily ugliness of a campaign Americans, almost universally, wished they too could escape. I would be home before election day, but I had voted absentee three days earlier, you know, just in case.

The previous night, the Cleveland Indians had taken a 2-1 lead over the Chicago Cubs in the World Series. I couldn't really say I had a favorite, and in fact, in the few moments I had spent watching the first three games between bouts of sorting food on the pool table and going through my backpack again and again, I couldn't always tell the teams apart, both having a "C" on their hats and uniforms that were mostly blue. I know that's a heresy to both sides, but it is true.

Crossing I-35 I bore east-northeast through a familiar progression of small towns on Texas' Blackland Prairie — Taylor, Thrall, Rockdale, Milano. An hour and change into the drive and I was sailing over the Brazos, Texas' third-longest river, which drains thousands of square miles in an enormous watershed that stretches across the state diagonally northwest to southeast like a beauty queen's sash. This was the post oak savannah, and two minutes later and I skirted the Little Brazos River, a tributary barely visible from the highway through a canebrake and a riparian thicket of oak and ash.

Here, I always tipped my hat to my Irish great-great-great-grandparents, who arrived on these banks in 1829, when this was still Mexico, built a little log cabin eight miles from the nearest neighbor, and laid claim to a few thousand surrounding acres. They came partly because the land was free for the asking, partly because rye grew wild here, and they saw it as the perfect place to fatten their free-roaming herds of cattle and horses. They lost two babies to malaria in that log cabin on the river and soon moved a mile up and out of the river bottom. But the Little Brazos would always hold a special meaning.

When I reached Bryan, I pulled over at a newly built heritage park to see a new statue that was just erected of Eli Seale, another third-great-grandfather, this one from North Carolina. The statue depicted three men, the other two being Sam Houston, who at 6'6" stood taller than the other two, and Methodist circuit rider Hiram Hanover. I judged the likenesses to be satisfactory, took a selfie with my bronzed grandpa, and headed again to the east, still driving in fog as I approached the national forest.

The mist would simply not relent, persisting for more than two hours. I wanted it to represent a mysterious spacetime barrier, a curtain that if successfully penetrated would lead back in time to something primordial. I was piercing a veil and coming out into Arthur Conan Doyle's *Lost World,* or else Sid and Marty Krofft's *Land of the Lost.*

Before long, I was crossing the final row of pastures before the farmland was suddenly overtaken by a wall of pine trees like a huge hunter-green tidal wave breaking over me. To cache my food bags, I had to drive near to the end of the trail to plant the last bag, then make my way, cache by cache, to the start. Siri took me northeast to Huntsville, then southeast toward Coldspring.

Four hours after leaving Austin I arrived at Cache No. 5, where the trail crossed a highway near Double Lake Campground. Being close to the campground, this bag was heavier than the others as it contained both the extra-large can of Spaghetti-O's (with meatballs) and the plastic jar of Nutella, which I was sure would pull me, as if a magnet, the seventy-five miles from Trailhead No. 1 to here. I overshot the unassuming trailhead, then made a U-turn and crept along the shoulder until I spotted it. Parking the truck half in the grass, I grabbed my old rusty shovel out of the bed with one hand and the two-gallon ziplock bag with the other and trudged across the grassy easement and into the tree line. I had come up with a default rule that I would try to plant each of the bags within ten paces of whatever sign or marker was there, just to limit the area I would have to search. Finding the sign to Double Lake, I went ten steps away from the trail into the thicket and started digging. With the bag in its shallow grave and covered, I found a stick and shoved it a few inches into the sand to mark the spot like a flag on a putting green, then headed back to the truck.

Turning the Jerry Reed CD off to better concentrate, I consulted the two pages of complicated driving instructions I had scribbled in pencil the night before and made it to the next cache point. It was only about ten minutes' drive from the last one, but in a week's time it would be a seven-mile, half-day hike involving a bridgeless river crossing.

The national forest is not a solidly contiguous area, and there were numerous ranches grandfathered into the system and little towns that the timber has had to thread its way between. As for that curtain of fog, I did not think I had gone back in time, *Land of the Lost* style, but I was definitely in a different world. The front yard of almost every farm house was bedecked with a "Trump-Pence" sign and occasionally, for good measure, one reading "Hillary for Prison." I was "not in Kansas anymore." On second thought, maybe I *was* in Kansas. At any rate, I was certainly not in Austin, which politically is often described as a blueberry floating in a bowl of tomato soup.

I buried the next bag in the same fashion, marking the spot with an upright stick, and continued to rinse and repeat. Parking on the shoulders of highways and dirt roads and walking in and out of the tree line with my rusty shovel, I'm sure I looked for all the world like a serial killer disposing of evidence, albeit in the most inefficient way possible. It took me the better part of three hours to bury all those bags, and I became quite nervous as I drove for twenty minutes here and thirty-five minutes there, at highway speeds, all the while imagining covering all that territory on foot.

But at last I reached Trailhead No. 1. I parked the truck, set the brake, killed the engine, and started scrupulously putting the contents of my pack that had strayed onto the seats back into their place. Once it was all on my back, I peered into the cab hard one last time, drew a deep breath, locked the door, and slammed it shut.

As a gastronomic last hurrah, I had planned to grab a hamburger in Bryan, or Huntsville, or Coldspring. But in my haste to get to the trailhead, I had not stopped anywhere and thus not eaten anything at all. I wasn't hungry, but with the impending scarcity of opportunities I felt compelled to eat. Wade had given me a package of BelVita crackers, apparently favored by runners, which he was and I was not, and I crunched them down as I paced nervously around the parking lot.

I extracted the telescoping selfie-stick from my front pocket, mounted my phone in its clamp and took a picture of myself in front of the hiker gate. I imagined this would function as a "before" shot, with me looking fresh, plump, and clean, all in contrast to what the "after" shot surely would show eight days hence.

A mother and her five-year-old were playing with the sand and pine needles in the parking lot, perhaps after a short hike of their own, perhaps waiting for someone to come out of the woods. I told them what I was doing and demanded the boy give me a knuckle-punch for luck. Proceeding to the kiosk, I dug through the inch-thick stack of hiker registration cards until I found a blank one, then filled it out with the golf pencil provided. Most of the cards I read there were older than three weeks, and I could not decide whether to be comforted by the fact that there had been no need to review them during that time or alarmed by the fact that they were so seldom collected.

A shot of self-satisfaction came as, in the blank for DESTINATION, I penciled in the words "THRU-HIKING ENTIRE LSHT." I stuffed the card in the box and proceeded to feed myself through the narrow zig-zagging hiker gate that marked the true start of the trail. The gate is designed to let hikers through but keep horses out. Almost stumbling, I took the first, hard step as if I were being birthed into the forest.

0.0

I fixed my eyes immediately on the first set of blazes, white metal rectangles, two-by-four-inches, nailed to the trees that mark the trail. If they are straight up and down, walk straight past the tree. If they are diagonal, look for the path to bend in the direction the blaze does or risk losing the trail. I have learned over the years the original meaning of the term "trailblazer" is known to almost no one, and I enjoy seeing the light of recognition in eyes who behold "blazes" on the "trail" for the first time. In pioneer days, trails were blazed by simply taking out the hatchet or the Bowie knife and removing a chunk of bark and cambium to expose a white strip that other sojourners could see and follow. On the opposite side of the tree, you notched out another one so you could spot it coming or going. But those notches weather and grow over with bark or moss, and so metallic blazes were what I became trained to look for, nearly subconsciously, every fifty yards or so.

As impressed as I always was by the wood when I first entered it — because I grew up in a land too arid for conifer forests and because of my urban/suburban existence generally — I can only imagine what all this must have looked like two hundred years ago.

In 1816, this was still part of Spain's vast New World territory. At that time it would have been truly primordial, touched only by the hands of the region's native tribes. They occasionally burned the woods to clear out understory thicket and flush game toward waiting hunting parties, but other than these changes, which were merely tweaks by modern standards, it was just the way God had made it back then, and its trees would have been 150 feet tall.

Sam Houston National Forest is a part of a region known as the Big Thicket, which is hard to delineate but which explorers considered the heavily wooded area south of the Old San Antonio Road, east of the Brazos River, north of La Bahía Road, which ran along the coastal prairie, and west of the Sabine, Texas' eastern border. Ten thousand years ago, the Big Thicket was roamed by mastodons, elephants, Taylor's bison, the American horse, camels and tapirs and giant sloths, giant beavers and giant armadillos and saber-toothed tigers and dire wolves. It's never been all that safe in here.

In the late eighteenth century the Alabamas and Coushattas began to settle on the northern and western fringes of the thicket. The first person to lay a personal claim to the area was Lorenzo de Zavala, whose 1829 Mexican land grant included the Big Thicket. But no Mexicans came, and the first settlers to move into the thicket permanently were Anglo-Americans in the 1830s.

Mexico's short rule of this land, barely longer than a decade, would at first glance seem completely inconsequential. But in fact, it was the turning point. It was said that during Spanish rule, not even a bird was allowed to fly across the Sabine from the United States. But when Mexico took over, the unstable, constitution-a-year government invited Anglo settlement. Before the Texas Revolution, some 30,000 Anglos had moved into the region known as Tejas y Coahuila, along with 5,000 of their slaves. The Big Thicket became a refuge for runaway slaves before and during the Civil War, but the core population of the Thicket was and as of this writing remains overwhelmingly white, Anglo, and Protestant.

By 1860 there were 200 saw mills in East Texas, which might sound like a lot. But it was nothing compared to the wholesale destruction of the forest that began in 1880. With the first push of railroads into the area, "the Bonanza Era" had arrived. In the half century between 1880 and 1930, lumber companies pushed steadily through the entire region, clear-cutting these timberlands and hauling the wood out on rails. By 1907 Texas was No. 3 lumber producer in the country, cutting 2.25 billion board-feet that year.

Lumber towns, isolated as they were from the outside world and monolithic in their raison d'etre, were virtually feudal societies, with company owners the lords. In the Angelina National Forest, just northeast of the Sam Houston, you can still see the remains of a lumber ghost town named Aldridge. In 1905 Hal Aldridge entered the area with ox-carts and built a wooden saw mill. The next year, the Burr's Ferry,

Browndel & Chester Railway built a spur into the mill. A rail spur was like a shot of growth hormone, and a town sprang up around the mill. By 1911 the town of Aldridge counted seventy-six buildings — houses, a hotel, company store, offices, a warehouse. That year, the wooden mill burned down and a new mill was built using concrete. The new mill with its updated equipment produced 125,000 board-feet per day. It ran continuously until 1923. When the surrounding forests had been converted to a shadeless plain, the mill was closed, and by 1927 the town was abandoned, the whole life cycle of the community lasting barely twenty years. But those concrete mill walls are still visible today, covered in spray-painted graffiti and surrounded by a ninety-five-year-old forest. Trees grow inside the buildings as if taking their deferred revenge on Hal, having the last laugh. Coming upon the scene feels like happening onto Mayan ruins in the jungles of Central America, but they are twentieth century ruins … again, think Planet of the Apes.

While 1907 was the peak year for lumber in Texas, the onset of World War I and the pine-based ship building that ensued kept demand artificially high throughout the 1910s. Lumber companies followed a "cut-and-get-out" business model, clear-cutting followed by complete abandonment. Eighteen million acres were cut during the Bonanza Era. The largest lumber companies moved on to rape the Pacific coast.

In the 1920s, some Texans looked around, realized that the East Texas of their parents' and grandparents' days was gone, and slowly started coming to their senses. The East Texas Big Thicket Association was formed that decade to preserve what little remained. Texas' first "state forest" was established in 1924. And in 1936, under FDR, this part of the Thicket passed into the national forest system to become Sam Houston National Forest.

Forty years on, the federal government started taking an even greater interest and in 1974 created the Texas Big Thicket National Preserve, protecting 84,550 acres north of Beaumont from the hand of man.

It was hot for late October, and I was fully loaded and soon dripping with sweat, but it felt good to be underway. As I passed mile marker No. 1, I stopped to take its picture with my phone, then continued winding my way along the trail. The rain during the spring and summer had been heavy, so the weeds and groundcover grew up high and close to the trail. Occasionally a thorny twig snagged my nylon sleeping bag, which for stability I preferred to roll in such a way as to make it twice as wide and half as thick around as normal.

We tend to forget that a mile is a pretty long way, 5,280 feet, to be precise, more than seventeen football fields. I typically walk a forest mile in about thirty minutes, and fifty-five minutes in I was passing mile marker 2. I again immortalized it with the phone camera, and in a few more minutes I had arrived at the pond where Wade and I had camped ten months earlier and had been visited at six in the morning by two woodland creatures capable of gripping sticks and knocking loudly on tree trunks. I took a selfie with the scenic little pond in the background and texted it to Wade straightaway with the caption: "Back to the scene of the crime." Odd to be heading into primeval forest and yet — with full cell coverage over the entire region — be thoroughly connected with civilization to whatever degree I desired.

Continuing to the southeast, I soon came to another small parking lot and trailhead kiosk, and I crossed a forest service road. I was now entering Little Lake Creek Wilderness, a section of the forest that had won a special "wilderness" designation in 1984 under the Texas Wilderness Act sponsored by Congressman John Bryant. It was here that I had brought my youngest son a year and a half earlier during a muggy and buggy May backcountry trip. It looked reasonably familiar despite the thicker groundcover, and I even spotted where he and I had tied our hammocks and eaten our Spaghetti-O's hobo-style (that's heated in the can next to the fire instead of over a camp stove in some high-falutin' cookin' vessel) and where we had marveled at the thousands of fireflies that lit up the woods all around us as we settled into our hammocks.

As I passed the mile 5 marker, I soon started hearing sounds fifty yards to my left through the understory of yaupon holly and American beautyberry and white oak. It was a banging, a loud, deliberate knocking that sounded like a person fashioning some piece of work with a hammer. At first I wrote it off as a woodpecker, but it didn't have that jackhammer speed to it, or the sound of any bird at work: *pop-pop-pop-pop* (pause) *pop-pop-pop-pop* (pause). No, it sounded distinctly human, irregular groups of knocking interspersed with irregular rests. Hearing it so clearly, not being able to see anything, and it sounding so ... opposable thumb-ish, the hairs on my neck started to stand out. I was on high alert.

I immediately thought: "nut-crushing stations." It was a term I had picked up from a research paper I had read earlier in the year by a group with the comically opaque name of the North American Wood Ape Conservancy.

The group's paper, titled *The Ouachita Project Monograph*, which was 228 fascinating pages, presented perhaps the most systematic and sustained study of sasquatches yet attempted. In 2011, a group of investigators learned of a valley in the Ouachita Mountains, just inside of Oklahoma near its border with Arkansas. This area had long been a hotspot for sightings, but there seemed to be one valley in particular, which came to be known as Area X, where sightings, vocalizations, trackways, and thrown objects had become routine. Here, in this remote valley on private property, the team set up a permanent observation post, and rotated in, with a new crew of four to six people coming in every two weeks or so ... for four years! Area X was not so named to be ultra-mysterious; the group had three areas they had studied extensively and had named them areas X, Y, and Z. Area X was this valley in the Ouchitas. Z was the Big Thicket National Preserve. And Y, Sam Houston National Forest.

The Ouachita team had a stated goal of "collecting a specimen," in other words, killing a bigfoot — just one — and using its body to establish its existence to science. The paper's abstract is arresting in the dry scientific language it uses to explore what is everywhere else the very embodiment of sensationalism:

> The possibility of an unlisted anthropoid species indigenous to the Ouachita Mountain Ecoregion was investigated on a protracted basis by the North American Wood Ape Conservancy (NAWAC). Surveys ranging from 60 to 120 uninterrupted days were conducted during the 2011-2014 field seasons in an area with a history of reported sightings of large ape-like wild animals. Observations recorded by NAWAC teams are described and discussed in this paper.

"Only one difficult and rocky road leads to the property, which is set in the midst of hundreds of thousands of acres of publicly and privately held forestland and mountainous formations," they explain.

During this quadrennial, the group logged forty-nine sightings. This might seem like a lot, but put in the context of the more than 12,000 man-hours of observation, here is what that tells us about the creatures' extreme furtiveness: "... generally speaking, 1 person out of a team of 4 might experience a 2-second visual contact, if the team remained on location for 10.2 days."

The team heard innumerable wood-knocks from the forest, often in apparent response to knocks they would make. They found massive, humanoid footprints in the woods and around their cabins. Rocks would continuously pelt the tin roofs of the cabins in which they stayed. And they discovered several "nut-crushing stations" throughout the valley, boulders where something with hands apparently used rocks to crack large numbers of walnuts and pecans.

For long hours, the team staffed an "overwatch" station, which consisted of a 10x10 pop-up tent wrapped in black plastic. During many cold winter nights, two snipers would sit in swivel chairs inside the tent manning high-powered rifles fitted with thermal scopes. Thus they could "see" through the plastic, but creatures outside the tent could not see in, presumably.

Two shots were taken during the project; one missed its target when a branch deflected the bullet, and another apparently hit its target, as blood was found in the vicinity in the following days, but the victim got away.

In the end, the project documented a number of facets of sasquatch life that many had known about or suspected before, but, falling short of its ultimate goal of collecting a type specimen, it was simply further evidence, not proof. Throw it on the already heaping pile.

But was I hearing a nut-crushing station in use now? The problem was, there were not that many nut-bearing trees out here that I could tell. It might have been a couple of juveniles, as the young of any primate species do not need a reason to bang sticks together, even if it produces noise that might give away their position. It was so humanlike I half expected to round a bend and see a hillbilly nailing together a platform for his still.

A fallen tree blocked the trail ahead so I decided to straddle it and rest for a minute. I took the pith helmet off, reached for my phone and switched to video mode before hitting record. The knocking persisted. I captured the audio but nothing showed itself in the video frame beside an understory of yaupon and hardwood saplings under a canopy of pines and snags.

After a minute of recording, I rose and continued down the trail, panning back and forth with my phone. I never saw the source of the knocking. That's one weird woodpecker, I thought.

Forty-five more minutes of twists and turns through the yaupon and I arrived at a long clearing. The map indicated that the hunter camp at which I needed to stay that night was just the other side of a forest service road. I studied the clearing and concluded that this must be the road in question, although it was only a "road" in the sense that the Romans might still have a few "roads" in England. There were year-old saplings growing up in the double-track's median, and waist-high weeds covered it in a haze of sage. Some blue triangles tacked to trees on the other side pointed my way left toward the camp, and after five minutes of bushwhacking along the "road" I came to a more conspicuous sign that led me off the path and a hundred feet into the vegetation, where I found the camp.

I knew there would be nothing to these camps, and indeed they lived down to billing. But I didn't need anything, and didn't particularly want anything. My first choice would have been to stay wherever I pleased, in keeping with the whole reason I began backcountry camping in the first place. But "open camping" was only available from January to September. During hunting season, archery or rifle, the Forest Service stipulated that all hikers stay in hunter camps. The experience of staying in hunter camps was virtually identical to an improvised camp because, as I said, the only thing they offered was an acre or less of cleared-out understory and perhaps a fire pit. The real impact of the rule was that you could not simply pull over and camp when you felt you had hiked enough; you had to cover a certain distance each day to make it to the next camp.

It was archery season; rifle season would not commence for two more days, but I was still required by law to stay in camps. There was a fire pit and two logs that had been sawn into the shape of a bench, and a kiosk announcing that this was a camp. That was it.

With the October days shortening and the shade of the woods piling on, I was losing light quickly. But I was hot from the fully loaded six-mile hike, and the day was warm and humid. Thoroughly convinced of my isolation, I stripped off every shred of clothing but the flip-flops I had brought along to wear in camp. A woodland creature observing me from a distance would have wondered at the pink figure moving around the site, with a short, gray crest and a blindingly white swath across its mid-section.

I hung my olive hammock between two small hardwoods and strung my olive tarp taut three feet above it to keep off the dew, insects, spiders, bird poop, acorns, and all other things that fall in the night. The sewn-in bug net would stop mosquitoes, and other invaders. I spread another tarp on the pine needles and leaf litter below the hammock and on that ground-cloth set my shoes, water bottle, and a sleeve of water crackers. As was my custom, I hung my backpack by a carabiner from one end of the hammock's suspension so that at least a little of it was under the tarp if it rained.

Despite the relatively short walk of the first day, I was good and tired. The questionable night's sleep before, my amped-up emotional state, the drive over, the complicated food caching, and the walk in on city legs had all added up. Ketosis had already set in, in which the body, having burned through all its blood sugar, begins to burn fat. With me, it is accompanied by a wretched taste in my mouth, and something that feels like a cousin to a fever. I would surely sleep well this night.

Alone and unarmed in sasquatch country, which was the smarter strategy for staying safe in camp: Was it conspicuousness, to make my presence known to one and all, building a fire and being loud? Despite their extreme elusiveness, they seem to have the primate's signature curiosity, and there is ample video evidence of them spying on human activities such as campfires, sledding, or shooting ranges from what they believe are hidden vantage points.

A fire had no appeal except to fend off regular woodland denizens like hogs or coyotes. But just as it would keep some animals at bay, it might bring others, those driven by curiosity, in. Was the wiser choice stealth, just blending into the woods? That was the strategy of most everything else out here. The downside of stealth was that something that otherwise might have stayed away could stumble into your camp unawares, forcing both parties into an encounter that neither wanted. In the end I opted for stealth, not least because building a fire took considerable effort, and fire had a tendency to be hot.

Of course, stealth completely flies in the face of dominant "squatching" practice, which is all about drawing them in. Two squatching techniques in wide circulation were trying to elicit calls by mimicking their calls, and trying to elicit wood-knocks by doing knocks yourself. While I had on earlier trips with my sons done a few calls and knocks just for fun and mainly to revel in the echo of the forest, I had sometime earlier stopped this, mainly because it occurred to me that we have no idea what we're saying to them. What if a howl to them means "deer down, time to eat"? They come toward the howl and don't find any deer, but they do find you. Then they think, "Well, he doesn't look very appetizing, but it's better than nothing..."

But was this even squatching? I wasn't even sure anymore. Was I out here looking for evidence? Yes. Was I out here looking for *Them*? Not anymore, I wasn't — not after the Torn-Up Camp.

My pacifist, law-of-attraction ideas notwithstanding (peace begets peace; defensiveness begets aggression), I could not help thinking of ways to deter visitors to my camp, and I had three items that served that purpose. The first was bear spray, which was a permanent accessory that rode on the front of my backpack's shoulder strap. The second was the GI Tanto knife, heavy, large, and sharp, but only effective insofar as something came within arm's reach, at which point it no doubt would be too late to do any good. And third, an item I had thrown in my pack on the final night of preparation, a roll of fishing line. With it, I could create an invisible fence around my immediate campsite.

So with my camp all made and hammock ready to accept my aching pink-and-white body, I retrieved the monofilament from my pack, tied it off to a tree trunk a foot above the ground and about ten feet from my hammock, fed a pencil through the hole in the spool to act like an axle, and proceeded to circle my entire site in a perimeter about ten feet outside my hammock. Once, a second time a foot higher, and third time at chest height, a fourth time at neck height, a fifth time at seven feet, and a tie-off at the end. I had no illusions about the efficacy of such a system against anything determined to get through it. It might slow down a hog and her piglets. It wouldn't deter a raccoon or armadillo in the least. A squatch would probably pause for second, curious about the strange substance, then swat it down like a spider web. But it made me feel a tiny bit safer, a little more insulated, fortified — a little.

I stepped through the gap like a ranch hand steps through a barbed-wire fence, kicked off my flip-flops onto the ground cloth, and sat in the valley of my hammock.

A sip of water, a handful of water crackers, and there was one thing left to attend to. I fetched the little audio recorder Wade had loaned me and hit RECORD. "This is Night One," I announced, "October 29th, 6:52 p.m. Too tired to eat. Gonna try to get some sleep." I set it next to my flip-flops.

With much unzipping and re-zipping, I entered my hammock and lay atop my sleeping bag, still hours away from needing it in the muggy heat of the close thicket.

Darkness fell, and despite what the calendar said, I was surrounded by a roar of insects befitting mid-summer.

I texted my wife that I had safely reached the first camp and had no company there. I texted her a picture of me smiling with a tube of arnica she had sent me with. Arnica and Tylenol were the twin pillars of my pain-management plan, and I had rubbed my feet, shoulders, and collar bones with generous amounts of the clear, sunflower-derived ointment before turning in.

All of this and more was captured on the audio recording, which I later listened to entirely in real time on headphones and logged meticulously, and so I can say with precision how the night unfolded. For instance, at 6:59, I heard barred owls start their otherworldly conversations.

It has been dark less than fifteen minutes when I start hearing what sounds like a helicopter in the distance. Hmm. Weird, I think. It's like they were just waiting for dark to send up a helicopter for some reason. Reminds me of how the military waits for darkness to begin operations, zero-dark-thirty, and all that. And it isn't passing over, as if going from Conroe to Huntsville with purpose; it is hovering low, circling, hovering some more.

Fifty seconds later, eight gunshots sound in the distance, either from a semi-automatic rifle or from multiple shooters, or both. At 7:27, a helicopter comes very close. Through my bug net, I can see its red tail lights flashing as it flies very slowly south to north about a quarter mile to my east. The chopper recedes, and again the din of a million insects fills the sound spectrum.

Now, perhaps five hundred yards away, I hear a desperate, hoarse honking over and over again. I know this sound. I heard it in a video of a whitetail deer being killed in someone's backyard by a bear. It goes for fifteen seconds, then stops. A deer has just been killed, silently, within a thousand yards, I think. Five minutes later, another one lets out two honks, then nothing.

I do not like this, not one bit. If the Others were hunting near my camp, this is what it would sound like. Bob Garrett says they are ambush predators. One will sit inside the yaupon at the end of a game trail while his fellow hunters flush deer down that trail with knocks or calls or just chasing.

When a deer passes the seated one, he simply reaches out into the trail, grabs its leg, and snaps it. From there it's an easy task to twist the head until the neck snaps or crush its windpipe with a squeeze of the hand. Is this what I just heard?

The night is young, and already I have heard not just a deer kill, but a slow-flying treetop helicopter and gunshots, all within an hour of nightfall. Of course, there were alternative explanations for all of these sounds. On the other hand, what are the odds that within an hour of dark, I would be surrounded by sounds that all supported Bob Garrett's conspiracy narrative?

My legs begin to shake, and I cannot control them. They shake like that poor bastard who saw one in the wee hours of 9/11 on the far side of Baker's Bridge; he shook for two days. If anyone else had been out there to see me, it would have looked like my hammock was outfitted with a vibrating bed.

Every twenty or thirty seconds, I hear something rattle the dead leaves around my camp. It sounds like stick breaks, but there is no walking pattern. Could be an armadillo. Could be a bird. It is the heart of autumn and acorns are falling, which make more sound than you would expect when they hit the ground and roll or bounce.

When I hear something that doesn't sound right, I hit the tree line with my Cyclops, a small spotlight with a pistol grip. I once found the Cyclops comforting and empowering. Now it just reveals a scary-looking Blair Witch woods, a forest transformed into a zebra of harsh white light and hard black shadows. And turning on the Cyclops is the one thing I do that is decidedly not stealthy. Something observing my site could see it between the trees for a half mile. It could be like a beacon guiding them into port.

The words of the Miller Document echo in my mind: "massive sternocleidomastoid musculature ... bone-crushing dentum. Omnivorous ... predacious ... opportunistic. Bone-crushing dentum .... Bone-crushing dentum."

As I lie in the hammock waiting for sleep to overtake me, I write a few lines in the journal I had packed: "Legs shaking uncontrollably. Don't know if I can do this for seven nights. Too frightening. Thought I could handle it, but don't think so. Will need serious change of heart to not get Ansen to take me to truck tomorrow."

I turn off the headlamp sewn into my tuke. I hold the Cyclops in my left hand, and in my right, I clutch the GI Tanto, sheathed, to my chest as hard as I can. I clutch it like I clutched a teddy bear forty-five years earlier in the terrifying dark of my bedroom. I should have brought a gun, or at least just waited until someone could have come with me. I should have brought a gun. I should have brought a gun.

As much as I had wanted to come out here and do this, I no longer thought I could handle it. Seven nights of this? I would sleep so little that I would not possibly have the strength to make the daily mileage required to finish in time. My adrenals would collapse. I would have a nervous breakdown requiring hospitalization.

Every time I would drift toward sleep an acorn would fall twelve feet from my hammock and skip through dead leaves. I would spotlight the woods and see only sticks, tree trunks, hard shadows. Distant coyotes sent up their alien chorus. Owls continued to hoot to one another overhead. Always, always, dogs barking at the night from a farm a half mile east. How could their vocal chords sustain such abuse hour after hour? And more importantly, what were they barking at? Deer? Hogs? Coyotes stalking their livestock? The Others?

Whatever it was refused to go away, because they barked, and barked, and barked. Could their owners simply not hear them? Or was it like a waterfall to them, something they heard the constancy of but that didn't bother them because it meant the dogs were doing their job?

As I lay contemplating everything going on around me, I marveled at how my experience would be so very different if I just didn't know. Why couldn't I be like Kenneth Kramm, innocently setting up my tripod and shooting my YouTube videos with my sidekick "Bear" and demonstrating primitive fire-building techniques before turning in for a night of great shut-eye in the fresh air under the stars? No, like Adam, I had eaten from the Tree of Knowledge, and this was no longer the Eden my sons and I played in only a year earlier. I knew what was out here in this wilderness, and what they probably were capable of doing, and what the government might be doing to them, and I could not unknow any of it.

I texted my wife: "I don't know, honey. I think this might have been a mistake. Deer was killed silently less than five hundred yards from me. Footsteps around camp." She wrote back that she'd support whatever I wanted to do. I could try again in the spring if I wanted.

I figured I was only about a mile from Highway 149. If I walked until I hit it the next morning, I could be back to the truck in two hours at the most. I could be home by noon, showered and watching a World Series game that night with a bowl of Blue Bell ice cream, and sleeping in my own bed surrounded by four brick walls.

My brother Ansen had not left San Antonio yet, and I didn't want him to drive all the way over here if I were on my way home. I texted him from my hammock saying I wasn't sure I was up for this and that I would let him know in the morning where things stood.

Eventually the helicopter and gunshots and miscellaneous crunching sounds around my camp abated enough that I drifted to sleep to the barking of dogs.

The tale of the tape, as it were, was even more interesting, because the audio recorder was not only picking up sounds from the forest night while I was asleep but was picking up sounds that were beyond what I could hear even when I was awake. Throughout the night there were more gunshots, stick breaks, and movement around the camp, a deer bugling a mating call, crazy barred owl squawking and talking, some spooky howls of indeterminate origin, and strangest of all, the sound of hooves galloping. Mind you, the recorder was on my ground cloth directly under my hammock, and three or four times during the night, including before I fell asleep, it recorded what sounded like deer running, I'm guessing one to three of them. And because the little recorder had left and right microphones, you even hear the deer running right to left or left to right in headphones. One of the first instances of this galloping was during the deer kill. I figured it must have been similar to when Plains Indians put their heads close to the ground to hear whether bison or horses were approaching from miles away.

Speaking of Indians, that night, the Indians beat the Cubs 7 to 2 at Wrigley Field to go up three games to one. For me, as for Chicago, it wasn't looking good.

8
What a Fool Believes

"The Lord said, 'What have you done? Listen!
Your brother's blood cries out to me from the ground.'"
—*Genesis 4:10*

6.5

FIRST LIGHT CAME AT SEVEN, and I was awake and thankful for that light. I slipped on my flip-flops, creaked and snapped to standing, walked out to the fishing-line fence, and peed through the most convenient of its spaces.

Returning to the hammock, I saw that the audio recorder's power light was off. I turned it on and noted that it had captured seven hours, thirty-two minutes, and three seconds, stopping for some unknown reason at 2:24 in the morning.

I reeled in the monofilament fence, circumambulating the hammock again and again as if chanting morning prayers around a shrine. As my thoughts turned to my morning *twallet*, I began to hear distant whooping that did not sound like coyotes. Was the forest being signaled that I was awake and on the move? I wondered if sasquatches had a relay system, like in the greatest scene of Peter Jackson's *Lord of the Rings* films, when the beacons were lighted one at a time on mountaintops from Minas Tirith all the way to Rohan. I could imagine the whooping starting from my hunter camp and relaying a mile at a time all the way back to my truck and, ahead, all the way up to Stubblefield Lake. "Watch for the loser in the pith helmet! You can go ahead and snap his neck! He's totally unarmed! Hahaha!" I turned my phone camera to video mode and hit record to capture the audio while I grabbed a purse pack of tissue and the GI Tanto, which you'll recall that I selected because it was sturdy enough to use as a shovel. Forthwith I answered nature's second call of the morning with alacrity.

I broke camp, getting every item folded, rolled, and wedged back into its allotted space in, on, or under my backpack, then walked out of the hunter camp the way I had come in.

Back down the abandoned jeep track I spotted the point where the Lone Star Trail continued to the east and threaded myself into it. It is at times like these, when the brush and branches crowd in on the trail from all sides, that I think of what a challenge it must have been to cut the trail in the first place. While the forest has been here for time out of memory, this trail has been winding through it for only fifty years. In 1966 members of the Lone Star Chapter of the Sierra Club were backpacking in these woods when they hatched the idea for a foot trail. Approval from the Forest Service came quickly, and in 1967 they began flagging and clearing the path. By 1972, with thousands of hours of volunteer work logged by the

Sierra Club and Boy Scouts, the Lone Star Hiking Trail was finished, though in 1979 it would grow a few more miles to its current dimensions. In 1995, the Lone Star Hiking Trail Club was formed to facilitate its use and advocate in the never-ending battle to keep bikes, horses, dirt bikes, ATVs, and all other manner of conveyance besides human feet the hell off of it. May it always be thus, but advocates on the other side are relentless, and nothing in Creation is permanent, leastwise things of our creation.

Soon I passed the Farm of the Barking Dogs. All was quiet, and so in retribution for the previous night's continuous loop of baying I began to sing loudly, then had an idea. Ready to share a little of the trail experience with friends, I extracted my phone and mounted it on the telescoping selfie-stick I carried in my left pocket. Holding the phone in front of me and almost to the ground, so that it captured me with the trees above and behind me, I launched into my best Michael McDonald impersonation, and loudly, and I mean loudly, belted 1979's Song of the Year, the Doobie Brothers' "What a Fool Believes." I knew I could be heard for at least a half-mile in every direction. Turnabout's fair play, and, just like I used to be a little louder than necessary in the mornings after a neighboring camper had kept me up with late-night noise, I hoped I was waking up those frigging dogs that had woken me up twenty times overnight. Payback's a bitch — that is to say, a dog.

I posted the clip on Facebook, and so it was that I inaugurated a new tradition I called trailaoke, in which I would post a song, and friends would request a new song in the comment section. I would pick one from their requests and perform and post it the following day. It was like Carpool Karaoke without the car, or the stereo, or the artist singing next to me. Singing in the forest is an incredible experience.

It is like singing in the world's biggest shower because the thousands of tree trunks reflect the soundwaves to each other creating natural reverb.

Now three bookmark-sized sticks of hardtack rode loose in the deep front pockets of the adventure pants, occasionally clicking against my keys as I had dispensed with the niceties of the ziplock baggie. As I walked, I broke off a chuck with my teeth, let it partially dissolve in my mouth, and then gave a few chews worthy of a pirate and swallowed the flour and salt down as a cursory breakfast.

And as long as we're on the subject of things you do on the trail that you don't do in civilized society, such as carrying food around loose in your pockets, there has ever been the matter of one's nose. I learned some years ago that it is simply an unsustainable practice to blow one's nose into a tissue the way I did fifty times a week at home and at the office. For one extremely important thing, Kleenex purse packs were my toilet paper, and it was critical to conserve them for that which only they could be used. For another thing, it takes time and energy to find a tissue, extract it, then, after blowing, tidily fold it up and then find a place to store it until you get to the next trash can. If you are asking what the alternative is, then you are not an experienced outdoorsman, because the alternative is "the shotgun," so called because of the nose's double-barreled structure. Holding one nostril shut and, with a deep breath, forcing all the air out of your lungs through the open nostril in one-tenth of a second does a splendid job of clearing out one's upper plumbing, and if there is cleaning of the fingers to see to, the next tree with smooth bark will suffice. Nothing to find, nothing to keep track of, nothing to throw away. It is also known as "the snot rocket."

The least romantic part of morning in a forest, aside from the activity just described, is the superabundance of cobwebs stretching across the trail. I could tell easily if any other hikers had been on the trail that day by whether there were trail-spanning webs. Most assuredly, there had not been.

If spiders are any indication of ecological health, then the Big Thicket must be the most salubrious ecosystem on earth. It seemed I could not walk more than twelve feet before taking another spider web in the face, often with the web's spinner coming along for the ride, then spitting and huffing, and pulling it off of my hat brim and out of my beard stubble, spitting again and then leaving a choice curse word on the trail with the web before trying to regain my rhythm. Twelve feet and I'd hit another. This does nothing for one's pace.

So it was I found a new function for the trekking poles. I fell into a rhythm in which I would plant the right, then the left, then with a flick of the wrist swing the right pole all the way out in front of me just over eye level, then mirror with the left. With the odd-looking flying saucer-shaped pith helmet, and with all of this flailing of my bamboo trekking poles, I must have looked like some giant praying mantis picking his way through the undergrowth on his hind legs and spoiling for a sissy-girl slap fight with his front. *GET 'em up! GET 'em uuup!!* At first, when I still had enough excess energy to feel compassion, a pang of guilt pulsed through me for taking apart an entire night's work with a single flick of the wrist, but it had to be done. I didn't begrudge them their daily bread, I just didn't want to be an ingredient.

I have found there are two main responses to the topic of sasquatches. The first is to say: this can't be, therefore it isn't. The second is to say: This appears to be, so how might it be possible? The first closes the door to knowledge; the second opens it. Of course, this is a pattern that exists throughout the history of scientific discovery. The first supposition, that something simply CAN'T BE, always assumes that we know more than we do. Earth *can't* be round or we'd fall off, therefore it isn't!

In a 1961 issue of *Science*, Bernard Barber wrote a wonderful analysis called "Resistance by Scientists to Scientific Discovery." The thrust of the essay can be gleaned from the major headings he used to organize it: "Scientists Are Also Human," "Religious Ideas," "Professional Standing," "Professional Specialization," and "Societies, Schools, and Seniority."

In fact, the history of science could be written as a long series of haughty dismissals, nearly always with a few mean-spirited insults thrown in for sport. In *A Short History of Nearly Everything*, my favorite living writer, Bill Bryson, recounts the woes of Swiss naturalist Louis Agassiz, who posited a theory that leading geologists thought was crazy: that ice — glaciers — could carve away earth. "Agassiz' theory found even less support in Britain, where most naturalists had never seen a glacier and often couldn't grasp the crushing force that ice in bulk exerts," Bryson writes. " 'Could scratches and polish just be due to *ice?*' asked Roderick Murchison in a mocking tone at one meeting. ... To his dying day, he expressed the frankest incredulity at those 'ice-mad' geologists who believed that glaciers could account for so much. William Hopkins, a Cambridge professor and leading member of the Geological Society, endorsed this view, arguing that the notion that ice could transport boulders presented 'such obvious mechanical absurdities' as to make it unworthy of the society's attention."

Alas, scientists are all too human. And physicist Max Planck was undoubtedly right when he wrote, "A new scientific truth does not triumph by convincing its opponents and making them see the light, but rather because its opponents eventually die, and a new generation grows up that is familiar with it."

In a little under an hour I came to Highway 149 in a full sweat and threw off my backpack for a quick rest in the dirt parking lot there. Three fleets of motorcycles roared past in formation, fouling the soundscape of the forest. I tried to summon any feeling of kinship with the riders, to think how fun and free it must feel to speed through a pristine wilderness at eighty miles per hour, without a muffler, but I failed, and I momentarily despised them.

A man in his fifties with flyaway gray hair and a Frisbee in his hand loitered around a dirty white sedan. A black dog came running out of the wood line. The old hippie opened the car door, the dog jumped in, and they drove away. Now that's weird, I thought. You couldn't pick a more challenging place in all of Texas to throw a Frisbee to a dog than the Big Thicket, but who knows? Maybe they had found a clearing a few hundred feet from the road that would allow a good catch. And whatever the quality of the sport, they had the playing field all to themselves.

Here, at Ansen's inspired suggestion, I divested myself of my sleeping bag, thermal pad, tarp, and pillow. If I were seeing him tonight, then he could drive me back here to pick up the camping gear before nightfall, so I wouldn't need to carry it all day long. All I really needed besides the clothes on my back was water, the water filter, a tiny bit of food, the first-aid kit, and my hammock, which I had decided to take in case I had a chance for a midday rest.

After unsnapping the roll from the bottom of my pack, I bear-hugged the unwieldy mass of gear and high-stepped back into the woods ten yards or so, planted it at the base of a tree, then buried it with a thin layer of leaves, sticks, and pine needles. It was probably no more than five pounds of gear, but without it I felt like I was flying, and losing the bulk of my sleeping bag mattered too, as I no longer snagged sticks and branches that protruded into the trail.

Looking both ways so as not to get mowed down by a lagging fleet of motorcycles, I crossed the highway and again disappeared into the tree line. Crossing Highway 149 was a little like crossing the Rubicon. I was now going sharply away from the truck, and thus committing to at least one more day and night of this. I was now in the heart of the Kelly Section and by day's end would have reached the middle of the Conroe Section — nineteen miles in.

Night to day was like throwing a switch in my psyche. It was never so clear to me as now that we had evolved as daytime creatures. This was our domain. The sun was shining and the birds singing as I headed into mid-morning.

In the same way that the passage of time had lessened my certainty about that first vocalization I heard in 2011, letting in the possibility that it might have actually been a coyote or barred owl or just a redneck letting out a rebel yell in the forest, the events of the previous night already were becoming gauzy memories full of doubt and borderline embarrassment that I had gotten so worked up. With daylight, the rationalist retook the controls inside my head.

First of all, about that deer I thought had been killed 500 yards from me — I wasn't actually positive that was a distress call. It was rutting season after all, and it might have just been an especially desperate mating call. (Hey, we've all been there.) The helicopter — it could have been transporting someone from Houston up to the state's maximum-security prison in Huntsville. Strange that it was so low, and awfully slow, but on the other hand maybe they were just doing night flying exercises, in case of a night rescue they might need to perform, or night fire-fighting, if that was a thing. And the gunshots, well, it was hardly the first time I had heard those after dark out here. When Wade and I were out in January, the night before the knock-and-response episode, we heard gunshots from dusk all the way to midnight. It could have been poachers, or maybe hunters going after raccoons. Could have been anything. Anyway, the day was beautiful, I wasn't in the office, and all was right with the world.

Just then, I saw two figures in the distance coming down the trail toward me. Now I could see they were two men, with strips of hunter orange here and there on their clothing and gear. Perhaps in their early thirties, they had mid-sized backpacks and hiking boots. When you haven't seen anyone else on the trail for a day, it is exciting to see another hiker, and while in the city, we truck right past thousands of people without even giving them a glance, out here, you tend to stop for a quick visit.

"How y'all doin'?" I chirped.

"Pretty good," said one. Then straightaway the other asked, "Have you seen anybody out here who looks like they might be seriously injured?"

"No," I said. "Haven't seen anyone at all, not since I left my truck at Richards yesterday." Then I corrected myself. "Well, there was one guy at the last parking lot who'd been playing Frisbee with his dog, but he left. Why?"

"Back there, where that loop meets the main trail, we found a pool of blood about like this," and he held his arms to form an oval in front of him big enough that his hands did not quite touch.

"Woah," I responded soberly.

The other man continued, "There was a blood trail going away from it down that loop trail that we followed for more than a mile."

I don't recall what I said at this point, but I didn't let on what I was thinking, which was *helicopter, gunshots*. Then the other one added, "And the ground looked like something had dragged a foot behind it, like this," and the man limped along dragging his right foot through the sand like Quasimodo.

"Guess somebody came out here unprepared," the other one said. I thought this a strange comment. How would one prepare for getting shot? Or was he thinking he cut himself? Neither scenario made much sense. You don't lose a pool of blood by nicking yourself with a Swiss Army knife.

"Hmm," I said, "maybe a deer," and then I added cryptically, just to see how they would react, "maybe something bigger."

I had learned that raising the subject of bigfoot in mixed company too abruptly is dicey, and so I had a tendency to ease into the topic if I went there at all, throwing out open-ended statements like that and seeing if the other party rose to the bait. It was similar to how early Christians approached each other in the hostile Roman Empire: one would draw an arc in the dirt with a finger or a toe; if the other was Christian, he would draw an overlapping opposite arc creating the fish symbol with which you are familiar. My two conversationalists did not complete the fish. "Well," I said after a few more seconds, "have a great hike, and take care."

"You too," they said, and continued on in the direction I had come from.

I thought a lot about that exchange over following days. There was something about those guys that wasn't normal. I mean, it was a Sunday morning, and I suppose it could have just been a couple of buddies up from Houston, getting in some steps. But there was just something about them that was both odd and familiar. They were in their thirties and were burly dudes — solid and stocky. One had a goatee. Their clothes and their gear were so put together. It's like someone had handed each of them a thousand dollars and told them to go to an outfitter and get a shirt, pants, and a pack. Top-of-the-line boots too. They were not packed for overnight — I could say that much. No sleeping bags, no tents. But if they were just out for the day, why wouldn't they have simply brought CamelBaks to stay hydrated?

And then it all gelled in my mind, their age, their build, the fact that there were two of them — partners, like in law enforcement — their similar-looking, high-quality gear. They reminded me a little bit of pictures I had seen of Special Forces. And the line of questioning — had I seen anyone who looked seriously injured? Someone dragging a foot behind them?

What if, just what if, these guys were out here "cleaning up"? What if they were the ones in the chopper the night before, or the ones who were shooting. They weren't armed that I could see, but they wouldn't be visibly armed and strolling down the most popular trail in the forest if they were part of the conspiracy. It would be concealed carry during the day. They would have backpacks that would carry break-down automatic rifles, break-down shotguns, or handguns. And the day-packs they were carrying could have concealed those.

Wow, I thought. Less than 24 hours in this forest and Garrett's conspiracy narrative is firing on all cylinders. And what's more, I might have just crossed paths, and had a nice little Sunday morning chat, with a kill team.

The whole thing made wonder. I certainly did not major in forestry, but to my civilian eyes, the Forest Service seems to take the most liberal approach possible to restricting public access to the land. Drought? Close the trails! Flooding? Close the trails! As I write this, the entire national forest has been closed to the public for a month due to Hurricane Harvey with no reopening date even speculated about. No doubt, many of those closures are for rock-solid reasons. But if there was as much "interesting" activity going on out there as I seemed to experience during nights and days when the whole forest was *open* to visitors, I couldn't help wondering what the sasquatch "management" activity level might look like during times when the entire forest was closed to the public for weeks at a time? It could turn into a war zone and no one but maybe a few scattered ranchers would even suspect anything.

If I had it to do again, I would have done a lot of things differently. I probably would have engaged them in a longer conversation. I might have even come right out and dropped the "s" word, as in "Y'all seen any squatches out here?" At a minimum, I would have turned off the Lone Star Trail where the loop trail fed into it and looked for the blood pool and trail they had described.

If that pool was as advertised, I would have soaked my bandana in it, bagged it up, and brought it back to Austin for DNA analysis. A pool that size would represent a treasure trove of DNA, more than any amount of biological evidence reported to date short of a body. So why didn't I? I guess I didn't because I was holding my goal front and center and didn't want anything, not even that, to sidetrack me. Ansen would be waiting for me at five o'clock at Stubblefield Lake Campground, and if I possessed any single virtue at all it was punctuality.

And after all, would DNA have made a difference? Eight years earlier a forensic geneticist up in Nacogdoches, Texas, by the name of Melba Ketchum had put out a call for purported sasquatch DNA samples and had received 111 of them. Most of the samples were hair, but there also was blood, a tooth, and some hide-covered muscle from one that had allegedly been shot in 2010 near Lake Tahoe.

In total, she claimed to recover enough DNA to sequence three whole genomes, and they all yielded the same result. There are two kinds of DNA — mitochondrial DNA, which passes from mother to daughter only along the female line, and nuclear DNA, which passes from father to son, only along the male line. Ketchum's results, which are available to read under the title of the Sasquatch Genome Project, claim that the nuclear DNA is a "mosaic" including human and an unknown primate, and that the mitochondrial DNA, from the mother, is 100 percent modern human. According to this study, sasquatches are hybrids of humans and unknown primates.

What's more, because of the steady rate at which DNA mutates, she claims to know approximately when the hybridization event occurred, and according to Ketchum, this species is not millions of years old, or even hundreds of thousands of years old. It began a mere 15,000 years ago.

Predictably, the publication of the study was met with howls of derision from mainstream scientists and some bigfoot researchers too. It's a long, complicated saga, but this was partly due to the unfortunate fact that in order to preserve the peer reviews done for it, Ketchum bought the journal and then published the paper, in effect self-publishing the study in an act of desperation brought on by the refusal of mainstream journals to touch the subject once they realized what it was claiming to describe. In a poorly attended press conference, she and a few of her financial and moral supporters sat at a table and presented the evidence to a handful of mainly local news outlets, who ran the item, of course, toward the end of the newscasts, in the slot that begins "AAAAND finally tonight…"

Nonetheless the Ketchum study's abstract makes for interesting reading:

> One hundred eleven samples of blood, tissue, hair, and other types of specimens were studied, characterized and hypothesized to be obtained from elusive hominins in North America commonly referred to as Sasquatch. DNA was extracted and purified from a subset of these samples that survived rigorous screening for wildlife species identification. … histopathologic and electron microscopic examination were performed on a large tissue sample. The mtDNA whole genome haplotypes obtained were uniformly consistent with modern humans. Of the 20 whole and 10 partial mitochondrial genomes sequenced, 16 diverse haplotypes were found suggesting that these hominins did not originate in a single geographic location. In contrast, consistent, reproducible, novel data were obtained when nuclear DNA was amplified utilizing various platforms. … Three of the Sasquatch samples were subjected to next generation whole genome sequencing, each of which independently yielded high quality complete genomes. … The totality of the DNA evidence suggests the Sasquatch nuclear DNA is a mosaic comprising human DNA interspersed with sequence that is novel but primate in origin. In summary, our data indicates that the Sasquatch has human mitochondrial DNA but possesses nuclear DNA that is a structural

mosaic consisting of human and novel non-human DNA.

I never knew exactly how much credence to give the Ketchum study. At a minimum I thought it a praiseworthy undertaking. The points at which it has been criticized are extremely technical and therefore something of a black box to me, not having the deep biology chops it would take to really assess it.

Her endeavor seemed plagued by a combination of real outside bias and unforced errors. Some of those are just aesthetic. The website on which the paper is now hosted is an explosion of strange fonts, garish colors, and for good measure, prominently features a cartoon in which a hand-drawn sasquatch pleads "We are humans 2." It's what one sees all too often across the online bigfoot world, and exactly what one does *not* see in the world of scientific journals. She then published a novel called *Mystic Forest: Wishes*. As I've said, stepping into fiction when you're desperately fighting to have something recognized as real doesn't help the cause.

But I don't know that a more sophisticated presentation or a lead investigator that stuck to non-fiction would have made a difference. Would it have changed the ridicule or the ultimate rejection of the study by mainstream science and media? I doubt it.

Of course, Ketchum's central claim — that sasquatches are more than half human — is richly supported by the non-DNA evidence: the shape of the foot, the shape of the hand, the variety of hair coloring, the pendulous breasts of females, their faces, featuring a hooded nose and more often described as human than as apelike, and the beginnings of symbolic communication, including some language and crude structures. For this reason alone, the study deserves better than the summary execution most sentence it to.

It was not long after the two middle-aged men disappeared behind me on the Lone Star Trail that I descended slightly into what would be one of the most intriguing portions of the entire journey, the Caney Creek bottom. It is astounding how such slight changes in elevation can shift an entire ecology. One minute, at 375 feet above sea level, I might have been in the foothills of the Rockies. The next, at 220 feet of elevation, I'm in Florida. The first sign that things were changing was the sudden preponderance of dwarf palmettos. These were not the first I had seen on the trail, but they now grew in larger numbers and began to dominate the understory.

Caney Creek had been an important feature of these woods. Just after the Civil War, the community of Dodge had formed on its upper reaches. And where it empties to the San Jacinto River, Riverside was founded in the 1870s as a station on the new railroad. German prisoners of war had been kept captive on its banks downstream during the Forties.

On my left, I noticed fruit trees. They were fifteen to twenty feet tall and ferocious two-inch thorns dared you to pick their round, yellow fruit, each just a little larger than a golf ball. I took them for wild lemons or limes, but they turned out to be trifoliate oranges, an invasive exotic from China. There were probably a hundred trees, with thousands of oranges on the branches and hundreds of thousands on the ground. For any wild creature that could get them open, this would be ground zero for sugar and vitamin C.

After twisting through the palmetto for a few more minutes I came out of the trees onto Caney Creek. Not seeing a blaze where I would have expected one, I reached into my adventure pants pocket for my trail notes — six pages of six-point type that described each landmark and turn on the Lone Star Trail. They were gone. Just gone. The adventure pants front pockets were purposefully deep, as adventures tend to challenge your ability to hold onto wallets and keys and such, and I couldn't imagine when or where the stapled and rolled-up notes would have jettisoned themselves from my front pocket without my noticing. But they were gone as gone could be, and this wasn't good.

The trail was well marked for the most part, and in nearly twenty-four hours out here, I had only consulted my notes once or twice. But when I had needed them, I had needed them. Getting lost out here is no joke, and I had learned how incredibly easy that was to do. It's not a featureless landscape by any means, but its features are thoroughly mixed. You can't look up and keep your bearings with a distant mountain range or the mega-contours of a massive valley. Here, it is as if hills and valleys and rivers have all been put into a blender and then dumped out so that all of those features are miniaturized and mixed and the landscape homogenized. If in every bite you get a little taste of everything, it's hard to know where you are in the meal.

When I was out here with my youngest son the previous year, I stepped off the trail to look at a little area that might have been suitable for us to camp in. He and I both left the trail and walked for thirty seconds toward the spot. It wasn't quite open enough for my taste, so we turned back around and took a few steps. I was suddenly and completely lost. A minute passed, then two minutes. I could not find the trail. Every direction I stared in looked like every other direction. Tree trunks, vines, fallen trees, little ravines. Even the sun was no help, being high overhead and sending dappled light through the branches to add even more confusingly dispersed contrasting detail. A stray bit of good sense overtook me, and

I stopped walking. I told my son to stay right where he was, and I began to circle him while looking for the trail. Twenty seconds or so later and I had found it. I called for him to come to me, and we were back on track, but I'll never forget the sensation of being lost so completely in less than sixty seconds.

After discovering my trail notes were missing, I reached for my phone and dialed Ansen. He had just left his house in San Antonio headed for the forest three hours away. I told him my predicament, and he made a U-turn, drove the few blocks back home, and printed out a new set to give me that night when we rendezvoused at Stubblefield Lake.

A few minutes later I came to a well-built footbridge that crossed Caney Creek and took the opportunity to filter some water. Flopping my backpack, helmet, and trekking poles on the bridge, I pulled my filtering kit out of my pack and scooched down the muddy embankment, coming to rest under the bridge like a bright orange troll.

There are two kinds of creeks in the Big Thicket — most are so muddy that you could not see three inches under their surface; the other kind, flowing over sandy soil, is crystal clear, and happily this was the latter. I suppose there is a third kind as well, "seasonal drainages," sometimes-creeks that flow only after a rain. Before my foray into backcountry camping, "seasonal drainages" would have suggested only the post-nasal drip I suffer from at the onset of winter allergies in Austin.

Affixing the hose to the hand-pump and then plugging the opening of my water bottle with the opposite end of the tubing, I began pumping water from around the minnows that curiously studied the intake hose. In the previous day I had only drunk the contents of my CamelBak bladder and one of my two Nalgene bottles, and so I filled the empty bottle and the CamelBak in about fifteen minutes, hoisted myself back up to the bridge and, now paranoid after losing the trail notes, studied the ground for anything I might be leaving behind: pith helmet, trekking poles, bandana, both water bottles, yes, yes, yes. I reached in my pockets and felt the comforting presence of my keys, wallet, and hardtack and decided all were present and accounted for. I crossed the creek and started the slow climb out of the Caney bottoms, leaving this strange and prehistoric land behind for a few days.

In a few more turns I glanced to my left, and something else caught my eye. There, perched on one of the radiating leaves of a palmetto and facing away from me — a perfect little green treefrog. Never before had I seen one of these in the wild. Two inches long, his smooth green skin was an exact match both in color and texture to the leaf he was perched on, with a couple of tiny, tan, grain-sized imperfections in his skin, making him even more camouflaged. The phone went onto the stick and I started clicking and smoothly moving the lens ever closer. At last my phone was only two inches from the frog, and still he held his ground, like a statue. It seemed everything out here understood the efficacy of freezing.

I started walking again and was simultaneously scrolling through the photos of the treefrog I had just taken when I rounded another bend and looked up just in time to see a large dark gray snake with small white spots rearing its head in the middle of the trail. I froze in mid-step as adrenaline coursed through me, just as it froze too. We studied each other with mutual respect, I like to think. I was not yet within its striking distance, so I took a slow step back. I had not brought a camera with a zoom lens, so I remounted my camera on the selfie stick and slowly moved it toward the viper as I had the frog. One click, two clicks, and it turned and slithered back to the right whence it had come and in a second was covered completely by fallen leaves and sticks. I looked out at an expanse of leaf litter in every direction and wondered what else was down there just out of view. Well, if I had not been studying the trail before then, it now had my undivided attention.

What with the wild fruit and the serpent and the crystal stream, the parallels to Eden were too obvious to miss. And sure enough, I was heading out of it, and heading east.

9
East of Eden

"There's more beauty in truth, even if it is dreadful beauty."
—*John Steinbeck,* East of Eden

AS I CLIMBED SLOWLY out of the Caney Creek bottom and gained an iota of altitude, the palmettos and hardwoods quickly yielded again to the pines. Crossing FM 1375 felt like an accomplishment. I had turned and was now entering the long, multi-day climb to the north. If you looked at a map and blurred your eyes, with the exception of an initial dip to the southeast, the trail formed a rainbow, although it wound so much that in any given hour you faced every point of the compass.

For a moment, my mind wandered to the multiple sightings on this highway to my east, where it crossed Lake Conroe — the guy who saw one as he pulled off the bridge to take a whiz in the wee hours of 9/11, the husband and wife who, independently, both saw a large male on the bridge just earlier that year. Where did that one hang out during the day, waiting to hunt the night? I might have walked right past him, bedded down behind a screen of yaupon, chewing on the starchy heart of the palmetto and finishing off the remains of an armadillo or a wild piglet or a chicken from a nearby farm.

Despite not having one in captivity (that we know of), these sightings and thousands more, along with photographs and videos, have given us a remarkably complete picture of what it is that still officially eludes us. Indeed it would be easier to dismiss the whole phenomenon if descriptions of the sasquatch were all over the board. But the consistency of the sighting record on subtle physiological points, and the convergence of evidence from film, video, photos, audio, and tracks supporting those reports, has shown us what we're dealing with.

First, among sasquatches, as among humans, there appears to be both conformity and individuality, and, we might conclude from the consistent reports of subtypes, some differentiation of breed or ethnicity, if not evidence of more than one cryptic species.

With the exception of their size, they appear to exist midway between ourselves and the great apes on a spectrum, physiologically, mentally, and socially. And the more we learn about their behavior, the more likely it seems that in some regard they resemble a very primitive version of ourselves. Some research groups, such as the North American Wood Ape Conservancy, have of course planted their flag in the "it's just an ape" camp. The problem with this is that the feet and hands are so close to human, to say nothing of the many reports that claim their faces are human too. Many a hunter has had one in his sights but has not pulled the trigger because they look too human.

On the other end of the spectrum, and underscoring this humanness, are Melba Ketchum and her camp, which hold that they are at least half human. "Forest people," they're often called. Based on her conclusions from DNA testing, she has even assigned them the scientific name of *Homo sapiens cognatus*, translating as "blood relative of *Homo sapiens*." That they are neither completely ape nor completely human is the source of all of their mystery and why their very existence is so unsettling to us. Most aspects of how they live are a mystery, but we do know what they look like:

Adult females are typically between seven and eight feet tall, as the creature in the Patterson-Gimlin Film, affectionately known as "Patty," was. Males are typically eight to ten feet. This size difference between sexes — sexual dimorphism — of course perfectly mirrors our own. These heights, as well as footprint sizes, conform to a naturalistic bell curve of distribution.

Their bodies are covered in hair three to four inches long, and this hair comes in all shades of human hair: black to brown (most common), auburn, blond (rare), gray (probable elderly), and white (probable albinism).

They are distinct from us not only in their height but in their huge bulk and muscle mass. Their shoulders are wider proportionately than humans', their limbs thicker, and their torsos appear as deep as wide. As seen in the Patterson-Gimlin Film, females tend to be barrel-chested and of a more uniformed thickness top to bottom, with chest and hips of about the same width. Pendulous breasts are apparent in females, another significant similarity to humans and a difference from apes. While female torsos appear with a relatively uniform thickness, the telling sign of a male (besides his external genitalia), is the unbelievable width of his shoulders, creating the visual effect of a V from shoulders to waist. Witnesses consistently report shoulders four feet wide, with the body ripped and shredded eliciting frequent comparisons to bodybuilders or superheroes. Their trapezius muscles, which connect the shoulders to the back of the neck, are so huge and attach so high on the neck that they create the appearance of no neck at all. For witnesses who see them head-on or from behind, this neckless look is compounded by their posture, the head low and forward, with its torso held at an angle about fifteen degrees shy of vertical.

Their arms are relatively longer than ours, and their legs relatively shorter. Whereas our arms are typically 40 percent of our height, theirs are close to 60 percent. This long-arm/short-leg body plan, suggestive of apes, allows them, according to many witnesses, to knuckle-walk and even run on all fours. While extremely fast on two legs, some have seen them go to all fours when they really want to turn on the afterburners.

Their elbows are farther down their arms than ours, and likewise their knees are relatively lower on the leg. You can see how this would create greater leverage and power by increasing the length of the biceps and triceps in the arms as well as quadriceps and hamstrings in their legs.

What's more, these proportional differences are exceedingly hard to fake and so are generally the easiest way to separate hoaxes from probably authentic photos and videos. Someone coming from the Halloween store in a gorilla costume cannot easily lengthen his arms nor adjust his arms and legs so that they hinge in different places.

All these factors — their height, their bulk, their disproportionately long arms, and their more advantageously placed elbow and knee joints — combine in an otherwise human body plan to create speed and power that can scarcely be imagined. In them, we see how powerful the human body plan can be when modified just a bit. Compared to us, their strength and speed appear almost supernatural. They push over trees at will. They pull trees up. They pull trees up, turn them upside-down, and drive them four feet into the ground. They've pulled chain-link fences out of the ground with the concrete footings still intact. Lifted and carried off full fifty-gallon drums. Witnesses describe them climbing straight up ravine walls and hillsides so fast it looks like they are flying.

Sasquatches' feet, which first betrayed their existence to popular culture, are remarkably human in form, the big toe having migrated fully into alignment with the others in contrast to the opposable big toe of the apes. While the top of the foot is hairy, the sole is covered by a thick gray pad, similar to a dog's pads, the better for trampling sticks, gravel, and other rough terrain. These "Ostman's pads" were first described by Albert Ostman, who reported being captured and held by a family for multiple days in 1924.

However, while their feet are similar to ours, there are significant differences as well, not only in size but in their apparent internal structure. They do not have a ball and arch, but are flat and apparently contain a "mid-tarsal break" that allows the heel to move vertically independent of the foot's front half. This break, as well as flat-footedness, is present in other great apes. When walking in mud, this hinge results in a signature "pressure ridge," a lateral hump across the width of the footprint created by the push-off of the forefoot after the lifting of the heel.

Like so many of their other traits, their hands appear to be midway between those of the great apes and our own, with a thumb that is opposable but not quite in the same position as ours.

Because of their massive shoulders and related muscles, especially in males, their heads often appear small in relation to their torsos. Their ears are small and close to the head, and one witness who claims to have examined a dead one reported ear canals the diameter of quarters — the better for hunting and long-distance communication.

What about that most mysterious and telling part, their faces? Their faces are especially mysterious because they are, compared to ours, quite hard to see at all. To begin with, their skin, under all that hair, is most often reported to be dark gray, often a close match to the hair itself, such that the whole head just appears to be black. This is exacerbated by an extremely heavy brow ridge. Sometimes their hair grows virtually from that brow ridge all the way up the forehead. Sometimes witnesses report a receding hairline, presumably in males. Other times the hair on the head is reported to be longer than the body hair as it is in humans and therefore hangs down like ours. The head often appears slightly coned, probably from a combination of the shape of the skull exaggerated by the upward-and-backward growth pattern of the hair on some. While they all have some facial hair, males can have outright beards and sometimes mustaches.

The eyes are large, as would be expected of a primarily nocturnal creature, with eyeballs probably the size of tennis balls. But they are set so deeply beneath the brow ridge that they are difficult to see except when they reflect light at night. The eyes appear not to have visible whites, again contributing to their featurelessness when seen at a distance.

Their faces are usually described as flat, indicating a nose that is vanishingly small in profile relative to ours, but often broad and with large nostrils. Their noses are small and flat relative to ours, but like ours they are hooded, with downward-facing nostrils, not upturned like those of the apes.

There is speculation that this adaptation allows them to swim, in contrast to other great apes. This feature, perhaps more than any other, probably adds to the perception of their faces as "human-like."

Their upper lip is longer than ours and has no cupid's bow. The mouth is often described simply as a long, level slit, hard to distinguish unless open. Multiple witnesses who have gotten a good look, some through sighting scopes, report they flip their top lips up to reveal their teeth; this is a warning, not a smile. Some but not all report pronounced canine teeth. Their jaws are extremely heavy and set slightly forward (prognathism) but not to the extent of the apes.

Lastly, another oft-reported trait is a strong, overwhelming stench. Witnesses often smell them before they see them. Theories abound, but it is so universal and so strong that it seems it must be the result of a gland not unlike a skunk's. Anthropologist Jeff Meldrum reports that great apes have glands in their arm pits that can likewise give off strong smells. The Miller Document purports that the northwestern squatches, *Cebidatelidae nerteros pacificus* if you like, have glands on their forearms, which he further claims as evidence of tree climbing and marking.

So this is what we think they look like in general. In East Texas, Garrett and his school recognize two distinct types: Type I, which he calls "blacks" for their jet-black coloring, have coned heads and are the more docile of the two. Type II, he says, are brown, have rounded heads instead of coned, and are far more predatory toward us.

It is no wonder that a creature so perfectly poised between the rest of the animal kingdom and humans is unsettling to us. Many have described it as a chimera — half man, half ape, but this is only because we have apes as a reference point. The first explorer to encounter the great apes of Africa might well have described them as "half man, half monkey," and so forth down the tree of life. It seems to simply fill a gap on that tree between apes and men, and, as such, offers fascinating potential insights into our own evolution, the transition from arborealism to earthbound bipedalism, communication techniques, and even the beginnings of structures. Developmentally, they appear to sit just before the dawn of what we would consider culture.

Many tracks and sightings occur near crude structures of snapped limbs — ground nests not unlike the gorilla's, but also lean-to's that seem to serve as shelters or perhaps hunting blinds. Other teepee-like stick structures appear to mark territorial boundaries or perhaps act as signposts leading the way home. They appear to use broken sticks and rocks to communicate with each other in clacks and knocks and to hurl at intruders. But they appear to have no real tools nor to use fire. This line between humans and the rest of the animal kingdom appears to remain bright.

And I was about to walk right up to that line and peer across.

10
Believing Is Seeing

"We have found a strange footprint on the shores of the unknown. We have devised profound theories, one after another, to account for its origin. At last we have succeeded in reconstructing the creature that made the footprint.
And lo! It is our own."
—*Sir Arthur Stanley Eddington*
Space, Time, and Gravitation

AS I CROSSED FM 1375 I ENTERED a new section of the Lone Star Trail, the Conroe Section, named for the lake the trail winds along and then crosses. Coincidentally, I also had entered a new county, passing from Montgomery County to the aptly named Walker County.

It was originally named for Robert J. Walker of Mississippi, who introduced the resolution to the U.S. Congress to annex Texas. But when the Civil War broke out and it was discovered that Robert was a Unionist, locals protested: "Did we say Robert J. Walker? We meant *Samuel H. Walker*." Samuel had the correct bonafides for the area, having served in the Texas Rangers in battles with the Comanche and subsequently having ridden into Mexico during the unpleasantness with that nation in the 1840s. In his *Notes on the Mexican War*, J.J. Oswandel writes that Walker grew ever more bitter against that enemy: "Should Captain Walker come across guerillas, God help them, for he seldom brings in prisoners. The captain and most all of his men are very prejudiced and embittered against every guerilla in the country." With Walker's mounted rifles in the lead, the army reached Huamantla, just northeast of Puebla, and during the brutal battle, Walker was either shot in the back or lanced to death.

I had some faint idea of how he must have felt. I was approaching twenty-four hours on the trail with only water and occasional hardtack, and my body was in ever-greater stages of ketosis. My muscles and joints were also beginning to complain. Every log that had fallen across the trail I took as sign from God that it was time to rest. I sat on the next fallen log and produced a clear baggie containing so many pain relievers it looked like a Border Patrol seizure. I swallowed two acetaminophen, stuffed the baggy back in my pack, and with a heavy sigh stood and continued winding along the trail.

The late morning was hot, and it seemed a long time that I wound through the thick, close stands of American beautyberry to the north and east. At long last a ribbon of sky blue at the horizon came into view and grew ever thicker until I had arrived at the western shore of Lake Conroe. The air was fresher and cooler, and the whole scene lifted my spirits. While I had stashed my sleeping bag, thermal pad, and other camping gear down on 149, I had kept my hammock, and for this very reason. I had walked farther already that day than I had walked on all of Day One and needed a break. I strung the hammock between two oaks right by the lake, kicking off my shoes and hanging the wool Icelandic socks on the ridgeline of my hammock in the hopes they would dry out a little.

Within two minutes of me lying back in the hammock, my site was overrun by three teenagers, two girls and a guy who, through the easiest job of eavesdropping ever, I deduced were from nearby Conroe, the city at the foot of the lake. My feet and back were thankful for the rest and the cooler air off the lake, but it was not as relaxing as I had fantasized it would be, as the three took turns walking out over the water on a log and the girls continually shouted good-natured insults and commands at each other and at the boy. "Shut UP!" one would scream as the other two would laugh. "She's like 'AAHHHH' and he's all 'OHHHHH!'" "You're such a DORK!" "You BETTER not push me!" "(mumble mumble) ... Shut UP!" And so it went for the entire twenty minutes I had given myself to rest. Not a care in the world, I thought, smiling at them from the hammock.

Those three screaming teens did make me feel old, of course, as many things did. But I was essentially happy to have seen them and spent those twenty minutes watching them scream at each other and push each other off the log, and to relive my own high school days for a moment, chicks and dudes using their new driver's licenses and newly acquired wheels to get to outlying places beyond the immediate reach of their parents and playing in and around water. Joshing and teasing and soaking in that hormonal stew that makes every interaction with the opposite sex ambiguous in its motive and its potential. Plus, and this might sound odd, it was refreshing to see any people at all. It is interesting how fast we miss them, even introverts like me, when they are gone.

Soon, the Icelandic socks were back on, and I was shod and coiling the hammock back into its stuff-sack and removing the straps and carabiners from the trees. "Y'all have fun," I said as I left them behind at the shore, and I meant it.

Now the trail led cruelly away from the lake, due west, when I wanted to get northeast, far enough for the water to be completely obscured again by the vegetation. Through this section, the trail had a tendency to wash out completely from underneath tree roots, so much so that, with the understory pressing in from both sides, I occasionally had no choice but to balance on the roots, as if walking on a ladder that was lain horizontal between two buildings. Again, the trekking poles paid their own way, helping me to keep my balance as I stabbed them into the banks on either side of the wash-out.

About a mile south of Stubblefield Lake Campground I started seeing them. Shapes, stamped into the sandy trail, bare spots among a thin bed of pine needles.

They were triangles, essentially, triangles with rounded corners — each side a different length and therefore each angle different as well, two acute, one obtuse if ninth-grade geometry still served me.

Something deep inside me knew this shape, knew what it meant. Usually the longest side pointed the way straight down the trail. The shortest side turned back toward me slightly, perhaps forming an inner angle of about thirty-five degrees. The final side angled on back and connected the short to the longest side through a lazy curve at the bottom. There was another, and another. Now two in a row. Triangles, triangles.

Some were traveling with me, others toward me. Occasionally they seemed to cross the trail as well. Even more interesting, they came in two distinct sizes. The larger size was about three inches longer than my shoe; the others were smaller, about half the length of my shoe, but the very same shape as the larger ones.

If I did not think of these as footprints already, now I noted they were distinctly left and right in shape. There were no slam-dunk trackways, but there were enough specimens to clearly see the symmetry one way at times, and then the other.

What little doubt I might have harbored began evaporating more quickly now. I had entered a hot area. Don't get me wrong — these were not clear prints, as are ones left in the snow or in mud that has dried to the perfect Play-Doh consistency. I could not really make out any toes, the essential component of any good track. (The advent of those running shoes with compartments for each toe was a serious blow to the sasquatch research world.) These bare patches in the trail would not even have drawn the eye of anyone who was not already looking for something, let alone convince someone who did not already believe.

But I did believe, and so I was looking, and so I saw. Some say seeing is believing. But sometimes believing must come first. Sometimes believing is seeing.

I had always been curious as to why God seemed to put such an emphasis on the need for faith. Why is faith even necessary? Why wouldn't God just take some corporeal form, land in Times Square, perform a hundred irrefutable miracles once the TV crews arrived, and we could all be done with the doubt and the debates around faith?

Maybe this was the reason — believing is seeing. If we don't believe, we don't look. And if we don't look, we rarely see. We don't see the Creator's signs — the beauty all around, the unlikely existence of love.

As I mentioned, the sasquatch mystery is a strong acid test that reveals how people approach mystery of any kind. It's my observation that it separates us humans into six categories:

1. The *Seeker* is at the beginning of his investigation. This was me twenty years ago. He is open-minded, which means he asks sincere questions and, being detached from preconceived notions and committed to the truth, is willing to follow the answers to those questions wherever they lead. As he is at the beginning of his journey he is not committed to belief or disbelief. He exercises "healthy skepticism" but is not only willing to be convinced but willing to put effort into his own independent investigation.

2. The *Rational Believer* has seen or learned enough to be convinced, believes in their existence but continues to look to explain various situations first by ordinary means before resorting to the extraordinary: It's a bear track until there's no way it's a bear track. It's a coyote until there's no way it could be a coyote.

3. The *Knower* is a subset of the Believer category, but he often eschews the term "belief" as insufficient. He does not need belief because he has encountered the creature first-hand in an unambiguous way. Many witnesses will say, "I'm not a believer; I'm a knower."

4. In contrast to the Rational Believer, the *Runaway Believer* becomes so intoxicated by belief that anything and everything not immediately explained by something else obvious is a bigfoot. To him, sasquatches are everywhere and responsible for every broken tree limb, every carcass, every ambiguous impression in the mud.

5. The *Skeptic* simply says "show me." His chief vice is laziness. The Skeptic, in my typology, prides himself on maintaining a sort of cynical pose, and so, unlike the Seeker, he will not lift a finger to investigate a matter sincerely for himself. Rather he leaves the matter of investigation entirely to others, and the Believer must overwhelm him with iron-clad proof before he will be moved. But at least he *can* be converted if that overwhelming proof is provided.

6. *Denialists* generally refuse to examine evidence at all. They group this topic with all other outrageous claims or forms of mythology: "I don't spend my time investigating the reality of unicorns, the Easter Bunny, or a living Elvis, either," they might say. When compelling evidence is shown to them, they eschew Occam's Razor and, in order to explain away a phenomenon they cannot make peace with, reach for explanations that are more outrageous than even the extraordinary reality. Denialists are Skeptics gone to an irrational extreme.

For Denialists, no amount of photographic, video, or audio evidence, and no supporting evidence such as footprints, scat, hair, or the like, even in the aggregate, is convincing. They cannot distinguish between the extraordinary and the impossible.

They would never acknowledge this, but their disbelief is actually a form of dogma, since they will never subject it to the evidence. To maintain their disbelief, this group accepts, without any critical examination, outlandish explanations designed to dismiss the phenomenon. A costume artist claimed to have been hired to dress up in a suit for the famous Patterson-Gimlin Film. And to the Denialist, it's *case closed*, without any critical look at whether his claim squares with the evidence on screen — whether even a state-of-the-art costume in 1967 could achieve the effect of biologically realistic muscle groups flexing and bulging under the surface of the skin, whether such a costume could achieve the odd limb-to-torso ratio seen in the film, with knees and elbows bending at points impossible for any normal man, and whether the man claiming the hoax in such a costume could achieve the height of the creature, which has been established by multiple methods at above seven feet.

Likewise, Ray Wallace claimed to have commissioned some wooden feet and faked prints over a period of years, and for the Skeptic and Denialist, that's good enough to explain away all footprints everywhere. "Case closed!" the news anchors proclaimed. Never mind the appearance of the creatures over the entire North American continent since well before European contact. And does it matter to skeptics that the wooden feet don't match any of the footprints that have been cast or photographed, let alone all of them? Not to the Denialist.

This willingness to accept lame theories that supposedly explain away a persistent phenomenon ("all UFOs are ball lightning or swamp gas") without real examination can only be explained as the result of three forces that are strong in the human condition and reveal themselves when humanity is challenged by either supernatural or preternatural experience: ignorance, arrogance, and fear.

Another hallmark of the Denialist is his shifting criteria of proof. The Denialist asks, "Why are there no clear photos of a sasquatch?" Show him a clear photo and he says, "This is obviously a hoax. It's too clear. Only a hoax would be this clear!" Show him something less clear and he complains, "Well this could be anything!" Whether consciously or subconsciously, he concocts criteria that can never be satisfied.

Had the triangles — the prints — really just started? Or had they been there all along? According to the sighting record, and especially Bob Garrett, the Others lived "from one end of the forest to the other." So was it like eyes adjusting to the dark? Did I simply have to put in eighteen miles before I started realizing what had been in front of me all along?

Because the larger impressions were a little larger than my shoes and the other prints were much smaller, my theory immediately was that I was tracing the path of a mother and child — a mother and a brother from an Other, as it were. I tried to picture the scene: the mother smoothly gliding along, as they are said to move, maybe looking like Patty, the subject in the Patterson-Gimlin Film. The child — maybe a little female, picking up the ways of foraging termites and pine nuts from her mother, maybe a little male, venturing too far away from the mother and earning a whistled scolding or a stick thrown at his head in reprimand for being too noisy.

About four o'clock I passed a family of *Homo sapiens* out for a walk. I knew I was getting close to my goal because no one had packs on and there were small children in tow, both of which meant I was probably within a mile of the campground.

The lake came back into view on my right now, and at last I spied a bath house on my left. I had reached Stubblefield. Crossing the asphalt camp drive from the bath house, I flung down my pack, trekking poles, and helmet on a picnic table, then rose and returned to the trailhead. There I spotted the stick rising up out of the sand like a tiny monument, and after a little probing with my index finger I clamped down on a corner of the two-gallon plastic bag and pulled. Out it came, a little dusty, of course, but otherwise no worse for the thirty hours it had spent underground. There was not much that could have happened to it, I suppose, but it was still a victory that my little system of food caching had worked.

Of course, that victory was tempered by the fact that I no longer really needed the system at all; Ansen would be here in a few minutes if he wasn't already, and if we wanted to we could drive into downtown Houston for filet mignon and Alaskan king crab.

I had done two days of the eight-day hike. Tonight would surely be better than Night One because I was surrounded by other campers. But I was insanely tired from the first nineteen miles of my trek and was not yet convinced I even wanted to do the whole thing. Ansen's arrival meant that I could tap out if I wanted to, and just that possibility kept me stirring the pot of deliberation and kept doubt alive. During the day's long hours of contemplation, I had resolved to adopt a one-day-at-a-time strategy so long as Ansen was game for picking me up when I had had enough.

And in that spirit I had decided to do one more day, and had agreed to Ansen's suggestion of him picking me up at day's end tomorrow and sleeping in the house he had rented in Montgomery. But beyond that, I gave myself no better than fifty/fifty odds of continuing the hike. I probably had bitten off more than I could chew. And at the end of the day, I was doing this for me and me alone, right? What was the point of burning a whole week of precious vacation time in pure suffering? Was the wiser path to bank the unused balance and try again in cooler weather, or when someone could come with me, or when it wasn't hunting season and I could camp wherever I wanted?

I returned to the picnic table but was soon overwhelmed by the stench of the restrooms upwind and so quickly resolved to find a site beyond their sphere of influence. We were now one day away from the start of rifle season, and hunters were starting to fill the campground. One group had pitched a truly palatial tent system that could have graced the centerfold of a Cabela's circular. I could tell they had really set up housekeeping and felt that to go to that kind of trouble they must be planning a solid week here.

I found a more olfactorally suitable site closer to the lake, and sat at a concrete picnic table waiting for Ansen. I had been off the trail less than fifteen minutes, and already my muscles were setting up hard. Each time I rose from my seat to do something or other, I moved more slowly and with increasing difficulty until at last all I could do was pivot like a gingerbread man or someone in a body-cast who was suddenly pulled to his feet and forced to walk to the hospital exit.

About then my phone rang. Ansen would be there in about twenty minutes, and he asked me if I'd like anything to eat or drink. Part of me wanted an A-1 Thick-n-Hearty Whataburger with cheese, add bacon, but the larger part of me still yearned to eat the food I had spent so long choosing, buying, bagging, labeling, and burying in shallow graves throughout East Texas. So I declined a meal, but hastened to add, "I'd kill a man for a Dr Pepper."

About a half hour later his red Ford Focus wheeled into the campsite. I collapsed into the passenger seat, and he handed me a gloriously cold 20 oz. bottle of that which I had requested and a crisp, fresh copy of my trail notes off his printer. We headed for the trailhead parking lot on 149 to pick up my sleeping bag and the rest of the gear I had dropped there. Thoughtfully, he also had gone through his medicine cabinet and bagged up anything that looked like it would be remotely useful for someone on a hundred-mile hike through a forest: a "pen" with an anti-itch ointment, a tube of diaper rash cream, mosquito repellant, sunscreen. He even brought a bottle of hydrocodone, wryly suggesting I should take it to barter with a hillbilly if I got into a tight spot.

As we sped west through the timber — and it did feel like speeding after an entire day of moving two miles per hour — the sun was getting low, and as if a seesaw, the lower it got, the higher the anxiety crept back up in my chest. I dreaded the dark. I was now a fully diurnal creature, crepuscular at best, nocturnal — not in the least.

After retrieving my gear, we returned to Stubblefield Lake Campground. Having eaten nothing but two handfuls of crackers and a stick of hardtack since the two taquitos that were the previous day's breakfast, my body had finally figured out that I was not in mortal danger, and I was at length ready for some sustenance. My first meal of the trip was ramen in a yellow plastic bowl, with a can of tuna unceremoniously dumped on top. And it was good. Ansen declined to break bread with me but did hang around until well after dark, talking, looking at and photographing the stars, and listening for howls.

He and I shared a strong interest in paranormal mysteries, which must either have been coincidental or genetic, because we did not live under the same roof long enough and during the right eras for him to have influenced that interest in me or vice versa. He had spent the better part of thirty years immersed in UFO phenomena, something I shared an interest in albeit not to his level of activity. And so our areas of interest were like yin and yang, mine being sasquatch, his being UFOs, with each of us, like the yin and yang dot, having a little interest in the other's field as well. Incidentally, there are those who believe these two most persistent mysteries of our time are related in some way; while this is not impossible, I'm not convinced.

But if this interest had taught me anything it was to reserve judgment. Don't like to be thought crazy? Don't think others crazy for holding to a theory a few clicks different from yours. In a subject almost completely shrouded in mystery, no one can say with any certainty what the Others are or where they came from, and inversely, what they are not. You see a connection to UFOs? I'll say it's not impossible. You think they have cloaking abilities or some other X factor that has enabled their preternatural stealth? That's not impossible either. Think they're a hybrid created by the Atlanteans before the Deluge? Sounds crazy, but so do I to most people. Work out a theory based on the evidence. Try to prove it, and Godspeed to you, I say.

Ansen drove me to the bath house, and I spent fifteen glorious minutes standing under the spray of near-scalding water. A choir of angels wouldn't have made it any better. I dried off with the Chilly Pad I had brought as a camp towel (something akin to a synthetic chamois) and donned my flip-flops, and he drove me the hundred yards back to my site before heading to his rent house in Montgomery.

As I made final preparations to retire to the hammock, what was this? Two kittens had taken up residence under my hammock. According to the park host, someone had brought them out there and just left them, and they were surviving and thriving on both the kindness and slovenliness of campers. They were cute (needless to say), but I was a hard-hearted and selfish quartermaster, and they got none of my tidbits from dinner.

Ansen's visit had delayed my bedtime to something more normal, for which I was grateful. Going to bed at seven p.m. can really play games with your sleep rhythms, and you wake up at two in the morning, refreshed and ready to go, with five hours of darkness to wait out.

163

In the black of the moonless night, I strode toward the lake a few paces for a final urinary salute, bade the kittens goodnight and told them to be careful out here, then, with customary unzipping, zipping and five minutes of wrestling my sleeping bag, pillow, and thermal pad, and spotlight, glasses, phone, GI Tanto, keys, wallet, and tuke into position, I lay still and listened to the night.

On my left, the lake — which was no more than 300 yards wide here at its head, and the dark, unknowable wilderness on the other side of it — and on my right, the rest of the camp and the forest beyond it to the west.

Though Bob Garrett never named this campground, I was positive from numerous inadvertent geographic clues he had dropped during his podcasts that this was a hotspot. Smoking hot. He said squatches come "right on through" this campground, and just across the bridge, at the Overflow Camping site, was where he located the woman screaming "a monster, a monster!" after one had apparently tried to enter her tent and grab her child. Wild claims, to be sure, but did I not start seeing footprint shapes just one mile south of the campground?

It was 9:38 p.m. when I started the audio recorder, and it proved to be a lively night, some of which I heard in real time, and most which, of course, I did not.

My proximity to civilization was ever evident, and I heard boats on the water nearly all night long, and cars on the road that traverses the lake. Now a car alarm in the camp, planes heading down toward Houston, lots and lots of planes, small ones down low, big ones up high. At 10:26 I hear the first gun shots of the night, something that had become as predictable as owls and coyotes. I was still awake at 10:40 when I heard a large splash down by the water, like a log being thrown into the lake. This was followed by movement of something through the brush at the shoreline. I listened hard — the understatement of a lifetime — but whatever it was kept to the shore, and nothing more came of it.

At eleven, what sounded like ravens began an odd conversation with owls roosting along the opposite shoreline. The audio recording told of more gunshots, a voice shouting, possibly something banging on a dumpster, and lots and lots of coyotes.

If North America were to be named for any single species, I think it should be called Coyotia. I can think of no other animal, including the human, that inhabits and thrives in virtually every single ecosystem on the continent, from the frigid reaches of the arctic circle to the scorching, arid Southwest. Great Plains, farmland, timberland like this, swamps. I've even seen them loping down the street in my suburban neighborhood, miles from any open countryside, running through driveways and leaping over hedges.

And if you are an American camper, or for any other reason regularly sleep out of doors, their other-worldly howls and yipping choruses provide you a haunting anti-lullaby each and every night, from the dunes of Boca Chica Beach outside Brownsville to the Canadian border and beyond in both directions. They are a fascinating creature in many ways including genetically. The eastern coyote is part wolf, and specialists have said that the concept of "species" in wild canines is "fluid." Various species can interbreed with other closely related species and the offspring will be fertile, unlike with other hybrids. I wondered if the same tendency of species "fluidity" might be responsible for wild hominids as well. It certainly was for Neanderthals, Denisovans, and Cro-Magnons.

On my recording, mixed in before, after, and during howls that are clearly from coyotes, there are several very suspicious howls, and several that reminded me of my first audible, in 2011. Some might say this argues for the 2011 howl having been a coyote; others might argue this meant that there were sasquatches across the lake. At one point something howled and then was joined by a chorus of coyotes that sounded clearly different.

At about 2:15 a.m., I recorded more gunfire in the distance, and in the three o'clock hour the howls really started coming in clear and suspicious. They were lone howls, and one of them, man! At 3:04 a.m., something let out a tremendous howl that ended strangely ... "waaaaaaaaaaaa *hoo!*" I wondered if that was the signal for the hunt being over.

Near the four o'clock hour, I recorded stick breaks and movement through the brush. At 4:45 a.m., there were steps around my camp. I know it was not me because there were no hammock zippers preceding them, and I could hear myself snoring through it. They did not sound like the steps of deer. Just for good measure, at 4:59 a.m. a large cat screamed in the forest behind me: *rrreeerrrrRRRR!* I don't believe it was a cougar. Some say a few have been spotted out here, but it did not have the signature woman-being-murdered sound they normally would. But it damn-sure wasn't one of those kittens. My guess is bobcat. Its volume and the echo produced by the woods was alarming, and it was eerie to think it was that close.

Of course, what I heard that night in real time was the log splash and brush movement, a few coyote choruses, a lot of owls and raven conversations, motor boats, and planes. The rest of it I remained oblivious to until hearing the audio weeks later at home.

Daytime in the forest is boring. Except for us and two or three other animals, night is when all the action is.

Oh, and Chicago eked out a 3-2 win in game five to pull to 2-3 in the series.

11

Gliding Forward, Ever Forward

"Life shrinks or expands in proportion to one's courage."

—*Anaïs Nin*

19.7

AT FIRST LIGHT, I labored out of my hammock, a strange diurnal animal emerging from its drab-green pod. It was Halloween, and the surroundings were apropos. The sky was gray, and thick fog blanketed the lake. The *caw!* of ravens in the forest across the water echoed through the camp. (Sam Houston, whose Cherokee name was The Raven, would have approved of this scene methinks.) I chugged my 5-Hour Energy in as many seconds and surveyed the campground. The concrete picnic table was a luxury I did not normally have when camping, and it was heaped with the contents of my

169

backpack, and on a bare corner of it I made a quick breakfast of peanut butter on a tortilla with dry oatmeal dumped in the middle. I drank as much water as I could hold, then with camp broken and all on my back, I sloshed toward the campground entrance, topped off my CamelBak and Nalgene bottles, and in the knowledge that I'd see Ansen again at day's end, I buried my sleeping bag roll in dry leaves at the base of a tree near the entrance. (Again I opted to carry my hammock in the event of a significant wait at my extraction point.)

Out of the campground I hung a right onto the gravel road, bearing into the rising sun that was still shrouded by fog, and crossed the Stubblefield Bridge. Four anglers occupied different stations along it, going for whatever they could catch but probably settling for catfish and carp. On the bridge's shoulder was a disappointing but unsurprising collection of beer and malt liquor cans and bottles, plastic grocery bags and Styrofoam worm containers. Bridge fishing is something of a class distinction, as any sportsman of means would be in a bass boat, a kayak, or at least an expensive pair of waders. On my right, Lake Conroe stretched for twenty-one miles down to the cities of Conroe and Montgomery. Stubblefield Lake, after which the campground was named, was created in the 1930s by the Civilian Conservation Corps, and the campground was the same vintage. Now Stubblefield Lake is merely an arm of the much larger Lake Conroe, which was filled on Halloween night, 1973, conceived as an alternative water supply for Houston. I wished it a happy 43rd birthday and kept walking. Nothing to make you feel old like having seniority over major geographic features of the region you are traveling through.

On my left was the San Jacinto River channel that fed the lake, the very corridor Garrett and company said the Others used on a regular basis. I glanced into the Overflow Camping area, of tent-invasion fame, and saw nothing of note. I would have gone into it and looked for tracks, but I had miles to go and was keen to funnel any and all energy I had forward and not sideways.

There was something about crossing that bridge that had an effect on me. As soon as I reached the eastern side, I also reached three fundamental decisions about this outing:

First, I decided that I would finish this hike, all 96.44 miles of it, if it was the last thing I ever did. No more fifty-fifty that I'd go on, no more playing it by ear, no more taking it one day at a time. There were several reasons for this renewed conviction, perhaps the biggest being that I didn't want to admit defeat to my boys, to my wife, all my other family, and, thanks to Facebook, the now several hundred people who were aware of my goal and were expecting to see how the movie would end. If I threw in the towel, I would be explaining myself for the next six months everywhere I went. Nope, I would go the distance or die trying. And that cliché had never rung quite so true as now.

But with the trauma of Night One still fresh, I secondly decided with equal conviction that I would not camp for the next three nights, Nights Three, Four, and Five. I couldn't do it. My adrenals couldn't take the stress. I really do believe I would have had a nervous breakdown with even one more night like Night One, let alone three. I would accept Ansen's suggestion and his host's hospitality, couch surf, and be happy that I had been given the means to finish the hike.

And third, I decided to camp on the final two nights. Night Six, after all, would be at Double Lake Campground, another developed camp like Stubblefield where I would have plenty of company, showers and the whole bit. As for Night Seven, well, I would roll the dice and finish like I started, like I had planned to do the whole thing, in the woods, by myself. If it was going to be another terrifying experience, well at least it would be the last night, and if I lived to see the sunrise, I'd have a hell of a story to tell.

As I said, all of these decisions sort of dawned on me at once as I crossed the bridge. FM 149 had been a mini-Rubicon; Lake Conroe felt like the real thing. On the other side of the bridge, nine vultures eyed me from the branches of a dead tree barely visible through the fog. What else did Halloween hold in store?

It was not long at all, less than a mile, before I started seeing triangles again in the sand. Going my way, going the other way, sometimes crossing the trail. They went on and on and on, as if to say, "Anywhere you can go we can go barefoot." I estimated they continued along the Lone Star Trail for more than ten miles that day, again, as if to say, "You do this distance five times in your life; we do this every night." Triangles, triangles, triangles. I wondered where they had been headed. To the creek for a nightly drink? Were they running from a kill team that had just choppered in? Or just strolling to pass the time while Daddy and friends finished the deer hunt? And as they strolled, did they talk? Many have heard what sounds like human conversation in the forest in places humans would never be, but to date it is an indecipherable language. Others claim to have actually recorded their speech, deep guttural explosions with definite vowels and consonants — other times rapid-fire "samurai chatter" or monkey chatter, as it's known. Triangles, triangles, triangles.

I freely admit that the sasquatch is an unusual topic to occupy the thoughts and the time of a grown man and a city-dwelling, white-collar professional. Any enthusiast of a paranormal topic admits it at significant risk to his own reputation, and at the very least lays himself open to ribbing, incredulous looks, eye-rolling, and whispered backbiting. But the volume of literature and TV shows on paranormal topics betrays a huge, if closeted, audience.

One thing's certain about embracing the reality of the Others: it permanently recalibrates your idea of what is interesting, and conversely, what is *not* interesting. When you accept — really internalize — the fact there are ten-foot hairy monsters running around all over North America, suddenly a whole range of things you might have previously thought interesting fade to trivia. We're accustomed to marching through our daily routines preoccupied by the pettiness of political races, celebrity hookups and divorces, what the Dow has done since noon, weight-loss plans.

Then, you discover that ten-foot hairy monsters actually exist, and suddenly the rest of it just doesn't seem to hold your attention. I often chuckle at myself during the day, riding the bus to work, sitting alone at lunch, head bowed during a worship service, or listening to an erudite lecture, and there it comes, a bigfoot walking along in a Homer Simpson thought bubble. It is never far.

Brad Pitt and Angelina Jolie are divorcing? Yes, and ten-foot hairy monsters are running down deer and killing them with their bare hands. Super Bowl coming up this weekend? I suppose that's interesting so far as it goes, but how interesting is it relative to a ten-foot hairy monster that was witnessed last weekend peering through the living room window of a mobile home in Oregon, or Florida, or Vermont?

And scientific discoveries? You mean a new subspecies of mole rat has just been discovered in Vietnam? Well whoop-dee-frickin-do! THERE ARE TEN-FOOT HAIRY MONSTERS RUNNING AROUND RIGHT OVER THERE.

RIGHT OVER THERE! How about we "discover" those, and *then* worry about the mole rat?

In truth, those other things that were now being outcompeted in my consciousness were usually vacuous trivia all along. This subject simply acted as a powerful new filter that actually helped sort the wheat from the chaff.

Of course, this kind of continuous recalibration in which everything else eventually pales by comparison — from pop culture to workaday science to geo-politics — can lead quickly to obsession, then consumption. And when you do manage to pry yourself away from the subject for a few moments and return to the things in which you used to be interested, a huge number of them seem to funnel you right back to the Others. Biology, anthropology, ethics, spirituality and religion, history, forestry, government, mythology, sociology, psychology? Pull me any topic, from rain-gutter installation to Jungian archetypes, and I can relate it back to bigfoots in fewer than three steps. Ask any of my friends or family members.

As I say, the obsession does have the side-benefit of helping to sort wheat from chaff, but is it wheat or is it itself chaff? I sometimes worry about this.

In the final analysis, of course, I think it is wheat. For one thing, it would be an earth-shaking scientific discovery. It's impossible to say at this point how many textbooks would have to be rewritten, but many, and not just any textbooks, but most likely the ones that talk about us, anthropology!

But you'd still be forgiven for asking why, in a world brimming with pressing issues — starvation and disease, political chaos, international economic crises, climate change, and energy decline — this really matters?

To me, over and above the scientific imperative, it is simple curiosity and wonder. I'm grateful to live in a world where there are still a few mysteries left, and frankly I don't understand anyone who is *not* fascinated by this. Of course, that is almost always to do with belief. Show me someone who is not fascinated by this and I'll show you someone who doesn't believe.

I have wondered whether, in some divine scheme, mysteries like this aren't meted out to act as intellectual catnip for humanity, teasing our minds along one maddening question at a time in order to stimulate our own development or to lead us to fresh insights about the world and ourselves.

A corollary to this pure fascination is a natural hunger for discovery. Every dent and bulge of the globe has been mapped to a fare-thee-well. Every continent has been not only charted, but much of it sold and fenced off. True discovery seems as though it has been pushed either out to deep space or down to the esoteric realm of quantum physics — either way, to places inaccessible to the average person.

But here, suddenly, a spectacular mystery — nothing subtle about it, something crying out for exploration that certainly doesn't require a graduate degree to appreciate. Geographic discoveries having been exhausted, adventure has migrated to the zoological frontier. And if part of it attracts the soul of the explorer, another part calls to the soul of the prospector. Any person in the right place at the right time can make a substantial contribution to our body of knowledge, if not land the mother lode, win the lottery — a body itself.

Moreover, this frontier is a highly democratic one. No need for wealthy benefactors to fly you to the Himalayas or Africa. One of the biggest revelations is that most Americans regardless of means are right now within a few hours' drive of a mind-blowing, society-shaking discovery. And while thermal sensors, night vision goggles, and drones can be useful add-ons, all you really need is a good pair shoes, a water bottle, and a camera.

So how do they do it? After, "Where are the bones?" the next question uninitiated friends ask me about the subject of sasquatches is articulated in many different ways, but all versions come down to: how? How have they escaped detection?

Of course, the first thing to realize here is that many thousands of them have *not* escaped detection. Remember our 10,000 sightings. That's 10,000 failures and mistakes by them — road crossings, skirting rural subdivisions, farms, campgrounds, riversides, mountaintops; hell, one came out of a trash dumpster at Bergstrom Air Force Base on the edge of Austin in 1980. On and on and on it goes.

Sometimes it's probably just a sasquatch "brain fart." On occasion they might be sick and inattentive to detail, or hunger might drive them to take foolish risks. Maybe it's just that there are so damned many of *us* now that they can't keep a distance.

But for a creature that is this hard-wired against human contact to nonetheless be seen and reported several dozen times each year, there has to be a dominant reason. If I were a betting man, I'd venture that most encounters are related to that supreme imperative of any animal, protecting its young. Think about your own life. Is there anything you wouldn't risk to protect your children from danger? Think about the rest of nature. What's the most dangerous animal on the books in North America? A grizzly mother when something has come between her and her cubs. Surely most impromptu meetings are because of junior.

But be all that as it may, it is still astonishing how seldom they are seen for being as large as they are.

If sasquatches exist, then they have successfully evolved in parallel to *Homo sapiens,* a species that has either out-competed or killed off all other competitor hominids on earth that we could not breed with. *Therefore, by definition, their greatest evolutionary adaptation must be elusiveness itself.*

Sasquatches seem to achieve this uncanny avoidance of humans in several basic ways:

First and foremost, they elude humans by living where we typically don't: in steep, mountainous terrain or in dense cover like the Big Thicket, and preferably both. They seem to understand what constitutes natural barriers to humans, and they put as many of those between us and them as possible while still eking out a living. Most sightings seem to be within or just outside of national forests, not surprising as these spaces allow for that combination of maximum isolation and maximum cover.

If the first pillar of their elusiveness is geographic, then the second pillar is temporal. Much of our segregation is achieved by them hunting, foraging, and moving primarily at night. Some of us fancy ourselves night owls, but watching late-night TV in our underwear on the couch is not exactly the same as hiking across rainy mountain passes and ambushing game at three in the morning. Try as we might, we are *not* nocturnal animals.

Simply living where we aren't and being active when we're not probably accounts for most of the remarkable fact that they are so seldom spotted. But beyond these two dominant factors, there are others:

Camouflage. Researchers have noted how their hair coloring and texture, and even the difficulty of making out a face because of the uniformity of color, all aid their ability to hide from us in plain sight. Forests are chaotic pastiches of light and shadow, and a dark, vertical figure is ideally suited to mimic a shadow.

Freezing. One of the most effective hiding strategies appears to be their ability to stand, squat, or sit motionless at the drop of a hat and for extended periods. I called to mind the wood-knocking episode of the previous January, when I listened for many minutes trying to hear footfalls but heard nothing. Freezing. It's been suggested that they evolved symbiotically with trees, and much of their hiding strategy involves blending into trees and even mimicking trees, standing stock-still, their coned heads looking for all the world at fifty feet like the top of a snag. The term "tree peeking" has been coined for a sort of fluid peek-a-boo hiding behavior caught on video and in thermal night images, and several have been filmed waving fronds in front of their faces in an apparent attempt to draw the eye to the frond instead of what's waving it.

Arborealism. Juveniles seem to live in trees, above our normal field of vision, where their long strong arms, obvious forest adaptations, allow them to lead the life of a gibbon. Naturally the great size for which they're destined prevents them from staying up there past adolescence, so it's easy to imagine a period of training whereby they're taught the ways of effective hiding before they reach a size that keeps them earthbound. However, even adults have been reported coming down out of trees that are up for the task of supporting 600-900 pounds. They might even ambush deer from trees by just jumping on them. Of course, this comports with the arboreal claims espoused in the Miller Document.

Aquaticism. While great apes cannot swim, it's been suggested that the sasquatch's hooded nose, like ours, allows it to. This would give them a world of mobility not available to other great apes. They could not only traverse streams and rivers but could swim through swamps and across lakes, perhaps even between coastal islands. Such an ability would open up vast wild areas of Canada, for instance, where the chances for contact with humans would be vanishingly small.

Put together, all of these factors — isolation through terrain, cover, elevation, latitude, nocturnal activity, camouflage, freezing, arborealism, and aquaticism — begin to paint a picture of how it might be possible for a highly intelligent and very versatile creature, *whose very evolution has been driven by the need to avoid detection by men*, to have escaped scientific cataloguing for two centuries.

But I can't conclude this section on their toolbox without addressing another possibility. It seems as though even with all of this working in their favor, there probably is still something else going on that we just flat-out don't understand yet. I call it their "X factor."

This is so controversial that many even within the already taboo field of bigfootology shun it as too crazy. But people who have studied them much longer and much more closely than I have believe they possess abilities that somehow cloak them from us. Bob Garrett himself has posted a puzzling video in which something transparent seems to riffle across the screen, a dwarf palmetto leaf radically swaying at the very same time, evoking memories of the *Predator* movie franchise. One researcher has theorized that they can use infrasound to manipulate the water molecules in the air in such a way as to momentarily refract light around them and cloak themselves. More than one witness has reported that they have seen one, clearly, in the daylight, vanish into thin air. Others have suggested that they can use infrasound or a presumably massive electromagnetic field to erase the short-term memory of those who see them, effectively forcing witnesses to "un-see" them.

I can neither endorse nor debunk any of these ideas. But I think it's important to always be modest about what we know and don't know. And if we are modest, we have to say: "We don't know. Maybe. Look for evidence. Look for patterns. Develop a theory. Try to test it." That seems like the way of progress, not, "That's nuts!"

This question, like the question of how dangerous they are, and the question of whether it is ethical to kill one for the sake of science, divides bigfootery into two camps. In this case, those camps are: 1. The flesh-and-blood camp, and 2. The woo-woo camp. I think this dichotomy is a hindrance to finding the truth. As researcher and author Christopher Noël says, whatever they are, we know they are *at least* flesh and blood. But that doesn't mean they are simply upright gorillas. At the same time, the fact that they might be capable of things we do not understand yet does not mean those abilities are supernatural; it only means we haven't figured them out yet. We must get away from this binary thinking that says either we already understand something or it doesn't exist. Or, to another set of people, either we already understand something or it is magic.

A final word on infrasound. It now seems to be widely accepted in this field that sasquatches can produce infrasound and that they use it to paralyze prey at a distance. People have witnessed deer freezing up, and a sasquatch walking calmly out of the tree line, picking it up under one arm and walking back into the woods.

Other people have felt the effects of this infrasound themselves when in close proximity to a bigfoot, becoming immediately weak or even paralyzed, dizzy, nauseous, and panicked — all before a sighting. This is known as "getting zapped." This might all sound far-fetched, but of course, these symptoms are known effects of infrasound on the nervous system, well established by science and experimented with by militaries. And we know that other large animals, specifically whales, elephants, giraffes, hippopotamuses, rhinoceroses, okapi, and alligators, produce infrasound. Tigers can paralyze prey with their roar. Some American Indians have long held that sasquatches hunt by "hypnotizing" their prey, which would be a good alternate description of infrasound "zapping." People wonder how sasquatches could eat enough to sustain their immense size. Imagine how easy hunting would be if all you had to do was get close to an animal, hum your lowest note in its general direction, and then just walk up and snap its neck. You could limit out every day.

Just as in religion, there seems to be no end to how many ways we can divide ourselves from each other in the face of a mystery that none of us can completely comprehend. In the bigfoot case, this division is usually expressed by the phrase "I was with you right up until ____." "As long as you were just claiming they were apes, OK. I was with you right up until you started with the 'part human' stuff..." "I was with you right up until the part about zapping..." "I was with you right up until the telepathy ... the cloaking ... the interdimensional travel." Virtually all believers tend to think they know just where the line of crazy is — the line between possible and impossible. Inside our own heads, we have staked out the conservative position, the science-based position, the common-sense orthodoxy. Perhaps the need to establish an "us and them" is especially potent in a group of people, all of whom are considered "them" by mainstream society. "We are the *mainstream* bigfooters; *they* are the lunatic fringe." I'm not saying there is no lunatic fringe; I'm just cautioning modesty about knowing for sure where the line should be drawn in a world where we are certain of hardly anything.

As I rounded a bend, a lovely pond appeared suddenly on my left. I didn't want to lose too much time, but I could not resist a quick survey of the eight-foot-wide mud bank that surrounded it. For all my gnashing of teeth about coming alone and multiple failed attempts to get friends to come with me, I now was glad to be alone, and for two reasons. First was for moments like this, when I could spend as much or as little time as I felt like looking for evidence of the Others without sheepishly explaining my rationale. If I wanted to spend three hours at this pond doing a grid search of the acre of mud that was here, I could; and if I wanted to walk past the pond and not even break my stride, as I did at the Overflow Camping Area — I could do that too. Human companionship is wonderful, even critical, but there is also something to be said for flying solo now and then. The second reason was that I would have probably spent 90 percent of my time on the trail wracked with guilt for putting anyone else through the ordeal, and the remaining 10 percent struggling to keep up with them.

If the Others are flesh and blood, the one thing they need above all else is water. And spring-fed ponds like this one are perfect watering holes. After my "knock-knock" encounter on that freezing, dark January morning the previous year, I had no doubt those two (or more) hominids were coming in for water before sunrise. We were blocking them from the pond.

Despite that, I found nothing more than a couple of frogs at this pond during my cursory survey of its muddy bank. I got back to walking, and after a while I left the triangles behind and came out onto my first road walk, Bath Road, a gravel lane that rose and fell gently over the next hour and a half. On my left passed the gates of Harding Historic Ranch, there since 1850. A few cattle, sixty yards out to pasture, eyed me warily. This was the only part of the Lone Star Trail on which my choice of shoe proved sub-optimal. As none of the woodland trail is rocky and is only occasionally steep (though there is more up and down crossing through creek beds and small ravines than I expected) I had opted for hiking shoes rather than hiking boots, and this meant that the soles of my shoes were more flexible. This allowed the white caliche rocks of the gravel road to poke uncomfortable into the bottoms of my feet, like the least effective reflexology treatment ever devised.

In ninety minutes on that road I never saw or heard a vehicle. I walked right down the center of the road at times, or on one shoulder or the other if one was shadier or looked smoother. A whitetail buck, probably eight-point, stepped out on the road 500 yards in front of me and stared at me coming toward him for two minutes before moving on. Every so often, I spotted a blaze on a tree beside the road, straight up and down; good of them to put my mind at rest that I was going right.

For the first time on this trip, I felt a breeze, a scintilla of cool air on my arms and face. As the trees swayed in that breeze, some of them finally having turned the colors of autumn and freeing a fluttering yellow leaf to sail across the deep blue sky, I thought I might cry. Then a rock would stab me in the sole. Not in this life, buddy! Dry it up and get back to work!

At last the lane T-ed into a paved road, and having no blaze to follow, I pulled out the new copy of trail notes. Up the unstriped paved road and again the Halloween theme held as I turned onto Cotton Creek Cemetery Road.

Deciding this was as good a spot as any for a lunch break, I found a patch of shade thrown from a sycamore tree, sat right in the dirt road, and used some of the hardtack that was still loose in my pockets to dig peanut butter out of its jar. I texted my wife, who was substitute teaching that day, and told her I was alive and well on Day Three. I then changed into my second and only other shirt, a long-sleeve, hunter-orange number, because the sun was high, and I saw more road-walking in my immediate future.

Before my muscles set up too much more, I struggled to my feet, clicked the backpack on and then used one of my trekking poles to flick the other one out of the weeds and up to my waiting hand. Here, I passed from the Conroe Section of the "trail" to the Huntsville Section, though, the trail being only a theoretical construct at this point, there were no signs or posts announcing this milestone. The only change is on the map. I was now entering the fourth of ten sections.

I headed around the corner and down the dirt road, but a good deed never goes unpunished, and my caution in changing shirts was rewarded by an immediate turn back into the woods. And with the breeze gone, I was hotter than ever.

Up and down and around I hiked. Yesterday had been about fourteen miles and today would be the same. In the long minutes between landmarks, when the world became a never-ending blur of yaupon, I adopted a mantra to occupy some small part of my mind and keep me from lumbering like an old man. I heard the mantra in the voice of Siri (American female version), maybe because I had just gotten a new cell phone two nights before the trip and this one was Siri-enabled. Or maybe because her voice reminded me of a voice on my wife's phone that was on a guided-meditation app for kindness she used most mornings. In any event, the woman's voice said in a soothing, sing-song statement of fact:

And I am gliiiiiding forward, ever forward.
I am gliding ever forward.

184

I would hear her say it in my head, and then I would repeat it, huffing and puffing under the weight of my pack and from climbing through dry creek beds and over and under fallen logs. "And I am ... gliding ... forward ... ever forward. (pant, pant) I am gliding ever forward." Other mental tricks helped as well. I sometimes pretended someone was sitting at the next trailhead in a pickup with a winch, reeling me in on an invisible line, almost dragging me forward by the belt buckle through the trail's countless bends and obstacles. I also spent a tremendous amount of mental energy calculating fractions in the pursuit of self-congratulations: "Hey! Once I pass this next mile marker I'll be one fifth of the way through today's mileage, after which I will be one-third done with the first half of this hike!"

Pines get all the press in this part of the world, which is most often referred to as "the piney woods of East Texas." But this overlooks the truly dominant tree in the region, which, in case you haven't guessed already, is the yaupon. For every pine tree I passed, I passed forty yaupons. The Catawban Indians called it yopún (*yop* meaning tree, and *un* denoting little). In a long, proud tradition of Anglo settlers butchering any non-English word they encountered, many locals reverse those vowels and pronounce it *YOO-PON*. The more standard pronunciations are *YO-PON* (what I prefer) or sometimes *YAH-puhn*.

It is one of the few plants I have learned about in which the Latin name is more colorful and evocative than the common name, and that Latin name is *Ilex vomitoria*. The *Ilex vomitoria* (it's just fun to say!) is either a tree or a shrub depending on its size. It can grow as high as forty-five feet but most are under twenty-five, having small dark-green leaves and gray bark with white splotches. The females bear copious amounts of brilliant red berries, giving it its last name, holly. It is native to the South, just about perfectly tracing the former Confederacy, from Virginia and Florida west to Central Texas.

In addition to being the most prolific tree in this forest, it also has the distinction of being the only plant native to Texas that is caffeinated, the stimulant being found in its leaves and twigs. The local Indians, of course, discovered this and created a ceremony in which they drank so much of it they had to then throw it up in order to ingest more, hence the Latin name. This doesn't sound like a ceremony that would tempt me much, but apparently it was a hot enough ticket to attract Indians from Texas' interior to the coast in large numbers every year to binge on the brew and then throw up. In a sort of historical echo, young people especially have been traveling to the Texas coast every year since the 1960s to throw up, usually in March, and on South Padre Island, though I doubt the experience is imbued with very much spiritual power in its current form.

In a few hours, a little subdivision came into view, Elkins Lake. As the name suggests, there is a lake in the middle of this upscale bedroom community outside of Huntsville, and that lake's name, for some reason I could never figure out, is Camellia Lake. I wondered if their motto was "Welcome to Elkin's Lake, Home of Camellia Lake!" Regardless of what it was called, I was elated to see its cool, still waters reflecting the pines and hardwoods around it. Where hikers first encounter the lake, there is a public bench and a tiny dock. I flung my pack and poles on the bench, shed my shoes and Icelandic socks and practically sprinted to the dock. Just before I sat down at its end, I heard a huge splash below me, which either had to have been a ten-pound catfish or carp feeding right by the dock, or, what it sounded more like, an alligator. It was not a far-fetched notion, I thought, as the creek leading out of the lake was called Alligator Branch. You might think this would have given me pause before thrusting my feet into the water, but they were an alarming hue of purple with the heat and stress of the miles, and I hesitated not at all in plopping down, rolling up the adventure pants, and plunging my feet into that glorious, cold, clear water.

After a deeply satisfying fifteen-minute soak, I resigned to press on before suffering the consequences of concretized muscles, and so reluctantly put the Icelandic socks and shoes back on. The quirkiest feature of the entire Lone Star Trail might just be how the trail's creators, with no other choice, had to route the path across a spillway. In times of heavier rain and flow, you would have to wade across, taking care not to slip on the algae and fall ass-first into the headwaters of Alligator Branch below. But today, the flow was no more than a quarter-inch deep, and I strolled slowly across the slippery concrete without incident.

Heading hard to the west along Alligator Branch, I crossed a small ravine on a fallen log and passed a few swampy areas that were looking their most scenic in the low afternoon sun. I now entered the stretch of the trail I had hiked only a year earlier with all three of my boys, when we did our "wilderness survival campout," with no tents, hammocks, or sleeping bags. I looked for the corridor along which we had departed the trail, or any of the old-school blazes I had notched into the trees with my Bowie knife demonstrating a lost method for the kids, but I couldn't spot it.

And I called to mind, about here, crossing That Old Fart, and the inspiration he provided — that if a retiree could through-hike the Lone Star Trail, surely a spry forty-nine-year-old could. I would spend tonight on a couch in Montgomery; I guess That Old Fart got the last laugh.

Perhaps Interstate 45 is so named because one starts hearing it a solid forty-five minutes — a mile and a half — before reaching it. Normally, I would have found this a depressing Superfund site of noise pollution, but today, because every additional decibel represented progress, it got a pass, and even enlivened my step the louder it grew.

You can hear it for an awfully long way, but you certainly cannot see it. I-45 appears suddenly through the last layer of trees. If you were deaf or wearing headphones it would be an incredible shock to the system, instantly going from the dark, dreaminess of the forest to the harsh light and blinding glare of the sun off of glass and steel and chrome, all roaring past you at eighty miles per hour.

I walked out to the tiny dirt parking lot on the I-45 frontage road the very instant that Ansen pulled up. We couldn't have choreographed it any better with two-way radios. I told him about the footprints I had been seeing for more than ten miles that day. Naturally he wanted to see one, and so we walked in a little way, but there were no good specimens within easy reach of the trailhead, and having just walked fourteen miles, I was not keen on backtracking very far.

A bright red dot shooting through a sea of greens and browns, we sped back to Stubblefield Lake to collect my stash of camping gear, then headed down to Montgomery.

I won't lie — I was glad to be in an air-conditioned car with a large Mexican dinner just moments away. But I did have to fight off more than a few feelings of inadequacy and failure, as this was my first time to leave the trail. Funny — thirty-three miles of hiking over two-and-a-half days was substantially more than I had ever done before. But this was not the plan, and so I resigned to a compromise that would allow me the greater of the two accomplishments, the hike. I vowed one day to redeem myself with a true through-hike.

For the moment, I salved the wounds of my compromised dreams with lightly salted nacho chips and picante sauce at a garish Mexican restaurant on the main strip of town that ran from Montgomery to Conroe and beyond. Even after only two and a half days in the wild, civilization was jarring. The non-descript five-lane blacktop carried moderate but non-stop traffic, an outer ripple of the nightmare that was Houston traffic sixty miles south. Gated communities on the waterfront. Low-slung strip malls carrying the full complement of goods and services required by a growing American suburb: auto parts, liquor, lawyers, Mexican food.

I scanned the waterfront to see if any of these subdivisions were ungated. Four months earlier, a man living in Montgomery had filed a report of two sightings right on the edge of the town. He traveled a lot and often returned home from the airport in the wee hours. He preferred to enter his subdivision from the "backside," an area bordered by thick forest that eventually leads to the lake. Twice during June he had come home between two and three a.m. Both times a large herd of deer were gathered beside the road. As he passed the deer, he saw in his rearview mirror that they suddenly scattered at high speed, moving away from the forest and into the subdivision. He then saw a large, brown biped emerge from the tree line and run toward his car for a few steps before turning back and disappearing from view. He also reported hearing howls at his home coming from the woods, "long and powerful." The subdivision was built about four years earlier on virgin land.

Our waitress, Svetna, explained to me in an incongruous Slavic accent that suggested neither East Texas nor Mexican food that I could have beef, pork, or chicken fajitas. I did not have the energy nor the heart to explain to the comely East European that a "fajita" was a cut of *beef*, and that therefore there could be no such thing as *chicken fajita*. As a South Texas boy who regularly ate *fajitas* (simply the Spanish word for skirt steak) long before the term was co-opted by mainstream American restaurants and corrupted to mean anything that can be wrapped in a tortilla from chicken to Portobello mushrooms — I had stubbornly held to the original definition for decades, boring many a dining partner with this little-known (or cared-about) fact. I ordered the fajita burrito, and Svetna brought it forthwith, whereupon I descended on it like starving hyena.

Just across the street was the gated community in which Ansen had found lodging via the Air BnB platform. Laurie, the homeowner, was a night-shift nurse who was gone for twelve hours at a time, and so it worked out splendidly that she left for work before Ansen and I showed up, and we left in the mornings before she got home.

She owned a small mutt named Tibley, who was none too pleased at first with his new roommate, and he made his lair in the crawl space beneath the couch.

If I was going to cheat, I was going to cheat good, and so I availed myself of every modern convenience on offer during the first hour of the stay: a hot shower was the most urgent order of business, followed quickly by laundry, as my clothes had already begun to reek of mildew. I had scrupulously packed no cotton attire, but rather technical, wicking fabric that would help keep me cool as it dried while I walked.

The problem was, *nothing ever* dried out there, ever. The terrycloth sweatband inside the pith helmet was soaked with sweat from Mile Marker 1 and never dried, not overnight, not in the sun, never, until I removed it from the helmet and put it through the washer and drier. From thousands of reports we know that one of the tell-tale signs a bigfoot is near is an overpowering stench. It makes witnesses' eyes water, and it has been compared to a skunk, a corpse, a wet horse, the monkey section of a zoo, and rotting garbage. In all likelihood, this colossal funk is the product of a gland similar to one possessed by gorillas, but living in an environment that never dries cannot help matters. If not for the showers and laundry I did along the way, I would have been making *their* eyes water right back. Just sayin'.

After starting laundry, I massaged arnica into my feet and collar bones and donned the shirt that wasn't in the wash. Ansen and I sat up and talked in the unfamiliar garden home. He downloaded my audio from nights one and two to his laptop, and we puzzled over the sounds of galloping hooves I had never heard while out there. We tried in vain to get Laurie's TV to work like a regular one, but in the end had to settle for watching YouTube on it, a long list of comedy desk-pieces about the Trump / Clinton race. I was tired and just wanted to watch TV; I didn't want to have to press play every eight minutes. American problems.

Ansen turned in upstairs to the room he was actually renting, while I powered off the TV. Tibley finally emerged from his lair and steadily warmed to me, first sleeping on the couch by my feet, and finally, making himself at home squarely on my chest, rising and falling with my every breath.

12
The Gray Walker

"I humble myself before God, and there the list ends."
—*Sam Houston*

35.0

AT FIRST LIGHT we were pulling into the Montgomery Whataburger for taquitos and coffee before making the half-hour drive back to the trailhead on I-45. We arrived just as the sun peeked through the pines that crowd the eastern edge of the highway.

As I mentioned, when you emerge from the forest here you are rudely jarred by the sight of the interstate that has been growing steadily louder over the past hour, and you see the eighteen-wheelers making the run between Dallas and Houston. At that point you might look to your left, north. And if you did that you might do a double-take.

There, on the other side of the highway and about a quarter mile to your left, a pure white face, statesmanlike and stoic, stares out across the interstate from a verdant backdrop. His receding medium-long hair is swept back and wavy, and mutton-chop sideburns extend nearly to his thin, clinched lips. The snow-white head sits atop a matching white body. All told the figure towers more than sixty-seven feet, higher than many of the pine trees that crowd around his back. He wears a long coat and full-length trousers. His left hand rests on his hip, and his right grips a cane, itself some forty feet tall.

In 1862, the citizens of Huntsville welcomed one who would become their most famous resident and the man for whom this metropolitan sprawl and this forest were named. A political overachiever if ever there were one, Sam Houston was the first and third president of the Republic of Texas, the seventh governor of Tennessee and the seventh governor of Texas as well as a U.S. senator. When he refused to take an oath of allegiance to the Confederacy, Houston left power and decided to live out his life, of which there was not a great deal left, in this little town, which he thought resembled his childhood home in Tennessee because of its hills. One assumes he might have wandered these very forest paths on one or two occasions, probably never imagining that these miles and miles of trees would someday be the exception instead of the rule.

I wondered what his attitude would have been toward the Others that call his forest home. Of course, it is not his, as its name would suggest; it is Theirs. I think he left a clue for us of what his attitude might have been. It's in how he dealt with the indigenous outcasts of his own day, the American Indians.

For his time, Houston was extremely progressive with regard to America's native population, not only tolerant, but often a fan and a booster. As you can imagine, this tolerance, nay affection, cost him dearly politically, but he was consistent in it. He admired the Cherokee in particular, so much so that at the age of sixteen he ran away from Anglo civilization altogether to live with Cherokee on an island in Tennessee's Hiwassee River. Later in life, after his first marriage fell apart, he again took up with the Cherokees, this time in the Arkansas Territory to which they had been exiled. He even entered into a common-law marriage with a half-Cherokee woman, Tiana Rogers, the niece of the band's chief, John Jolly. Chief Jolly adopted Houston as his own son and bestowed upon him the name of The Raven.

If he was OK with those others, perhaps he would be OK and even admiring of these as well. And who's to say he didn't know of them? One thing's for sure — in a forest with some especially tall residents, he will always be the tallest.

Sunrise of Day Four ushered in the least romantic stretch of the entire hike, a stroll along the frontage road of Interstate 45. Fortunately, it was slightly downhill, and with a good night's sleep under my belt, I was practically jogging. In twenty minutes I was making a left turn under the freeway and proceeding due east on a paved and striped two-lane. As I came to a T in the road, I thought it high time to record my next trailaoke performance. So I turned north and, with logging trucks whizzing behind me, gave Billy Joel's "You May Be Right" everything I had.

I did a quick quality-control check of the video, then posted it to Facebook. About the time I put my phone back in its clip and collapsed the selfie stick, I had a feeling of shakiness about where I was. I took a few steps farther into the weeds, stopped, and pulled the trail notes out. Sure enough, for a quarter of a mile, all the while I was singing my heart out, I had been hiking the wrong way.

After a U-turn and half mile to the south, I left the city of Huntsville and tunneled back into the forest off Elkins Road. I now left the Huntsville Section behind and entered Section 5: Phelps. Like most everything else over here, the Phelps community developed around a train depot and telegraph station established in the 1870s. They say it was probably named for the Phelps-Dodge Construction Company, which built the railroad. Connecticut businessman Anson Green Phelps started a saddlery in the early nineteenth century. He founded Phelps, Dodge & Co. in 1833 as an import-export business with his sons-in-law William Dodge and Daniel James as partners in Liverpool. Dodge had a nearby town named after him too. So although I didn't know it at the time, as I was hiking away from the town of Phelps, I was also getting the hell out of Dodge.

In another half hour I passed through the hunter camp I had originally planned to stay in the previous night. It felt remote, and a chill went up my spine at the mere thought of what it would have felt like twelve hours earlier. But it was a pretty section of trail, and a beautiful morning. I felt good, and I was free and doing exactly what I wanted. I stopped and texted my wife: "I'm loving this. Thanks for allowing me to do it."

An hour east of the interstate highway, I started seeing them again, the triangles. And once again, big ones and small ones, all of the same shape. I now found significance in something else: they were *re*appearing. If they had been everywhere, then who knows what they might have been, probably just natural bare spots in the sand where wind, water, or squirrels had pushed the pine needles aside. But their absence for long stretches told me they weren't naturally occurring. I was seeing the intermittent presence of a something, because I was also noting the absence of it.

I also noticed that they did not start until I was almost out of earshot of I-45 traffic, just as the triangles had *stopped* on the other side about the time I *started* hearing the traffic. If these are the tracks of the Others, this seems like evidence that perhaps there are two distinct populations in this forest — one west of I-45 and one east.

No doubt they *could* get across the highway if they wanted, and they probably did from time to time, darting beneath an underpass at four a.m. But I would be willing to bet that for the most part, they pick a side and stay there. Logging roads, county roads, even two-lane state highways pose no challenge at all to them. Hundreds of eye witnesses say they usually cross a road in three steps. But an interstate? I measured it later on satellite photos, and anyone contemplating getting across that is probably looking at a minimum of 400 feet of exposure: an easement cleared of trees and mowed, a two-way access road, a median, two southbound lanes, another median, two to three northbound lanes, and occasionally another access road and easement before hitting the tree line again.

There's overwhelming evidence that the Others occupy every section of Sam Houston National Forest, as Garrett says, "from one end all the way to the other." He even claims that the population is on the rise, and that there's a general movement in the region from south to north due to the explosive growth of Houston's northern suburbs such as The Woodlands.

Folks used to live in The Woodlands and commute to Houston. But The Woodlands has grown so much that there is now a significant counter flow of people living in Houston and working in The Woodlands — to the point that there is no longer any such thing as a "reverse commute" in north Greater Houston.

In September 2007, at two a.m., a security guard saw a dark figure more than seven feet in height strolling through the construction site of a Fox Sports News facility in The Woodlands before it walked into the tree line. Like any other wildlife population, they're losing habitat and so moving into the sanctuary of the national forest, where some development was grandfathered in but where, in the forest proper, development is now finally arrested.

As I was now east of I-45, my thoughts turned to a sasquatch Garrett and friends had witnessed on more than one occasion and claimed to have actually videoed. They called it the Gray Walker. It was big (if that's not stating the obvious, but big even for a squatch), a male, and, they speculated, probably the alpha male of his group that likely ranged through the southeastern section of Sam Houston, from Coldspring down to Cleveland. And, as the name suggests, he was gray all over. He was probably to the Others as a silverback was to a troop of mountain gorillas. He was the silverback of the squatches, an older one who had survived decades of encounters with humans, who knew this territory inside out. For a bigfoot, just making it to "gray" means you're strong, fast, wary, smart. Being the silverback of the Others would put you at the apex of apex predators, a stone-cold badass.

The public story goes like this: In 2013 an acquaintance of Bob Garrett and those in his research group, one Wyatt, was out in an area that I believe is near the town of Shepherd and was doing a test flight with a camera-rigged drone. In an attempt to achieve maximum scientific research credibility, he and a friend were doing what they called a proof-of-concept flight, just checking the equipment to see what sort of image it would render if the copter was at a given height. The two stood in the trailhead parking lot as Wyatt, a certified drone pilot, directed the craft into the woods over a creek. He flew a pattern at the prescribed height, recording 4K-resolution video, brought the drone back, and downloaded the footage to his laptop.

As the two watched it back, his friend caught something moving in a part of the screen away from the focal point. They backed it up, and there, a gray figure, walking calmly away from the drone through a clearing for several seconds before turning slightly to the left and disappearing back under tree cover, presumably upon hearing the craft.

The two went in later and recreated the drone's pattern and altitude but used a tape measure and themselves to gauge its size. They concluded that the Gray Walker covered nineteen feet with three and a half steps, and that he was wider than both researchers standing side-by-side. The definition of the video is purportedly so high that you can even make out the bottoms of the creature's feet as he raises them in the distinctive way the Others do while he steps through a swampy area with six inches of standing water.

So where is this amazing video that those who have allegedly seen call the second best in existence after the Patterson-Gimlin Film? In the podcast that covers this subject, the proprietors are in no hurry. They want to present it with the utmost scientific context. Over and over they refer to "proof of concept" and not rushing the evidence into the public sphere. "We don't want to release the footage because we want to be right. We want to ensure that we have a quality piece of evidence that we bring to the table." To be sure, they have not rushed the process. At this writing, more than three years on, they are still sitting on it.

Garrett, of course, claims to have seen the bigfoot a couple of times and thinks the Gray Walker once threw a log at him. "This fella is just massive."

When I heard this story, I couldn't help but think of a photo I had seen a few years earlier. In 2008, blogger Melissa Hovey received a photo that, if authentic, would certainly rank as the clearest photograph of a sasquatch ever taken; it looks like it was taken at a distance of about four feet with a full flash. The reason it is not more well known is that it was taken of the subject's back. The shot is at night, and according to the anonymous photographer, it was taken with a 35mm film camera mounted on the side of a house and fired by a remote trigger. The only other visible object in the photo is a loquat tree that the subject is facing. These Chinese imports with sweet orange fruit the size of a large grape are common ornamental trees throughout the South including in Texas. One further indication that the shot might have been taken in Texas is that the URL of Hovey's blog contains "txsasquatch."

In the picture, we see the back of the subject's head hunched forward atop a back and shoulders that despite their rounded posture appear massively muscular. The most striking feature of the individual is the silvery hair, perhaps four to six inches long, that covers the head and back uniformly, with many patches of bare skin visible through the unkempt mats. Is this the Gray Walker as well? How many gray sasquatches could be in East Texas? No one will ever know, but it could be many, or it could be one. And if there is but one, then this is probably him. If only he had been facing the camera. If only.

At mile 40, I was in a thick section of yaupon and hardwoods when my eyes were drawn by a strange phenomenon to my left. There, a yaupon with a trunk about two inches thick was bent into a perfect arch. There were lots of yaupons doubled over in the forest, and a look around soon showed me why — pine needles falling from above would gather in their topmost branches, and when the rain came, those needles would get soaked into a heavy mat that, like snow load in other forests, forced them over. But there was something about this arch that was a little too ... intentional. In fifty more feet, I spotted another just like the first. If they had been a little closer it would have looked like a primitive McDonald's had been opened there in the midmost heart of a forest wilderness. I started getting quite suspicious when, in another interval about the same as the first, I found a third arch. I stepped off the trail and inspected this one more closely.

Sure enough, the top of the tree appeared to have been pinned by a log. It would have been easy enough to write this off as a naturally occurring phenomenon but for one fact. The yaupon was alive and well, and the log pinning it was the rotten trunk of a tree that looked to have been dead at least five years. In other words, the top of the tree had been pinned down not by a tree that fell on it, but with a log that had to have been placed on it.

These three arches formed a line that called to mind a Renaissance-style portico like those around the university campus where I worked. Despite how it may seem, I was not simply seizing on any odd sight I came upon in the forest and attributing it to sasquatches. These looked very much like a subcategory of a well-established phenomenon in bigfootery, "tree structures" or "stick structures" in areas where sasquatches are known to live. The most common are pinned arches, X's, and teepee-like structures in which logs or whole trees are pushed over in opposite directions to form the skeleton of a cone. Of the three, researchers are only relatively sure what one type means. X's mean "keep out." (It is sasquatchese for "POSTED.") Perhaps this is the very beginning of symbolic language. Hold your forearms up and cross them in front of your chest. Could there be a more universal symbol for "You are not welcome beyond this point"?

But the arches, who knew? Maybe they meant "Come right this way." "Come on in!" "This is the way home." Or maybe they were delineating territory in some other way. Perhaps they were just the work of young ones playing, just a primordial doodle in wood. I found myself looking through the arches to see what they might frame. Nothing but tangled forest lay beyond, a never-ending sea of yaupon dotted with other mixed trees, shrubs, and vines.

Here, I did something I don't recall doing anywhere else on the trip — I left the trail. I wanted to see what was to my east off this trail. Was there a meadow back there like Garrett described? Or maybe a spring-fed pond, or an especially thick stand of young pines that could constitute a daytime fortress against the prying eyes of the Forest Service and other invaders and colonial overlords? As the trail crossed down through a dry creek bed, I made a hard left and followed the shallow ravine for a hundred yards or so, careful to keep my bearings and keep the trail in sight. My eyes scanned the horizon in all directions for any anomalies in the landscape, any snag that looked too hairy, or stump that looked too large, or odd mass up high in a tree. And alternately, I looked down at the sandy floor of the creek bed for prints that might be more defined than the triangles I had been seeing.

In a few more minutes, the voice came to me, the Siri-like voice, however now she was not soothing me, but with the same words reprimanding me for the side-trip. "And I am gliding *forward*! Ever *forward*! I am gliding ever *forward*!" she said, starting soothingly, then sort of passive-aggressively ratcheting up the edge in her voice. OK, OK. I said. With an about-face, I regained the trail and began looking for Mile Marker 41.

I emerged from the forest on the same road I had entered it on and started a long stretch of road-walking.

The world looks different from your feet than it does from a car seat. This seems obvious, but we forget it if we don't walk every now and then. With just three full days on the trail behind me, and even having just been in a car a few hours earlier, it felt very us-versus-them. I immediately sensed a kinship to everything in the world that was not a car or in a car. The way cars and trucks sound and the rush of air as they roar past you is terrifying and feels like a vexation to all of nature, an abomination. Righteous judgment swelled in me at once, and my inner monologue dripped with disdain: Yoooou ... *people*, in your .... *cars* and ... *trucks... Yoooou make meee SICK!* Of course, I was one of them, but not that week, at least not at that exact moment.

I only suffered this particular highway for thirty minutes or so before, at 42.6 miles, I turned and bore due east on a long, straight, paved country lane called Four Notch Road. I had noticed, while driving this area to plant my food caches on Day One, that there also was a Three Notch Road close by. Apparently these roads trace pioneer trails that were blazed with three notches or four notches, respectively.

I resolved that I would later on amuse myself by making a compilation video of dogs attacking me on the road, and so as the first two came after me from a farmhouse on Four Notch Road I powered on my body camera, a Go Pro knock-off I had duct-taped to the chest strap of my backpack, and walked briskly toward them as they snarled. *"I'm* the predator," I thought, and might have even spoken aloud.

A Shetland pony and chestnut quarter horse lent a pastoral calm to an otherwise hostile setting of snarling dogs and a foreboding wood, and I departed the road briefly to take the horses' picture across the barbed-wire fence. We can only wonder what these mute beasts might be able to tell us about the cryptic company they might keep if they could talk. One story that haunts me is an account of a filly in Iowa that a randy male sasquatch tried to mate with. I'm not sure if "rape" is word we can use in an animal context, but the alleged event was not consensual, and reportedly resulted in an ugly outcome that required much antibiotic ointment inside the horse and, due to extensive scratch marks along the poor animal's torso, outside too. Sounds outrageous on a first reading, but such behavior would be all too typical for a primate deprived of a more normal outlet, whether chimpanzee or the human.

For more than two miles I walked this road, sometimes up on the grass and sometimes down on the pavement, with only an occasional car or truck passing me, often with the driver raising an index finger off the steering wheel in a salute of friendship.

The road passed pastures of cattle and, on a hunch, I veered away from the asphalt to stroll alongside the barbed-wire fence. There, along the top of the three wires, black hair. It was coarse and four-to five inches long. Now, let me hasten to say, before you strain your eyes from rolling them, that this was probably not sasquatch hair, but it got me thinking about the many hair samples that have been found in places less readily explainable than this. It was odd to me that the hair did not match the cattle I saw feeding on the lot, which were not black at all but brown, but who knows how long they'd been pasturing there and who the previous tenants were.

Aside from being a source of DNA, sasquatch hair is said to be distinguishable from human hair because it has no medulla, a structural center line within the hair that shows up under magnification. I thought this black coarse hair was probably from that tuft of hair at the end of a cow's tail caught in these barbs while swishing flies next to the fence, but I pocketed a few handfuls of it anyway just to put it under my son's microscope when I got home, and in case there was another call for possible tissue samples.

Chief among the many reasons to walk is that you see things walking you don't see at any other speed, not even cycling. As I was walking along Four Notch Road I narrowly missed stepping on a little furry mass the exact color of the asphalt. I leaned way over to examine it and found it was not a mouse, as I had first thought, but a Southern short-tailed shrew, dead but not the least disfigured, like it was taking a little nap in the right-hand lane. It looked wholly unharmed except for a speck of blood on its exquisite, flesh-colored wrist. Like another creature to which I had recently been giving a lot of thought, the shrew was seemingly everywhere — millions burrowed through the floor of every forest and garden in the temperate world — and yet I had never seen a single one before that moment, and, nearly a half-century in, it was reasonable to assume I might very well never see another.

These are extraordinary creatures on numerous levels. Their nature stems from their incredibly small size. This species weighs less than half an ounce. And during the winter, the Southern short-tailed shrew can lose up to half that mass, even shrinking the size of its bones, skull, and internal organs. Because of their low mass and the correspondingly high ratio of their surface to that mass, they lose heat at a phenomenal rate compared to larger mammals, and therefore have evolved a metabolism that simply defies belief. They breath 152 times a minute, and their hearts beat 800 times a minute, *at rest*. To power this unimaginable feat, they must eat every hour or risk starving to death in less than a day. This results in them consuming *two to three times their body weight every day*, mostly worms and insects they have hunted and killed but pretty much anything is fair game. For me, this would be the equivalent of waking up in the morning and sitting down to a breakfast of 150 pounds of meat and bones, then doing the same thing at lunch, and again at supper. And of course, as one biologist, points out, I would have had to hunt and kill all of it as well.

This ferocious appetite, experts agree, makes shrews, gram for gram, far and away the most ferocious mammal on the planet, natural-born killers if ever the term applied. While most are insanely territorial, driving off rivals and only coming together to mate, the Southern short-tailed shrew is genteel by comparison, social even to the point of sharing its burrow systems with roommates.

But woe to the roommate who outstays his welcome. These shrews are venomous and secrete a toxin from grooves in their sharp buck teeth to paralyze their prey. Shrews' appetites are such that, in one experiment, when a glass cover was put over three of the beasts, two of them immediately killed the third and split the proceeds. An hour or so later, having burned through those calories, the two survivors went after each other, Thunderdome style, the lone survivor now having eaten twice his own weight. But a shrew's appetite never sleeps, and when it was time to feed again, it turned to the only meat left under the glass dome, his own tail. He ate his tail, and then proceeded to eat his own hindquarters, until bleeding out. He ate himself alive — to death. Take from this gruesome tale any analogy you please about mankind's insatiable appetite for natural resources and how we too might be eating ourselves.

But backing out to the physiology of the shrew, there was something in my later research on them that caught my eye: Food supply must be proportional to skin size, not weight, which explains why men can eat less than 2 percent of their weight daily on average, while mice (despite the insulation of their coats) must eat 25 percent of theirs, and shrews 200 percent!

What did this rule portend for the sasquatch, something so massive that its surface — its skin — is drastically *less* in relation to its mass than it is for us? Think of a tennis ball and a basketball. Both are perfect spheres, so our intuition tells us that as the sphere scales up, everything about it should scale up in proportion, but this is wrong. As it scales up, its volume grows faster, *much* faster, than its surface. As you can see below, a basketball's surface is 14 times bigger than a tennis ball's, but a basketball's volume is *54* times bigger:

	Surface	Volume	Surf : Vol. Ratio
Tennis ball	19.63 sq. in.	8 cu. in.	1 : 0.4
Basketball	279.71 sq. in.	434 cu. in.	1 : 1.5
Increase	1,424%	5,425%	

The shrew requires an enormous amount of food relative to its size. And by the same token, an animal bigger than us might require more food than we do but not *proportionally* as much.

Here is one of the most profound benefits of the sasquatch's size. Because its surface area is so low relative to its thick and hearty volume, it can withstand much colder temperatures, even with the same amount of insulation, because it is the mass that generates and retains the heat and the surface that radiates it.

In biology, this principle is expressed in Bergmann's Rule, which dictates that, generally speaking, the farther north an animal lives, the larger it is, because its sheer size protects it against cold. Think of black bears in the American South, now of grizzly bears, now of Kodiak bears, and now of polar bears — the farther north, the larger. While sasquatches are hairy, there is universal agreement that they are covered with hair and not fur, with skin often visible through the hair. And while even a light layer of hair can go a long way in protecting something against cold, the real biological strategy that allows them to live outdoors year-round across North America, naked, is being bigger than hell.

Homo sapiens evolved in East Africa with a body plan maximized for radiating heat. Until they wandered out of Africa, surviving cold was the *last* thing our ancestors had to worry about. Neanderthals, on the other hand, sported a stockier build optimized for colder climates with more mass per square inch of surface area. The sasquatch takes the human body plan and pushes it to one extreme, with three strategies to prevent heat loss: being hairier, being stockier, and being just plain bigger than any other primate on the planet. Squatches don't seem to give a tinker's damn about cold. A snowy mountain pass with a stiff breeze probably feels about right to them. If they are physiologically challenged at all, it probably is in the hot and humid forests of Texas in summer. Bob Garrett believes they spend much of their days in summer soaking in the region's paltry rivers, most of which wouldn't be deep enough to submerge a deer, let alone a bigfoot.

I had tucked the locks of black hair into the pockets of the adventure pants and veered back down to walk on the road when I heard a car slowing behind me and to my right. I looked over to see the driver's window lowering on a gray Toyota Corolla. The driver, a beautiful woman of about thirty, with dark brown hair pulled back in a head band, flashed a wholesome smile. "Are you walking the Lone Star Trail?"

"As a matter of fact I am."

"That's so cool! We have a place up here at 405," and she pointed up the road to the right. "It's a disc golf course. We have hot showers if you want one or just need a place to soak your feet."

This seemed too good to be true. Was she a mirage? Or had I been hit and killed by a speeding pickup, and was she my angel-guide leading me on to my customized paradise? I harbored higher hopes for the afterlife than disc golf, but if that's all I deserve I won't argue with it. Or, was she a demon, tempting me to set down the cross I bore and to leave the trail with its hardships and trials? I shouted "Get behind me, Satan!" Actually, I thanked her profusely and told her I sure wished I could but still had eight miles left that day and so had better keep stepping. She smiled, waved, and receded into the forest ahead as suddenly as she had appeared.

At last I turned left and reentered the forest. Here I completed the Phelps Section and, somewhat nonsensically since I had just departed Four Notch Road, entered the Four Notch Section of the trail.

The sky had been growing gradually darker for the last few hours, and thunder in the southwest was becoming louder and more sustained. It had been rumbling since just after noon, booming through the forest hills and gulleys like a call and response with the sound of rifles, as this was November 1 and the first day of deer rifle season. Gunfire was on all sides of me but was distant enough that I wasn't overly concerned. Nonetheless I did cover the crown of my pith helmet with my orange bandana, making an odd sight even odder and certainly more festive.

Finally, at three p.m., a light rain started. I pulled off the trail and fished my rain suit out of my backpack. The blue, paper-thin waterproof pants went on over the adventure pants, and, suffering from the heat and humidity, I stripped off my shirt before donning the matching rain jacket.

Now the thunder really started finding its voice, and I marched on somewhat nervously through the brittle trees. Gliding forward ... *boom!* ... ever forward ... *crash!* ... gliding ever forward ... *kabooommm!* I had wanted an adventure, I thought, and I am getting one. The rain never came hard, but the forest got good and wet.

Mile Marker 48 was in most ways no different from the rest, a brown strip of metal emerging from the forest floor with mailbox stickers enumerating 4-8 at the top edge and a long sticker beneath them with icons depicting all the modes of transportation that were banned on that trail: a car, an ATV, a motorcycle, a bicycle, and a horse and rider, each with a forbidding red diagonal slash through it. But it was a special marker nonetheless, because it meant that I was halfway through with my hike. I did not just take its picture like all the rest; I bent over for a selfie with it, even kissing the corner of the marker. In the photograph I wear a bright orange do-rag, my silver-rimmed glasses, and a four-day beard that is mostly white — picture the original Aunt Jemimah, only white, male, middle-aged, homeless, and topless, as I was now too hot for either a shirt or raincoat.

I was nearing the end of the day's work when I reached the bridge over Briar Creek. You've heard of a bridge over troubled waters; this was a troubled bridge over no water. I'll explain. There are creeks — seasonal drainages — without number out here, and a huge variety of bridges put up by either the Forest Service or as Eagle Scout projects. At one end of the spectrum is the iron bridge, of which there were about four along the Lone Star Trail carrying hikers over the more permanent bodies of water. If maintenance on them ceased today, they would still be there in 500 years. At the other end of the spectrum, a bridge could be nothing more than four treated two-by-sixes laid side by side and not so much as tacked to each other. (I am not including on this spectrum logs that have fallen over ravines and serve as bridges.) The bridge over Briar Creek was on the hardier end of this spectrum — a good five feet wide, with hand rails, and lots of lumber.

But meaty as it was, it was a sad sight and a case study in failed engineering. Here is how to picture this affair: Take a bridge and snap it in half laterally, so that a pedestrian would have to make a 90-degree turn to the left halfway across. Now take the entire thing and push it to the right so that the posts holding the bridge up are 45 degrees to the horizon. Then put police tape across the rails in an attempt to discourage its use. A wiser man would have simply trudged through the dry creek bed, but adventure beckoned, and I wanted to cross the bridge. So with the Indiana Jones theme blaring in my head I gingerly traversed down the first angle, then, holding fast to the upstream railing, fully expecting the whole apparatus to collapse under its newfound load, I made my way around the corner and back up the far side before reaching terra firma.

I texted Ansen to tell him I was about twenty minutes out. He was coming back from meetings in downtown Houston, was stuck in traffic, and told me I'd likely beat him there today. I emerged from the forest and collapsed in the red-dirt pullout next to the trailhead to await my chariot. Desperate for the comfort of any sort of cushion, and my backpack offering the only prospect of some, I thought it a splendid idea to lie on top of my backpack as if it were a mattress. But as I eased down on top of it, I heard a great crunch as it bore my full weight, and I slid off. I opened the backpack and there found my pith helmet completely stove-in. I had forgotten it was not on my head, and I almost cried at what appeared to be a total loss. *Pithyyy!!!!* But it's a tough old bird, and with a little patient work it regained its intended shape, more or less. The divots here and there that would never come out now simply bear false witness to admirers who assume they came from tumbles I took into ravines in the Congo, and not from the time my fat ass tried to mount my backpack on the side of a road while waiting for my ride.

This day, Day Four, would prove to be my longest day, 15.4 miles and more than 44,000 steps. My father-in-law's voice echoed in my mind's ear: "Meriwether Lewis walked 25 miles every day." Yeah, well not with a forty-pound pack!

Interestingly, it was some 5,000 more steps than the next longest day, which was only one-tenth of a mile less at 15.3. I figured this to mean that road-walking encouraged or enabled shorter steps than striding along a dirt trail.

This was the farthest I had ever walked in single day. So it was humbling to think that when my ancestors had come to Texas from the Carolinas, they had traveled sixteen miles *every* day for months at a time. I should say, I walked nearly sixteen miles, and their *oxen* walked sixteen miles, so it wasn't quite apples to apples, although riding in an ox cart along what passed for roads back then, with all the bouncing and wrenching that went on, would have been almost as much of an athletic achievement. Sixteen miles being the distance a family could travel in a typical day and still make camp, throughout the South white men who had married Creek women would operate "stands" that were spaced every sixteen miles. These were like a combination KOA campground (for those of you who remember them) and truck stop that would sell a traveler anything they needed, at a premium.

Ansen appeared shortly, like a dying man's vision, and hoisted me and my crumpled pith helmet off the ground and into the Focus. He drove us to New Waverly, and we homed in on the only cafe in town, Waverly House. He went on in as I hobbled across the parking lot in my now-familiar man-in-a-body-cast gait, pivoting from side-to-side like a sentient gingerbread man without the full use of any joint in my body.

Inside, under dim fluorescent lights, we found a Formica booth, and I kicked off the order unapologetically with a chocolate shake, then chased it with a chicken-fried steak, mashed potatoes with gravy, green beans, and a dinner roll. You could say I ate in honor of the dead shrew; it wasn't *quite* equal to my body weight, but an "A" for effort. Ansen saw my chicken-fried steak and raised me some purple-hull peas and a side of fried okra.

After we had eaten our fill and I had finished the chocolate shake and washed it down with a pint of ice water, I hobbled back to the front door toward the cash register and reached into my front pocket for my wallet. What I pulled out was a mass of black hair. "Hmm, I really need an envelope for this," I mumbled in Ansen's direction. The young man at the cash register did not seem the least bit curious about it. Perhaps his customers routinely offer remuneration in the form of sasquatch hair samples. Nothing would surprise me anymore.

Back in Montgomery I repeated the previous night's protocol, with a hot shower, some labor-intensive television, and Tibley and me reunited on the couch and blissfully drifting toward sleep.

Strange things were afoot all over the continent. The Cubs even took Game 6, 9-3, to tie the Series.

13
The Big Woods

*"Always in the big woods when you leave familiar ground
and step off alone into a new place there will be, along with
the feelings of curiosity and excitement, a little nagging of
dread. It is the ancient fear of the Unknown, and it is your
first bond with the wilderness you are going into."*

—*Wendell Berry*

50.4

SINCE MONTGOMERY LAY IN THE southwesternmost
part of the forest and I was traveling each day mainly east,
Ansen's and my commute to the drop point became longer
every day. From big arteries to small ones, we burrowed into
the forest. Highways, exits, forest highways, turns, and miles-
long dirt roads finally found us at the previous day's
extraction point. On the drive out that morning, apropos of
nothing, we had spent a fair amount of time breaking down

what it was, exactly, that made Steely Dan so great, and as I walked into the woods, I sent one out to him with "Deacon Blues" belting with all I had. It echoed out into woods for at least a half mile, and at moments like that I always wondered if the Others were as puzzled at our sounds as we were at theirs. I often wonder what animals in general think music is. What does my dog think I'm doing when I'm singing? And out here, what do the squirrels and raccoons assume is making that otherworldly racket? They probably think it no different from the coyotes' cries or the squatches' howls — long-distance communication: I'm over here. Deer down. Supper's on.

Now I came upon a fungus colony that stopped me in my tracks. It was an exquisite collection of feather-like fungi covering a downed log, each lobe sporting dozens of concentric wavy colored rings of browns and grays, black, and white and creams. Called "turkey tail fungus" and actually a kind of mushroom, it made me think of how beauty will find a way to manifest itself in every kind of lifeform, and in every kingdom, even the lowly fungus that we work so hard to stamp out of our daily lives, from athlete's foot to elderly toenails, to mold and mildew that we wipe away with household cleaners. Out here, all forms flourish just as they should, and, especially if you can train your eyes to go small, there is wonder around every corner and in every crevice. On one stretch of the trail, way back in the Kelly Section, I think it was, palatial clusters of mushrooms sprang from the middle of the trail every twenty feet or so. They were like tiny St. Petersburgs. At one point I saw shelf-fungus growing up the length of a five-foot snag, looking like a miniature of Minas Tirith, Tolkien's gleaming capital of Gondor. Fungus here ranged from plain and unassuming to fancy and even naughty.

A half hour in, I arrived at the hunter camp where I originally had planned to stay. Like the others, it had a fire ring and a kiosk. Unlike the others, this one also had a wooden sign, which read: Karolyi Primitive Camp. I could not see it from here, but I knew from satellite images that only a thousand yards to the south was one of the great curiosities of Sam Houston National Forest, the Olympic training camp of Bela and Marta Karolyi. The Karolyis defected from Romania in 1981 and after a brief stint in Oklahoma moved to Houston to join a gymnastics venture pitched by some Houston businessmen. The Karoylis bought the "ranch" in 1983, and built an empire in this piney wood miles from the nearest paved road. The ranch itself is well marked and branded to a fare-thee-well with U.S. Olympic signs, and I imagined many a gymnast's parent incredulously driving this eternal dirt road to drop their children off for summer camp. As Ansen and I had come in that morning, a Porsche had followed us down the dirt road. I couldn't see the driver, but figured it was Bela or Marta coming back from a coffee run to New Waverly.

In this hunter camp, I imagined Mary Lou Retton, Kerri Strug, Aly Raisman, and Simone Biles coming through on a short nature walk between workouts, maybe even taking a breather on these logs around the fire ring. I chuckled when I considered that here in the heart of the Sam Houston National Forest, some of the world's tallest humanoids might be living a stone's throw from some of the shortest.

In mile 53, I crossed a forest service road and was greeted by a disorienting sight. Before me, across the road, vertically down the trunk of a large pine tree in white spray paint were the capital letters: F-U-O-C-K. Hmmm, I thought. I guess that's an especially unfortunate code the Forest Service uses for trees that are slated to be harvested. Then it dawned on me that this was simply graffiti. I was glad to see that the high school youth of Huntsville were getting outside and enjoying nature, although the sight did fill me with the conviction that it was high time we returned to a robust teaching of phonics. Since I was stopped anyway, I decided to take a drink, and after fussing with one of my Nalgene bottles, I glanced back the way I had come and saw its companion tree, this one spray painted with a four-foot-long upward-pointing phallus and testicles, and a dotted line being ejected from the tip, lest anyone not understand the pictograph. I offered a silent prayer for the future of humanity, shook my head, and glided forward.

Soon I was dumped out on another road and took the opportunity to record the day's installment of trailaoke, the Muppets' "Mah Na Mah Nah." It was good to have a request that didn't require me to learn or remember lyrics.

54.4

"People get killed in there."

That's what Bob Garrett had said of the Big Woods Section of Sam Houston National Forest. And in case you just picked up this book and turned randomly to this page, he was not talking about falling trees or flooding or mountain lions. He was talking about sasquatches.

There was no way of proving or disproving this unsettling claim, because, according to him, if someone went missing or turned up dead, authorities would concoct a cover story, usually a hunting accident.

On the other hand, in my mind's eye there was always YouTube's smiling Ken Kramm, perhaps as a video inset, innocently riding his trail bike through the forest with backpack and Bear, showing off his newly fashioned haversack to an admiring online fan base. These two realities were ever at war in my mind. Which one was the reality I would finally subscribe to? Would it be Bob Garrett's "People get killed in there"? I had reserved judgement until I came out here and saw for myself, and so far, Garrett's reality was firing on all cylinders. Or would be it the innocent reality of Ken Kramm and of Karen Borski Somers, she who wrote of the neighboring Four Notch Section I had just left that it was "very popular with Boy Scouts"? Or, terrifyingly, was it both?

I crossed a forest road, and the Big Woods Section began with a brown wooden sign and routed letters filled with yellow paint announcing the LSHT Big Woods South Trailhead 8.6 miles to the southeast. If the Lone Star Trail was like a rainbow, I had summited and was now on the downhill side. It was more or less immediately obvious to me that if two roads diverged in a yellow wood, *this* was the road less traveled by. It was not as if any part of the Lone Star Trail was really parklike or groomed, but this stretch was especially scraggly and struck me as unkempt, with far more downed trees and overgrown obstacles. Of course, all of this played right into my fears about the Others in this area.

The Big Woods is high and therefore dry. All guide books and trail directions note the lack of water in this area, and so I rationed my intake even more strictly than normal. A few times I spotted a leaf on the ground filled with rainwater from the previous day's thunderstorm, and saying aloud, "Don't mind if I do," I squatted down, lifted it up carefully, and drank it down.

The trees in this section did not strike me as particularly big; perhaps they once had been, before the Bonanza Era. Rather, I supposed it was the size of the uninterrupted forest itself that earned the name. The dry understory was frequently brown and looked like it would make tremendous fuel for a fire if one got started out here.

With the brittle, sandy soil seemed to come a higher number of downed trees. At one point I came to three trees lying across the trail with about ten feet between each one. The first was just off the ground, requiring me to climb over it like I did many times a day with other logs; the second was too high to climb over but too low to walk under, and so it forced me to my hands and knees, my backpack scraping the trunk above me; and the third then forced me over again. It was nature's American Ninja Warriors course.

But the worst thing about so many downed trees was that many of those trees still had blazes nailed to them. Leaving me no idea which way to go. And some of those trees fell along the trail, obscuring my vantage point to the next blaze. While I could count on one hand the times I had lost the trail before Day Five, in the Big Woods I lost the trail no fewer than eight times in those 8.6 miles. On every occasion, I would stop and begin circling the last blaze I could find, my eyes scanning out to spy the next one, my blood pressure and anxiety steadily rising with each pass of the widening gyre.

Through the Big Woods I climbed across very long rises and descended equally long falls, on which I could look out at what seemed like millions of pine trees of identical size. This section of the forest was a strict duoculture. While pines dominated the canopy, covering the understory were equally endless fields of American beautyberry, their wide leaves obscuring the trail so completely that at a distance I would have looked to be wading among them up to my waist. Also in this section whoever had plotted the trail had taken to putting blazes on tall metal stakes, perhaps because they were more likely to remain vertical and visible this way than on one of the top-heavy trees. The featurelessness of it gave me the sensation of being at sea.

On either side of these long, pine- and beautyberry-covered hills, the hegemony of the yaupon reasserted itself with a vengeance. At points it grew over the trail, forcing me into green tunnels that would have veiled me from a tyrannosaurus six feet away let alone a sasquatch. I did not glide, but hacked angrily with my trekking poles, thrashing thorny vines and spider webs out of my way. Here too the beauty of the pith helmet was fully realized: when a modest limb or vine protruded into the trail, I did not stoop to avoid it, but merely bowed my head like a billy goat and rammed it at full speed, twigs and leaves scraping along the resin of the brim and crown until whipping back to their original place, now behind me on the trail.

The thousands of spider webs also testified to how few hikers came this way. It was late afternoon now as I started passing mile markers in the high fifties, and yet elaborate webs across the trail told me I was the first hiker of the day, perhaps the week.

At one point, I was glancing at the ground instead of in front of me and came face to face with what is perhaps the most spectacular creature I have ever directly encountered in the wild, the marbled orb weaver. This spider, a little bigger than a quarter was so exquisitely decorated that, upon seeing photos of it, several of my friends insisted it was fake. The eye is first arrested by a large yellow midsection with black markings that made me think this spider was wearing a natty hound's-tooth jacket. Had exhaustion given rise to delirium? What next — a cricket in a tuxedo? This yellow and black part, according to the website that later helped me identify the species, is known as the "butt." It had a big one, and I cannot lie — I liked it. I would have thought a more scientific name was available to us, but to each his own, and it does, after all, convey the body part. (I don't want to get all technical on you, but for the record, scientists call it the "abdomen.") Above the butt, the rest of its central body was bright orange. For their part, the legs looked like eight skinny pieces of candy corn, starting at the body with bright orange the shade of candied orange slices, then white, then black, then white, black, white, with smaller striping all the way to the tips of the legs. Because of its larger size, this one would have been a female *Araneus marmoreus*.

I confess I did not then know it was a marbled orb weaver, and like most other things in these pages, it had to be looked up later. They do not actually weave three-dimensional orbs as their name suggests, but large circular webs. Spiders, though we are somewhat hard-wired to be repulsed by them — and I am — are astonishing creatures. I cannot begin to imagine how they do what they do. These orb weavers, after completing their elaborate circular traps, run a "signal thread" from the center of the web to what is essentially a hunting blind of dead leaves beside the trap. When the signal thread vibrates, it's dinner time.

The previous day, a friend had requested a trailaoke performance of Leonard Cohen's "Hallelujah," a departure from the light pop fare I had specialized in to date, but I took the challenge and suspended the cheesy facade I used for most of my pop covers to render a short but earnest version, a verse and a chorus echoed through the woods.

Leonard Cohen died three days later; I hoped I didn't bear partial responsibility.

Across the Big Woods Section, and indeed across the entire forest, I saw the sign of hogs, soil dug up and plants toppled as if a plow had been dragged through. This is a familiar sight to any outdoorsman in the southern United States. These are invasive exotics, brought by the Spaniards, and state wildlife officials are only too pleased when they are killed. According to the state, "they may be taken by any means or methods at any time of year. There are no seasons or bag limits." They are so prolific and successful, that we must kill 60 percent of them every year just to keep the population flat.

In the 1930s, Texas sportsmen and ranchers introduced Russian boars, which were Europe's feral hogs, to Texas for sport hunting. Most escaped from game ranches and cross-bred freely with the Spanish hogs resulting in what we have so abundantly today.

Despite their ubiquity and their great numbers, and despite my very considerable amount of time outdoors in the past twenty years, I had never once laid eyes on one in the wild. I did see a young one crossing a highway once out east of Austin, but never had I seen one in the wilderness. Think about that. Our best estimate at this writing is that there are two million feral hogs in Texas, two million! And at forty-nine years old, I had only ever seen *one* with my own eyes. A statistic like that tells you just about everything you need to know about why we don't see more sasquatches.

I had about two hours left in the Big Woods when I heard a piglet squealing in the brush. There one was — a wild hog. I could hear it clearly no more than 200 yards away, but I couldn't see it. I sat on a footbridge over a creek bed, drank water, and listened to its funny grunts and squeals. Dropping my pack, I even took a few steps in its direction, but I knew actually getting a glimpse of it would require a lot more effort than I could afford to expend and would take me off the trail and away from blazes, always a dicey proposition.

I rose from the bridge, clicked my pack back on and started southeast again. The sun was getting low now, a sight that instinctively triggered dread, and right on cue, here came the triangles on the sandy trail. I decided it was time to pick up the pace and get the heck out of the forest. I was so worn out though, an observer would have thought I was a crippled man who was using two canes for support. The sight of the triangles, however, and the low angle of the light put more spring in my step than any energy drink ever could have. *And I am gliding forward, ever forward! I am gliding ever forward. I am gliding ever forward! I am gliding ever forward!*

When I reached the parking lot of Big Woods South Trailhead, I collapsed on the dirt and waited for that red Ford Focus to make its appearance, that angel that flew from Montgomery. As I waited, I updated my status, posting: "This was the day the Trail asked, how much do you want it?" I now had a section that ranked as my least favorite. I had started later than normal and compounded that with a snail's pace from getting lost so much.

As I lay in the dirt, I decided then and there that if I wanted to finish the hike strong I needed a day to heal. A day on the couch in Montgomery would be just what the doctor ordered. I finished my Facebook post by proclaiming this my plan. I would sit in the bath for hours tomorrow and soak in Epsom salts, a bit of folk wisdom I trusted even if I didn't understand how it worked.

Back in Montgomery, Ansen and I wheeled into a Walgreen's to get a few essentials — deodorant, the aforementioned Epsom salts, muscle cream. Doubled over at the waist, I pushed a shopping cart in front of me for no other reason than that I needed it as a walker. As soon as we got in line, we noticed the gentleman at the counter, two customers ahead of us, seemed to be paying for sixteen dollars' worth of cigarillos with hundreds of pennies and nickels. Being legal tender, the coins had to be accepted, and so for ten full minutes the cashier counted them out, occasionally losing his place and having to start over on this or that dollar grouping. I was so tired I laughed to keep from crying. Though the shopping cart now bore nearly 100 percent of my weight, I wondered if it would really be so wrong to just collapse on the floor. And I would have done just that if it didn't mean I would have to get back up. Or maybe I could have just been left in peace to spend the night on the floor of the Montgomery Walgreen's, the night manager pulling a light sheet over my snoring body before locking up.

At the end of the excruciating transaction, our hero had come up twenty-five cents short and so asked the longsuffering cashier to put the last pack back. Seeing the potential of another delay, Ansen quickly dug into his pocket, extracted a quarter, and plunked it on the counter.

"Thanks!" said the customer.

"This must be your lucky day," the cashier chirped.

"Yeah," said the cigarillo aficionado, and then, apropos of nothing, added, "I just hit a deer!"

To this Ansen replied, "What — and a bunch of change fell out?!"

That night, the Cubs, once down three games to one, won the World Series, by one run, 8-7, in extra innings, and broke a 108-year drought. This was a fact we would learn later, as we still could not figure out how to work the TV. Truly, the world was still full of mystery, wonder, and even the occasional miracle

14

The Magnolia Alpha Male

"Knock and the door shall be opened unto you.
Seek and ye shall find."
                                        —Matthew 7:7

AT DAYBREAK, TIBLEY climbed off my feet and retreated to his lair beneath the couch. I won't lie — the couch felt good. But the notion of sitting around the house all day no longer appealed to me nearly as much as it had the previous evening.

I was surprised to be moving with near regularity, no worse than the creaks and snaps that accompanied any normal morning. Ansen and I returned to the 105 Cafe for a leisurely breakfast of waffles with butter and syrup and scrambled eggs with butter and syrup and sausage patties with butter and syrup and coffee and orange juice and water.

There in our booth on his laptop, Ansen joined a Facebook group devoted to snake identification and uploaded the photo of the reptile I had taken on Day Two. Within ten minutes, his membership was accepted and we had a friendly but unadorned reply from the admin in Australia: "Buttermilk pacer - nonvenomous. Thanks!" What a world we live in.

As empty plates began accumulating and mid-morning became late morning, the hostess became visibly worried we were never going to relinquish our booth. Ansen floated the idea of returning to the trail and me doing some of the road-walking that was next on the map, something easy, just to keep the joints oiled. Though I hated the idea of him driving me all the way out there for just a few miles of walking, I agreed it would feel good to stay in the game.

62.8

Around noon he dropped me at the same parking lot at the end of Big Woods where he had scraped me off the dirt the previous afternoon. Refreshed by a morning off and itching to strike a blow against the trail that had struck me first, I set a smoking pace right down the center of the dirt road as his little red car disappeared in a cloud of salmon-colored dust ahead of me.

James Taylor immediately sprang to mind, and I extracted the cell phone and selfie stick and trailaoke-ed both "Walkin' Man" and "Walking on a Country Road" at the top of my lungs. I hoped I wouldn't be shot by a local for covering the songs of a known liberal, and out of an abundance of caution, I followed those quickly and loudly with something from Charlie Daniels' early catalogue.

At the side of the road I spotted a large gray-brown feather, probably a duck or goose tail-feather, and, in a stray moment of whimsy, stuck it under the band of the pith helmet. Granted, nothing in creation weighs less than a feather. Still, taking on any weight or bulk at all that wasn't purely utilitarian was, I thought, uniquely human. Old Horace Kephart wrote about this very phenomenon, little non-essentials that we choose to pack for miles and miles through the wilderness solely because they bring us a little comfort, nostalgia, or entertainment. For me it was a perfect keepsake from the trail: free, easily obtained, and light as... well, itself. Kephart's own nonessential was a porcelain tea cup that he especially liked to sip from — hot coffee and, I imagined, a cocaine pill.

I passed the Huntsville water treatment plant (scratch it off the bucket list!) and then on the opposite side of the road, an imposing black steel gate reading Big Woods Game Ranch.

It seems almost silly to note that there were again loose dogs on the road, like noting there was sky above me, or that gravity was still in effect that day. The dogs came racing off their owners' property snarling viciously at me as I trucked ever forward, occasionally taking a sudden step toward them to show them I was not the prey in this scenario but the predator. Oddly, being so utterly helpless in the context of a potential sasquatch encounter made everything else in creation seem at least manageable if not always trivial. Head getting twisted off by something nine feet tall? That's scary. Lab mix with an attitude? Suddenly not so much.

And at certain times out here, even though I still thought of them very much as the Others, I felt a certain pride of kinship as well. Maybe it's the way coyotes feel about gray wolves, frightened of them, but emboldened by being a miniature version of them. Coyotes are just a little more badass because wolves exist and coyotes are a lot like them. Those friggin' dogs had better be scared of me. I'm like a small sasquatch. And we know what their body plan is capable of — running, climbing, kicking, throwing, twisting. I'm 6'2" with a wingspan the same, I'm sporting nearly 200 pounds of mass (though not much of it in places that are helpful, but still). *I'm the predator in this deal, buddy! You'd better run away!*

I passed the town of Evergreen, where my trail notes said the Baptist church offered its spigot on the back of the building to hikers in need of hydration. It seemed Baptists had 100 percent market-share of believers in this part of the world. Even Sam Houston himself succumbed and was baptized into the denomination at the age of sixty-one after fourteen years of persuasion by his wife. My grandfather had been a Baptist preacher, and though my mother had scandalously strayed into Presbyterianism, I had some measure of genetic affinity for Baptists. And whatever affinity I might already have had shot up considerably upon learning of this spigot on the church and their generosity regarding it. However, I was moving so fast I had no need of it at the moment and was still as loaded with water as a fresh camel.

I doglegged through the little town, crossed the main highway between speeding logging trucks, and headed south along FM 945, a two-lane blacktop traversing gently rolling hills. It wasn't long before I had gained the attention of a gray pit bull and a black lab mix who raced off the property and came closer than any of the others to actually attacking me. Heart accelerating, I turned to face them and swung my trekking poles as hard as I could so that they whirred through the air. I screamed "HYAH!" The pit bull thought better of it, but the black lab mix bared his teeth and snarled, not ready to back down. A groggy shirtless man appeared on the porch and yelled something incomprehensible at the beasts, who finally retreated toward the house. *I'm* the predator.

A bit later, I came upon a ranch whose entrance the owner had adorned with two of the most random sights of the trip: to the left of the gate sat a square stone face, eight feet tall and ten feet wide, a weathered concrete head that looked like an angry Mesoamerican god. It struck me as perhaps the landowner's daughter's idea twenty years ago. Across the drive sat a two-seat helicopter without doors, windshield cracked and holding so much dust I couldn't see through it, with short flat blades drooping toward the grass. I have no idea, but at least it occupied my thoughts for the next ten minutes.

As I mentioned, the Lone Star Trail, without any of its ancillary loops, is 96.44 miles long, but I never hesitate to round up to 100, mainly because of how many times I crossed this highway either to avoid oncoming traffic or to get into shade. If you took that zig-zagging path and straightened it out, then you took all the circling I had to do in the Big Woods from losing the trail, then added in the half mile from walking the wrong way outside of Huntsville while singing trailaoke, you would get to the century mark easily.

Ansen had gotten the bug to see what this forest hiking thing was all about, and so, to kill time while waiting for me to finish my road-walk and to get a few photos, he had parked his car where we had planned to rendezvous and then gone two miles into the forested portion of the Magnolia Section away from me. I texted him that I was running ahead of schedule, and he turned back immediately but was still deep in the thicket. I passed a few more one-room Baptist churches and a cemetery, and when I reached the parking lot, I stashed my backpack in the weeds in front of his car and headed in to meet him.

67.4

For myriad reasons, this stretch, the Magnolia Section, had my full and undivided attention. While all of the road-walking

I had done that day was technically included in this section, the forest trail measured just under eight miles from here to Double Lake. And this ecosystem, in which magnolias grew plentifully along the long, creek-riddled descents to the San Jacinto River, was only about six miles wide.

To begin with, I was virtually certain this was the section in which Bob Garrett claimed to have had an extraordinary encounter nineteen years earlier. He and his son had just pitched camp and the sun was about to go down when they were ambushed by an irate female sasquatch. He said the creature had a complete "meltdown," circling their camp and screaming at them all night long while pulling up small pines and throwing them at the two from just beyond the light of their rapidly growing campfire. At one point she came at him through a stand of small pines, and from a kneeling position he planted his shotgun in her midsection before she backed away. This story has become known as his "Scary Night on the Lone Star Trail," which he tells in detail on *Sasquatch Chronicles* and which you can hear him reference off camera during the Torn-Up Camp video. Despite the attack, which he said put him into a kind of shock that prevented him from going back into the woods for nearly a year, he kept coming into the area to do research, and he said he witnessed her in here continuously for fifteen years. (He even left squeaky toys for her, which she would take, break, then return to the gifting spot for replacement.) He said when the gas company put in a new pipeline and an accompanying road (which I figured for Freeside Lane), she left the area. But he said it was common knowledge back then that you do not stay in there. "If you go in there," he said, "go *right* on through." And going "*right* on through" was exactly what I planned to do.

I also found it fascinating that in her guidebook *The Lone Star Hiking Trail*, Karen Borski Somers had this comment regarding this exact location: "It is best not to camp in this area." She continues, "Several large oil and gas fields lie just north of the national forest." While this helps confirm the location of Garrett's story, it is not at all clear if this sentence is supposed to act as elaboration on "best not to camp in this area." She plows ahead with just the facts: "At 69.3, pass another fence corner and cross over the creek..." Whatever the case, she and Garrett seem to agree on the imprudence of calling this place home even for one night.

I entered the forest of the Magnolia Section with nothing but my trekking poles, pith helmet, and the clothes I had on. I didn't even take a water bottle, as I knew I would be back out to the car in just a few minutes and had no impressionable Cub Scouts tagging along to witness this arch-sin of outdoorsmanship.

Less than fifty yards down the trail a familiar shape caught my eye, a rounded triangle with sides of three different lengths. I came to a full stop and lowered my face to see it better. This one was different from the hundreds I had seen over the preceding days. First, the quality of the print was of an entirely different order. It was much better defined than anything else I had spotted so far. It was a right foot, heading back toward the parking lot. Most critically, a big toe and a second toe, both in perfect proportion to the rest of the foot, were clearly visible, impressed in the topmost layer of the sand and rendered a slightly different color by varying degrees of moisture. Pine needles were scooted and crushed into a parabola that defined the heel best of all. In the middle of the print were a few dead sweetgum leaves.

What's more, the shape conformed perfectly to the anatomical details I had read about and seen in photos through the years. There are obvious similarities between our feet and theirs: the general oblong shape, the rounded heel, the five forward-pointing toes in contrast to the opposable big toe of the great apes. But there are clear differences as well, and those are just as significant. One difference is that the Others are all flat-footed. The delicate arches most humans possess, designed to carry the gracile, running creatures we evolved into in East Africa, would be no fit for a creature that can reach 1,000 pounds. And sure enough, the print was clearly from a flat foot, showing no sign of a ball and arch but rather being well defined to its edge all the way around.

Beneath the toes it widened out to a meaty nine inches before slowly narrowing toward the heel. While human feet are generally one-third as wide as they are long, true to the overall thickness of the Others' body plan, their feet are nearly always half as wide as long, and this one was right on the money: 2:1. While the shape of the print was what argued most loudly against this being some sort of a hoax, another significant factor was its subtlety. Ansen, who is highly observant and has won awards for his nature photography, missed it not once but twice. The only reason I saw it was that I had spent sixty-seven miles fine-tuning my vision to spot anomalies in the trail. Again, think eyes adjusting to the dark. If someone were trying to get attention by stamping impressions in the sand on this trail, they sure were taking a lot of time and care to create something the vast majority of people coming through here would never spot.

The quality was astonishing, but nothing was more astonishing than its size. It was *much* larger than the other prints and clearly out of the human range. I placed my men's size 10-½ shoe next to it like I had the others, and it looked like a toddler's shoe. The print was essentially twice as long as my foot and more than twice as wide. In fact, the footprint was as wide as my foot is long. The well-defined big toe was nearly half the length of my foot!

Heel to toe, the impression measured eighteen inches.

If it had been a human and had gone to get fitted for shoes it would have worn a men's 32, 11E. One friend to whom I later showed the picture was incredulous, saying, "But ... it's so big!" as if that were a mark *against* its authenticity instead of a point for it. Another said, "I never expected a bigfoot print to be so ... *big*."

"Yeah," I replied, "they don't call them that for nothing."

I later found a research paper in which someone had attempted to extrapolate the height and weight of sasquatches from the length of their footprints. This was mostly based on Patty, the creature in the Patterson-Gimlin Film, who had left a trackway and been filmed in such a way as to establish her height. For the record, her footprint was 14-½ inches long, and her height was established with photogrammetry at 7' 3-½". Using the video evidence and biological best estimates, her weight was ball-parked at 500 pounds. This table put the height of a similar creature leaving an 18-inch print at 8'4" and 770 pounds. And just in case you have lost sight of this particular reference point, the ceiling of a standard American home is eight feet from the floor. Look up at your ceiling; the eyes would be about there, the head breaking through the sheetrock. An adult male sasquatch could stand beneath a regulation basketball hoop, reach up, and, flat-footed, grasp the top corners of the backboard.

How the print was actually made was something of a curiosity to me, because it was difficult for detailed prints to take in this needle-covered dirt. I concluded that this print probably came in the aftermath of the rainstorm I had hiked through two days earlier through the Four Notch Section. If the creature's feet were wet, then when it stepped on this trail, which was lightly coated with pine needles, it would have simultaneously broken the topmost layer of sand with its immense weight, then lifted off a layer of needles, which would have stuck to the bottom of its foot. If true, this meant the print was less than forty-eight hours old.

Because in the days running up to this I had been seeing shapes that, barefoot, were about three inches longer than my hiking shoe, as well as small ones, I had postulated I was seeing the prints of females and their young, primate behavior being nearly universal in this respect, ourselves included. Now, I was even more sure this is what I had been seeing because this — this was the male. I came to call the maker of the print the Magnolia Alpha Male. I wondered about so much — was it a Type I — jet black with coned head? Or a Type II, brown or maybe auburn with a more rounded head? Could it even have been the Gray Walker himself?

The discovery of this print was another turning point in my journey from curiosity to belief to knowledge. If everything else I had experienced and ascribed to the Others could somehow be written off to coincidence, or to an overactive imagination, or to confirmation bias, this simply could not be. This was clear. This was real. This print was as real as the earth under my feet, as real as the blood in my own veins, as real as the chair you are sitting in right now.

Wow. There it was. One of those gigantic, hairy, unimaginably frightening ... *monsters* ... stepped *right here*, right where I stood. We had stepped on the very same pine needles and sweetgum leaves. We had breathed the same air. We had brushed past the same yaupon leaves. It's true — it's all true.

I came to regard the print of the Magnolia Alpha Male as a sort of gift, a reward from the universe for having the courage to go out there, alone and unarmed, and for persevering, for continuously scanning every inch of that trail for 67.41 miles. Saint Augustine said it best: "Faith is to believe what you do not see. The reward of this faith is to see what you believe."

No matter what happened now, I would always have this. If bigfoots were never "discovered," never admitted to by our government and the scientists that do its bidding, this print would still be real, and I would still have a very good photograph of it that I took with my own hand and that included my own foot. I would still possess this knowledge. I would know in my bones they were real, and not just believe out of a preponderance of evidence in the aggregate, topping out at ninety-nine percent. If I died tomorrow, I would die knowing. All of the friends and family members who had humored me over the years and who had listened to my wild beliefs only out of politeness, or who had dismissed it before I could even get to the strongest evidence — they would now have something else to contend with besides just my word.

But as with everything else in this odd journey, this did not come as a thunderbolt. Even as it was a turning point, it came upon me as a dawning, a fact that wasn't fully seated in my consciousness until days, even weeks, later, after many hours of studying the photos on my computer and on my phone and showing them to friends and texting them to family members. An onlooker would not have seen me falling to my knees dramatically like the winner of match point at Wimbledon, thrusting my fists to the sky as hot tears of joy and relief streamed down my cheeks.

No, they would only have seen me pause for about sixty seconds, take my phone off my belt, and stick my foot out at an odd angle. I took three pictures of it, one with my left foot against it, one with my right next to it, and one with my right foot inside of it. For an additional thirty seconds they would have seen me looking around for other similar prints that might have formed a trackway with this one. The woods, a vast yaupon monoculture that stretched for more than a mile, were extremely thick on either side, growing right to the trail. But an observer would have seen me move on, finding none. Gliding forward, ever forward.

Five hundred more yards down the trail I decided to just sit and wait for Ansen. Three minutes later I noticed a red tick making its way up the thigh of the adventure pants and so decided being on my feet was not the worst fate I could suffer after all. I continued strolling east toward Ansen.

We met at the mile 68 marker, and being more than a mile beyond the car now, I wondered aloud if there were any spot at which he could pick me up; fatigue had made me greedy, and now I was loath to walk a hundred feet without receiving full credit. The phones came out, and on a map search we found Freeside Lane, a little half-mile dirt road that the trail crossed where Ansen could get in to pick me up. You'll recall I had left the trailhead without as much as a bottle of water, so he gave me his, and I gave him one of my poles to free up a hand.

As we split up and headed in opposite directions, I called back to him, almost as an afterthought, "Hey, look for a big print about fifty yards before the parking lot. Pretty good!"

"I will," he said. He looked, but he never saw it.

Soon I emerged from the yaupon monoculture, and the forest opened up to reveal the most beautiful stretch of the entire Lone Star Trail. Maybe it was the angle of the sunlight. Maybe it was the fact that I carried nothing but one pole and a half-full bottle of water. Maybe it was the print I had just seen, which might have discouraged wiser men from forging ahead alone and unarmed into this total isolation. But it was absolutely magical. I crossed a few scenic creeks on bridges that were no more than a few two-by-sixes lain side-by-side, and the magnolias proliferated. Then I came to the hunter camp, which I figured for the site of Garrett's "Scary Night on the Lone Star Trail" nearly twenty years earlier.

The beauty of the trail notwithstanding, I noted a modest puddle of diarrhea directly on it, and of course, took a photo of it, with my shoe safely to the side for scale.

So it was that this throw-away day became a respectable seven-mile afternoon walk, nearly 20,000 steps that took me halfway through the Magnolia Section, into the most scenic stretch of the whole trail, and rewarded me with by far the trip's most enduring image to that point, my trophy, the print of the Magnolia Alpha Male.

Ansen extracted me on that skinny gravel road. The following day would be our day to hike together, and therefore we would need both vehicles to set up a series of shuttles. So we headed toward the setting sun and Lot No. 1 near Richards to retrieve my truck. It was odd seeing that old girl again. It seemed like it had been a long time since I had sprung out of that driver's seat with fresh legs and flung on the backpack. But at the same time, it was days sooner than I originally had planned on seeing her again. Oddness all around.

I pulled the rusty shovel out of the driver's seat and lobbed it into the bed. To my relief, the engine cranked on the first try, and Ansen and I caravanned south through the forest.

We returned to Montgomery and — why fight it? — to Seven Leguas Mexican restaurant. Ansen had taken a picture of the diarrhea puddle too, and we compared photos and laughed at our predictability as we ate chips and scanned the menu.

I felt the eyes of fellow patrons on me as, clad in only a T-shirt, the adventure pants, and flip-flops I hobbled comically slowly toward the restroom, again like Tim Conway's Mr.

Tudball. After I had powdered my nose, seen a man about a horse, or acted out whatever euphemism you prefer, I washed my hands and prepared for the long, daunting journey back to our booth.

Looking in the mirror to check my teeth as I habitually do in bathrooms, my eyes were drawn to my neck and shoulders. I had given myself a haircut less than a week earlier and distinctly remember "cleaning up" my neck at that time. But now, it seemed the hair was back, longer and coarser than ever. I had sprouted like a Chia Pet. Was I going feral?

In turn this made me think of epigenetics, the phenomenon by which organisms change not by a shift in their genetic code but by means of their genes being turned on or off, stimulated or suppressed by elements of their environment. The most famous example was the domesticated hog, which, according to some accounts, could manifest physical changes within a few weeks of escaping a farm and entering the wilderness, as many did. It was like a combination of *The Call of the Wild* and the Incredible Hulk. Their hair grew immediately longer and coarser, their tusks — or "tushes" (rhymes with "rushes"), as they're known to old Texans — grew from barely visible on the farm to dangerous daggers in the woods. Even their skulls took on a different shape; and mind you this was not from one generation to the next — this is within an individual. Was I witnessing some miniscule version of this in myself? Was my neck and back hair furiously springing forth to protect me from the elements as a result of hormones released by twelve hours of sunshine and fourteen miles of walking every day?

In fact, epigenetics played a central role in one particularly intriguing theory of the sasquatch. It is articulated in the book *You Are Sasquatch*, and, as the name suggests, the theory holds that there is no significant genetic difference — no speciation — between us and them. In a nutshell, the authors theorize that sasquatches are to us as wolves are to dogs. The parallels are compelling: wolves are generally larger, furrier, tougher and more resistant to the elements, especially cold, more nocturnal, and howl to communicate over great distances. By contrast, dogs are more social, are diurnal, bark instead of howl, and appear much more diverse despite being highly similar genetically. The theory says that sasquatches are the original human form, and that over millennia, modern humans "self-domesticated" and in the process became more social, living in larger and larger groups, become physically smaller, smoother, diurnal, and diverse in appearance.

Such a situation would neatly explain why many tissue and blood samples suspected to be from bigfoots come back from the lab as "100 percent human." The geneticists volunteering their services for these TV specials explain to crestfallen submitters of the tissue that it cannot be a sasquatch because the results show it is human. Or that it must have been contaminated because it is showing human. Well, maybe they're contaminated, or maybe, as far as these tests can see, they *are* human, with an extreme case of epigenetics, an extreme case of back hair. One obvious difficulty with this theory is the scarcity of fossil evidence. If this were the original human body plan, one would expect to find some really big human bones here and there, and perhaps there are good reasons we don't, but I applaud the boldness of the theory. We have to start somewhere.

Supper was the ground-beef burrito.

It was my last night to get a shower, and to share the couch with Tibley, and to try to watch the TV neither Ansen nor I nor Tibley could figure out how to operate. Tomorrow night I would be back in the forest and once again alone and armed only with an audio recorder, a big black knife, and a roll of fishing line.

15
Little River, Big Creek

"We can't have full knowledge all at once. We must start by believing; then afterward we may be led on to master the evidence for ourselves."

—*Thomas Aquinas*

I ROSE IN THE DARK OF THE NOVEMBER morning and bade a final farewell to Tibley, the scruffy little mutt who had been a comfort to me and had shown me that, even if your memory is so bad that every single time you see someone it is as if you're meeting them anew, you can still drop your defenses and warm up so fast that you wind up sleeping with them every night. Ours was a romance that was evergreen, a perpetual whirlwind courtship; every night was a first date that went all the way.

I did a final look-around, behind pillows and under couches and in the washing machine and on the kitchen counter and in the shower, making sure I had every food bag and battery charger and Tylenol bottle I had come with. For the first time since this all started, I drove myself into the forest, as the streetlights blinked off and the black night turned to gray dawn.

I returned to the parking lot near the Magnolia Alpha Male print with a tape measure I had put in the truck for just such an occasion, and I took a few more photos with my phone. The print had deteriorated badly from the previous afternoon, bolstering my theory that it was no more than forty-eight hours old when I first had encountered it. I pulled the food cache I had buried near that intersection and headed for the spot where I would start that day's work. On Butch Arthur Road, the paved two-lane that roughly paralleled the trail I had walked the previous day, I spotted a gated property with a large sign over the entrance reading "Monkey Ranch," and I wondered how it had gotten that name.

A few minutes later I pulled off the skinny gravel Freeside Lane, stomped the parking brake, dummy-locked my steering wheel with The Club (remember those?), and extracted my pack from the cab.

69.9

What would today hold? For one thing, in fairly short order I would have to cross the San Jacinto River, the bridge over which had been washed away at least five years earlier in a flood and never been replaced. This could get interesting. For some time I had harbored romantic notions about what this river crossing would look like, certain I would have to strip naked and hoist everything in my pack over my head as the river rushed past my chest. A few hours would tell.

The race-walking pace that had become customary for my mornings was aided now by a long downhill run toward the river bottom. Down and down I gently went, eating up a hundred yards at a time with my bamboo sticks, head on a swivel, looking down for prints and snakes, up and out at the gradually obscured horizon for odd dark shapes or movement or stick structures. Ears attuned for wood-knocks or whistles or oofs or howls, nostrils ready for whatever pungent smell might waft across the trail.

When I reached the San Jacinto, it curiously was no larger than many of the creeks that fed it, and I crossed it with a twenty-second stroll over a half-submerged fallen tree trunk. Didn't even have to take off my shoes, let alone strip naked and hoist my belongings aloft.

With that anti-climax behind me, it was all uphill, literally. A gradual, forty-five-minute climb out of the river bottom, and I finished the Magnolia Section in fairly short order, emerging onto a highway in the eleven o'clock hour. I crossed Farm to Market 2025 and angled into the trailhead on the other side. There I made a hard left off the trail and found my last food cache, the one I had buried first.

My luck with the caches, although I did not really need them as it turned out, had run its course. Tiny ants had found the bag, chewed through it, and through another one, going for the tortillas. *But* ... the Nutella was safe.

The walk from here into the Double Lake Campground was the easiest stretch of the entire Lone Star Trail — a wide, airy trail with a soft, uniformed bed of pine needles that finished up on a levy that had once held a logging tramway. You couldn't design a trail any easier.

One of my friends had commented online that for my next vocal selection I should "bring it down," so I here recorded my very best rendition of the Eighties slow-skate "Lady in Red."

(Fade to a female squatch behind a log. She closes her eyes and sways, moved to her very soul.)

The trail led to a dam that created the area's namesake lake, and on the other side of the dam, Ansen was flagging me down. We refilled water bottles from the drinking fountain and drove to get the truck, relocating it from the middle of the Magnolia Section to the south end of the Big Creek Section. We returned to Double Lake and embarked on our joint hike. It was odd but nice to be walking with someone else.

75.0

The Big Creek Section, the ninth of ten sections of the trail, was the first area I had ever seen at ground level in the Big Thicket region. It was the section I had hiked with Andrew five years earlier, when we heard the howl, and when I told him about Santa Claus, but it now looked completely unfamiliar. Back then it had been in a drought of record (recall: we were not allowed to camp on it because of that drought), but now it was grown-up and scraggly. And at any rate, I supposed out here you never really saw the same area twice. Nature is always churning, destroying, overtaking, reshaping. And we are too, with our clear-cuts and controlled burns and levies and dams. I could go into this forest every year for the rest of my life and would see a different wood each time. Even without that change, I would see something new. As we looked down in mile 76 we saw a magnolia seed cone, looking like a pine cone festooned with fifty bright red kernels of corn. As many times as I had been out here and as many miles as I had already walked, I had never seen one of these before.

Around mile 77, we passed beneath a magnolia with a three-inch-thick trunk that was bent into a perfect arch over the trail by nothing I could discern and threaded between two other closely spaced trees. As soon as we had cleared that arch, a familiar object caught my eye right in the middle of the trail. It was a nearly black stool with human shape and dimensions. Well, not shaped like a human, but, you know what I mean, like a human's stool. It was not terribly large — you have made bigger on special occasions — but it was not from a human unless that human had a habit of eating fur-bearing animals whole. What's more, it had been dropped right in the middle of the trail — not that humans are completely above doing that, but it seemed unlikely. It might have been from a coyote, but it would have had to be the largest one west of the Mississippi. And of course, it could have been from a juvenile squatch. We snapped the requisite picture. With my growing portfolio, I briefly considered the possibility of a glossy coffee table book: *The Feces of East Texas – A Scatalogue.*

As we headed back down the trail, I looked to my left and stopped for the third time in five minutes. "Hold … everything," I mumbled.

Ansen looked at me then turned his head to follow my gaze.

"Hold everything," I repeated incredulously, and stepped slowly off the trail to our left. There, only thirty feet away, a stick structure. It was not huge, as some of them are when whole trees laid against each other; it was probably only seven feet at its peak. But it was definitely a teepee structure, and the clincher in this case, was that at least one of the logs had no stump or roots below it, and thus had been placed there by something. All around the teepee, the earth had been trampled to mud. No one knows, of course, what function these structures might serve or what meaning they might carry. This one would not have served as a hunting blind, as it was only a tripod and anything could see right through it. A few obvious possibilities were that it could have served as a territorial marker, one squatch or family group warning off another squatch or family group: "This is our hunting ground … keep moving!" Or it could have been a signpost, signaling the way back to camp: "Turn at the teepee to get back home, Junior." Or it could simply be playing, doodling with wood, the very beginnings of architecture, or art.

All of this together, the magnolia arch, the stool on the trail, the stick structure in a thoroughly trampled bog, had a cumulative effect. It definitely felt like we were in a "hot" area. As a matter of fact, we were probably now within only ten to twenty minutes of where the Gray Walker had been videoed by drone. Hell, he could have been watching us the whole time from just behind a yaupon screen or crouched beside a snag.

We now had to have been within the "Scenic Area" of the Big Creek Section, a wildlife sanctuary where camping is forbidden, although I found it strange that the northern boundary of this area was not marked on the trail. How is one supposed to know he has passed into a no-camping area without any sort of signage? This is the one area in the entire Sam Houston National Forest where camping is never allowed. I must say I did not find it any more "scenic" than the portions of the forest I had hiked earlier in the day. I had heard this area called "the birding area" as well, although I noted no more birds here than elsewhere. Of course, the whole thing was fishy to me.

As we hiked along the banks of the winding Big Creek, one of the more impressive streams I had seen in this relatively dry forest, we encountered a meaty dark gray snake, much thicker and more dangerous-looking than the buttermilk pacer I met on Day Two. Mean-looking as he was, the serpent was not interested in us; to the contrary, he reared up, then beat a hasty retreat through the leaf litter to hide under a large stump. Damn right. *I'm* the predator.

At last we left the Scenic Area and turned right to head nearly due west for a mile on an arrow-straight path built atop an abandoned tramway levy. We reached the truck, and Ansen agreed to set up one last shuttle that would allow me to travel another two miles without my pack.

As I sat on the tailgate of my truck and peeled off the Icelandic socks to let my feet breathe for a minute, Ansen walked around the front of the truck, messing with his camera.

He stopped. "Did you hear that?" he asked.

I hadn't. He had heard a howl, distant and powerful, from the southwest. That seemed to be the pattern with this stuff. I had heard the tree knocks so clearly in January, but Wade had been down inside his sleeping bag and hadn't heard a thing. I had seen and photographed the Magnolia Alpha Male track, but Ansen had walked past it twice without seeing it at all. It all showed me again how limited our perception of the world is, even with two able-bodied people right next to each other, one will see, one will not; one will hear, one will not. It reminded me of Michigan J. Frog, the Looney Tunes character who would belt fantastic vaudeville numbers in front of his owner, even high-kicking with a top hat and cane. But when even a single other soul was present, it was only: *"Crrroak."*

I also was impressed by how little of the forest I had actually experienced, even after walking in it for more than eighty miles. Staying on the path and gliding ever forward, I knew that I had seen far, far less than one percent of Sam Houston National Forest. I had seen probably an average of 100 feet on either side of this one tiny artery. Saying I had seen this forest would be like a blood cell that had traveled once from the heart to the toe claiming it had seen the human body. With the understory screens of beautyberry and tunnels of yaupon and the trees that even in an "open" forest environment incrementally obscured everything within a quarter mile, whole worlds existed within a stone's throw of me, worlds of which I remained oblivious, worlds above me in the canopy — squirrels and butterflies, worlds below me within the forest floor — shrews and anoles and snails and snakes, worlds at eye level but beyond the reach of my view, worlds at the insect level I only saw when they appeared directly before my eyes in the form of cobwebs, and of course whole galaxies at the microscopic level that I could never appreciate without high-tech instruments. All of these realms remained invisible to me, all this effort notwithstanding.

I told Ansen I'd see him in an hour, took one pole and one Nalgene bottle, and headed in. As I disappeared into the green, I told him to record video, and I belted my wife's teenage favorite, "Jesse's Girl," into the forest reverb.

82.3

Having reached the penultimate trailhead of the Lone Star Hiking Trail, it was time to again go it alone, and to tackle my last night in the woods. It was time to say goodbye to Ansen, who was collecting a large sack of pine cones off the ground for one of his wife's art projects as I fussed with my gear. I got my pack on and, as my voice broke, I said, "I don't know how I'm ever gonna thank you for all this, but I'll find a way."

He smiled. "It was my pleasure to help you succeed."

I walked halfway across the highway before realizing I had forgotten my poles in his backseat. I jogged back and retrieved them, then tried again. Before I disappeared into the forest on the opposite side of the road, I turned, shrugged my shoulders, and gave him two victory signs with outstretched arms. "Nixon ... Marine One!" I shouted, just in case my impersonation wasn't adequate.

With a mile to camp and just forty-five minutes of daylight, I took off in a fast-walk into the Bayou Section. The undergrowth immediately crowded in on me from both sides like a neglected version of the hedge maze in *The Shining*.

When I reached the mileage marker that indicated my camp, instead of a camp, I saw another wooden sign that read: HUNTER'S CAMP .6 MILES" with an arrow to the right.

At any other time of day I would not have considered .6 miles — fifteen minutes — a burden, but when you're cutting it close and encounter something that is not as advertised, it hits you as a huge imposition. I strode so quickly I would have been disqualified from a race walk, until the trail simply ran out with nothing that resembled a camp in sight. Darkness continued to fall. I did a 180, headed back to the main trail, and improvised a camp a hundred feet from the intersection of the two paths — stringing my hammock and tarp between two pines and nestling them as far underneath the wide leaves of an American beautyberry bush as I could get. There was no debate in my mind this time; like everything else in this forest, I was going for stealth. If I had gotten there earlier, I probably would have thrown some branches on top of my tarp and piled a few around the edges of my ground cloth for good measure. But now it was dark, and I was out of energy from a full day's walk and a whole lot of car shuttling. That night I did not bother stringing the fishing line "invisible fence."

I reclined into my hammock and ate a handful of water crackers and tried to stop sweating. Shortly after dark, at 7:02 p.m., I turned on the audio recorder. As I lay there, I heard faint traffic noise from FM 2025 a mile and a half to my west.

Every five minutes I heard another airliner carrying hundreds of passengers from all over the world into Bush International. I heard distant dogs and cattle, but nothing like a vocalization.

There was no moon. Solid cloud cover put the pines in silhouette against a charcoal night sky, partially grayed by light pollution from Shepherd and Cleveland and Conroe.

Woop. A text came in, and I pulled my phone out of the mesh bag that hung from the ridgeline of the hammock above my chest. It was Ansen: "You'll do fine," he wrote. "Just picture the forest during the day."

I replied: "And in its underwear."

Then I slept.

16

Occam's Razor, Pascal's Wager, and Arby's Super Roast Beef Sandwich

> *Roads go ever on*
> *Under cloud and under star,*
> *Yet feet that wandering have gone*
> *Turn at last to home afar.*
> — *Bilbo Baggins*

AFTER ALL MY WORRYING LEADING up to my last night, it was mercifully uneventful in real time.

But the audio, as it always is, was far more interesting. Five weeks later, I sat at my desk listening to the twelve-hour recording of that night on headphones, volume cranked.

Beyond the many airliners in and out of Houston and the occasional barking dog at a distant farmhouse, there were definitely stick breaks and was movement around my camp.

It could have been hogs, could have been a raccoon or a hefty armadillo, but I most definitely had visitors.

For the most part, I could hear nothing on the audio but hour after hour of crickets and snoring and the aforementioned airplanes coming in all night long, albeit with lower frequency between midnight and five a.m.

But there was something that occasionally broke the din of crickets and planes. It was like whisper — *pah ... pah .... pah ...* a rhythmic popping sound, one every three seconds or so, that would last for five or six minutes and then go away. It was very faint. For a while I thought I might have been hearing myself, a glottal stop in my breathing; I do hold my breath sometimes in my sleep, but it is for much longer than two seconds. Moreover, this pop carried with it the forest's echo, telling me it was very distant and therefore necessarily very loud at the source. I thought it might have been distant gunshots, as those seemed to be a nightly occurrence, but these pops were too regular. And would there be sixty in a row, regularly spaced, at three in the morning?

Was it that sawmill over on FM 2025? It certainly wasn't a saw, and if they were running some sort of equipment at midnight, and again at 3:03 a.m., and again at 5:38 a.m., and it was loud enough to make it all the way to me, then it would have been deafeningly loud at its source, and the mill's neighbors would have never slept, and never stood for it. At my computer, I pulled up a satellite map of my location and looked around for two miles. I saw nothing.

What ... *thee* hell ... were those pops?

After many hours of pressing the headphones tighter to my ears, listening to these popping sessions, and mulling what they could have been, I landed on a theory. Like any theory, it could be wrong, but it's the best I have:

I know the Others are out there. And this was one of the most remote expanses I traveled through. In fact, the following morning, it took me four hours — eight miles — before I crossed a road of any kind. And these sounded like tree knocks, but not like any I had heard before. Certainly not the "knock-knock" of the previous January's highly *un*funny knock-knock joke. Tree knocks are always reported as coming in ones or twos, or maybe threes, but not three minutes of continuous rhythmic knocking.

But now imagine this scene: In a remote meadow surrounded by a thicket of yaupon and blackberry bushes, a family of four Others has bedded down, lying low during the day, foraging and hunting at night. Perhaps a few closely related adult males are hunting deer. Perhaps the young ones are exploring on their own. Then, with the snatch of a leg and a twist of the head, a deer or a hog is killed, and it is time to eat. The clan is widely scattered, perhaps over an area two miles square. If the mother hit a tree once to call them in, they would have one chance to fix her location. If she slowly hit it five times in a row, she gives them five times as long to lock in their heading and find her. If she hit that tree for four minutes, that gives them an even better chance of finding her quickly. Maybe this is what those pops on the recorder were. And just maybe, this was how music began. A hirsute mother, swinging a hickory branch against the trunk of a pine, scanning the woods with pupils the size of half-dollars letting in the faintest of light, *pounding, pounding, pah ... pah ... pah ... time to come back, kids ... Home is over here now ... and it's time to come home.*

83.3

It was time for me to go home too.

I awoke before first light, at 5:55. It was Saturday, I was pretty sure. I ate water crackers and looked at Facebook and waited for any bit of light to my east. I broke camp for the last time in the dark, loosening my overhead tarp and coiling and frapping its six thin guy lines, wadding up my ground cloth, turning my sleeping bag, thermal pad, and pillow in a single roll and clicking it in beneath my pack. Rolling the hammock and pushing it into its stuff-sack.

First light came at 7:05, and I was on the move as soon as I could see my hand in front of my face. I set a long-striding pace southwest along Tarkington Bayou, which was mostly a muddy trickle of a creek, but nonetheless scenic and Jurassic.

An hour or so into my walk I spotted another possible stick structure — two mid-sized trees leaning into a larger standing tree to form a tripod. Next to them a twenty-five-foot tree with a three-inch-thick trunk was bent into a perfect arch. I had little doubt I was still among Them.

As I continued with the bayou on my left, I heard a crashing and saw a large black mass spring suddenly into view. If I were a video editor at *Finding Bigfoot*, I would cut to commercial right now, but I am not, and will tell you right away that it was a big black hog running through the dry creek bed. He must have been moving thirty miles per hour as he cleared my field of vision in about eight seconds. How about that? I finally saw one. I hiked eighty-five miles before I saw one, but there one was at last. This seemed to be the way discovery works. You see their sign first — in the case of hogs, plowed up soil, and poop. Then, if you stay at it, you hear them next, like I heard that piglet squealing in the Big Woods behind a thicket screen on Day Five. Then, if you stay with it long enough, you see one. Were it a squatch, this would have been known as a Class A daylight sighting, and a great one.

My sasquatch encounters have taken a slightly different order: vocalization first, then knocks, then prints. I still await a sighting and am not at all sure I want one. There is nothing in the world to compare a sighting with, and no matter how much one might already believe in them and how much one thinks he is psychologically prepared, there is no predicting your response to seeing one. It might be blissful amazement. There might be a soiling of adventure pants. There might be clinical shock. There might very well be a fatal heart attack, or an emotional trauma so severe that I would give up outdoor pastimes immediately and permanently. There are hundreds of reports to go on, and all of these reactions have been documented (though of course the heart attacks remain speculation).

Though I had begun this hike as a purist, reluctant to take shortcuts or to ease my burden in any way, once the original concept of through-hiking had been corrupted by coming off the trail and succumbing to the siren song of Mexican restaurants and showers, I was now all-in on the whole shuttling and caching concept. My plan was to drop all gear except my poles and water at the first road I crossed, then come back for it when I had wheels. Eight miles later, at eleven a.m., I still had not crossed a single road. That distance notwithstanding, it says something about how thoroughly we have carved up and gridded out this enormous state when four miles is the absolute farthest I could get from any road. When I came out on my first road, a little gravel lane that accessed a small subdivision, I rejoiced, raced across it, and giddily hid my gear at the base of a tree, throwing a few dead leaves on top in a half-hearted attempt to camouflage it.

Weary but significantly lighter, I crossed the San Jacinto's East Fork yet again on an iron bridge, and the area now became swampier with generous stands of palmetto. Long, broken boardwalks intended to keep hikers' feet dry through this low area during wetter seasons spoke of untold Eagle Scout projects long ago or else of Forest Service maintenance projects of the lowest possible priority. I tried walking on them, just for the novelty, but wound up hopping off and trudging along the sandy trail when their gaps and collapsed sections became more work than I had bandwidth for. A hundred miles was enough of a workout without adding in a man-made obstacle course in the homestretch.

I spotted a fuzzy yellow fruit on the ground — another trifoliate orange — and pocketed it. I decided to give it to my wife, as we had a habit of bringing each other little souvenirs from the solo trips we went on. There was no gift shop at the end of this particular tour, no Christmas ornaments, no T-shirts or sweaters, no earrings, not even a postcard. Mainly just raccoon poop. And this little bright fruit, so the fruit got the nod.

As the final mile markers clicked by, it seemed the end of the trail might be an asymptote. If you go into hypnotic regression and recall your tenth-grade geometry, an asymptote is a function that forever grows closer to a line but never actually reaches it, and this seemed to be what I was on, always closer to the finish line — the truck — but never quite reaching it. There was a certain rhythm that had been established over the previous ninety-five miles that continued apace, and I now seemed to be in a never-ending hologram in which these landmarks were just randomly generated and accompanied by my trail notes: "... you will cross a forest service road, cross a utility cut, cross a boardwalk, cross an abandoned jeep track, follow the blazes and turn left, and turn right, and stay straight, and cross a firebreak, and cross a bridge," and on, and on, and on.

My hike itself was now mirroring these damned mysteries we keep trying to solve — bigfoots, UFOs — every year more and more evidence, but never the proof. Always getting closer to the finish line, but never quite reaching it.

I passed a couple on their way in from the trail's western terminus. "It's a great day," the man enthused. "Did you come all the way from Parking Lot 11?"

"I came from No. 1," I said pridefully, then added for good measure, "eight days ago."

"Wow!" the man obliged.

"Congratulations!" the woman added. I saw a subtle glint in the guy's eyes, and I could tell right away that the torch had passed, that to him, I had become ... That Old Fart. At least I hoped so.

At last, I perceived the surest sign I was near a parking lot — the sound of children. Sadly, they were not my children, but they were a symbolic stand-in for them. I was coming to the end of my time alone, my time as a free-roaming, predacious, increasingly hairy alpha male. And, in a break from nearly all the rest of the natural order, it was time for this male to head home and share in the duties of child rearing.

In the sasquatch, perhaps we see as clearly as we will ever be permitted to the natural state of a hominid. I admit this is only a theory, but allow me it for the moment. He hunts. He communicates, the better to hunt. He hides. He mimics nature. He owns territory. He intimidates. He mates. He nurtures and defends. And life continues generation after generation with no discernable advance. Morning follows night. Spring follows winter. Death follows life. Life follows birth. Birth follows sex. This is the natural man, free of self-knowledge, man before eating from the Tree of the Knowledge of Good and Evil, man before being visited by Prometheus.

We, on the other hand, are messy, are we not? We are the ones with only one foot in nature and the other resting on a moving object, the destination of which we can only guess. We have priests and temples and bureaucracies and armies. We have laboratories and symphony halls, microchip manufacturing cleanrooms and online shopping. We split the atom and go to the moon if we want (at least as of this writing).

We also become enslaved by a buffet of addictions, we foul the planet with chemicals we only half understand, and we are subject to so many vices and perversions that we often appear pitiable in relation to the rest of nature. We are at once better off and worse off than these, our country cousins. But in us there is that most curious and mysterious of all phenomena: civilization. Rise and fall. Art and religion and science. In short, we have potential.

Might the Others simply be us without this Y factor, and perhaps *with* qualities we do not so readily possess, an X factor? As the blind person has more acute hearing to help her compensate for her lack of sight, perhaps their minds have evolved in a different direction to fill a different ecological and mental niche — a different kind of body and consciousness that gives them almost preternatural advantages over us and everything else in the forests of the earth. The more we learn about them — and let's modestly remember that we are certain of almost nothing — it seems increasingly like they are yin to our yang.

Taking nothing away from the Others and whatever their virtues might be, we might see our true essence in a starker relief because we have them — so close to us and yet so far —

with which to compare ourselves. And if they can say the same about us, let them, and so be it.

Many people have puzzled at the Book of Genesis and speculated that its casual and bizarre reference in the sixth chapter to "giants in the earth" — the Nephilim — is an early reference to sasquatches. But there is another Genesis story that often springs to mind when I think of our relationship to these creatures, and that is the story of Jacob and Esau.

For those of you who skipped Sunday school or synagogue that week, Jacob and Esau were brothers, sons of the Semitic patriarch Isaac. The two were night and day. Jacob was physically smooth, mentally clever, and preferred the life of the tent. Esau was exceedingly hairy, not nearly as clever as his younger brother, and much preferred life in the field. Alas, Esau was the firstborn and so would get Isaac's birthright inheritance. One day, a hungry and not-so-bright Esau sold his birthright to Jacob in exchange for a bowl of stew. Then Jacob (in cahoots with his mother, who favored him) covered his arm with wool and approached his blind father, masquerading as Esau. The trick worked, and Isaac gave his blessing to Jacob instead of the hirsute, outdoors-loving Esau.

Might this be the most apt allegory for the modern human and the sasquatch? Perhaps we are merely those very different brothers, and we smooth ones who prefer the indoors — perhaps we cheated our Father out of the inheritance that is dominion and civilization, art, science, and religion, contract riders and plug-in air fresheners and season finales. Perhaps this was the meaning of the Jacob and Esau story all along, an encoded explainer, waiting to be cracked in the fullness of time.

William of Ockham was a Franciscan Friar in England in the late 1200s and early 1300s who wrote extensively on logic, physics, and theology. He is remembered by most as the namesake of Occam's Razor, a principle — also known as the law of parsimony, succinctness, or economy — that holds that when looking to explain a phenomenon, we should always opt for the answer with the fewest causes, factors, or variables. In the case of the Others, I long ago concluded that Occam's Razor favored their existence.

This started with the fact that there were simply too many reports for all of them to be attributable to hoax, hallucination, or misidentification. And the reports were not limited to the last few decades, the period of the pop culture phenomenon of "bigfoot"; they went back well into the nineteenth century, and before that are part of numerous American Indian traditions. We have the Patterson Gimlin Film, now more than fifty years old, the credibility of which deepens the closer and the longer it is scrutinized. There are footprints by the thousands, many examined by anthropologists and found to be subtle and credible in ways virtually no one could fake. There are hundreds of photographs and video clips of likely specimens, artifacts of natural history that agree on such a wide range of subtle anatomical points that dismissing them all would require more twists and turns than could be performed by every gymnast who has trained in this forest from Mary Lou Retton to Simone Biles. Occam's Razor reverses and shaves away the arguments of the irrational skeptic — that American Indians, who have spent thousands of years on this continent, can't tell the difference between a bear and gigantic humanoid; that the subject of a film that shows muscle rippling under hair with every step is really a costume that could have been made in 1967; that hundreds of people across North America and over a period of well more than a century have been conspiring to make footprints deep in the wilderness in the hopes that explorers and travelers might find them, and that those hoaxers are experts in primate and anthropological anatomy, and that they took time to create hundreds of nearly microscopic dermal ridges on each print. Believing these outrageous scenarios requires an epic contortion of logic, many more assumptions than Friar Ockham would have had patience for.

On the other side of the scoreboard, the assumptions on the side of belief are, in short ...

1. That humans have not discovered and catalogued every remarkable animal on earth. This is manifestly true. The point has been made many times that no less a zoological superstar than the mountain gorilla was only "discovered" in 1902. Indeed, more than twenty primates have been discovered since 1990. Even megafauna are discovered on a fairly regular basis.

2. That humans are not presently capable of dominating the vast wilderness areas of the northern hemisphere so completely as to rule out the existence of a smart, reclusive creature with vastly superior wilderness adaptations.

3. That an animal that is mostly nocturnal, supremely well adapted to forest living, has finely tuned instincts for evasion, and possesses intelligence that could rival our own could not evade us except for a few dozen instances each year.

Again, which scenario does Occam's Razor favor?

In short, as hard as it might be to believe in bigfoots, it is easier to believe in them than to believe that some 10,000 people from all walks of life, including practicing psychologists and active-duty police officers with nothing to gain and everything to lose by reporting such a thing, are either wildly misidentifying bears or recruiting NBA players to travel into incredibly remote areas of North America and parade around in gorilla costumes through the roughest sort of terrain.

Hoaxes have occurred, for sure, and many misidentifications too. But ultimately, nonbelief impugns too many credible, corroborating witnesses. While there still is no *proof* in the public domain, the mass of testimonial evidence has simply grown too great. Put another way, *the simplistic nature of the dismissals is no match for the sophistication and volume of the evidence.*

But even while Occam's Razor, for me, points to their existence, it is worth asking one final question about all this:

What if I'm wrong?

After all, an awful lot of my thinking on this geographic area in particular has been shaped by Bob Garrett, who claims, in addition to everything I've already attributed to him:

That the Forest Service or an affiliated law enforcement agency caught him conducting bigfoot expeditions in Sam Houston National Forest without a commercial permit and is using the threat of prosecution to coerce him into censoring his own video evidence of the creatures

That his cell phone communications have been hacked by law enforcement

That his personal computer at home was remotely hacked by a government agency that deleted a video he had just downloaded from his camera to his computer (The video allegedly showed sasquatches chasing hogs.)

That he has videoed one of them in "stealth mode" showing their ability to become momentarily invisible

And that he was possibly rescued in Colorado by a sasquatch, who might have carried him out of a remote wilderness while Garrett was delirious with a fever

Now— that's a lot to swallow. What are the possibilities regarding Mr. Garrett? Is he delusional? Is he a full-time and life-long hoaxer? Has he experienced some strange things but embellishes for the sake of a good story? Or has he lived one of the most extraordinary lives in the history of all of humanity?

I do not know which of those is the case. Some people *do* lead remarkable lives; they are the ones who get off the couch, who go outside, who take the road less traveled; maybe he is just one of those people. I don't know. I have talked to others who have been with him on expeditions, and they are impressed by his authenticity. I have listened to him for many hours, and he sounds very honest; I still think that's worth something. Before I left on my hike I attempted to contact him for some pro-tips on where *not* to camp, but he never replied. In his defense, if government agents really are after him as he says, then I wouldn't blame him for not returning the email of a complete stranger.

So again I ask, what if we're all wrong, all 10,001 of us, and there is some mundane explanation for everything I've read about and now seen and heard? What if, on this very trip, everything could be explained away? The deer was killed by an especially quiet coyote. The helicopter was on a night training mission of some sort, and all the guns were simply rednecks poaching deer after dark. The triangles on the trail were the work of squirrels that just didn't like to get too close to I-45. The stick structures and arches were just things that happen in a forest where trees are always falling every which way, and like a sylvanic Rorschach test, I saw bigfoots in the meaningless tangle. The scat was from a gigantic coyote. The howls overnight were all coyotes too, even the one that went "waaa-hoo." And the print of the Magnolia Alpha Male — it was just somebody having fun with me, subtly rubbing the sand just so, then arranging leaves and pine needles on top of it to make it look like a natural print. It was all one big eight-day, hundred-mile exercise in confirmation bias.

Even if it could all be explained away, would that make me a fool? Would it make me a fool for going out there and for looking and for trying to answer the question through direct experience and independent investigation? Would it mean that I had wasted thousands of hours of precious life?

Blaise Pascal, the seventeenth century French philosopher and mathematician, came up with a famous device in logic I seemed to invoke all the time. It's known as Pascal's Wager, and it posits this: If I live my life as if God exists, and He does exist, then good for me. I guessed correctly, and (according to the popular theology of Pascal's day) I am bound for heaven and not the other place. If on the other hand I live my life as if God exists and it turns out God does not, then I am no worse off for having believed and having lived as if He did. Indeed, even setting aside any consideration of heaven or hell, I am *still* better off because of the blessings that Godly behavior bestowed on my earthly life, the blessings of clean livin'.

What in the name of the Mary Ann, Ginger, and Ha Ha Clinton-Dix does this have to do with bigfoot? is what you might be asking. It is this. Whether or not I am any closer to the truth than when I started, indeed whether the Others exist at all, I have gained a lot from the search: I have learned about forest ecosystems; about genetics and epigenetics; about river systems and wildlife corridors; about intraguild predation; about optics and acoustics; infrared, infrasound, and biological electromagnetic fields; about anthropology and primate behavior; about metabolism and surface-to-volume ratios; about dogs and coyotes and wolves; and about government agencies. The search has led me on a journey of discovery through multiple pinch-points of theology. I've met interesting people and formed long-distance friendships because of this. And the search has gotten me "off the couch," led me outside and kept me outside more than otherwise would have been the case — "camping with a purpose," as some squatchers like to put it. And isn't that all to the good? Just as with God, living as though they existed has led me into a richer life. Pascal's Wager has already paid off.

At the age of thirty, British Columbia newspaper reporter John Willison Green began researching the bigfoot mystery. The subject captured his imagination, and he followed the evidence wherever it led. Over the next fifty-nine years he built a massive database of 3,475 reports the old-fashioned way, by clipping newspaper articles and interviewing people who claimed to have sightings — thousands of file cards, loose-leaf notebooks, and maps. He was eighty-nine when he died in 2016, five months before my hike. There is a video of him I love at a bigfoot conference five years prior, at age eighty-four. Tall and broad-shouldered with swept-back white hair and smiling eyes, he stood at the podium for thirty minutes gamely answering questions and recounting stories. Finally someone in the audience asked him if he felt like he had paid a price for being a public figure associated with this taboo subject.

Without missing a beat, Green, with twinkling eyes shot back, "No— I've had a ball." The audience thundered its approval. I did too.

The idea of the sasquatch cuts to the heart of our place in the world. It cuts to the question of that good but seldom invoked English word from the Book of Genesis, *dominion*. Who has the right to live where? Who has the right to exist at all? And who decides? Me vs. the spiders vs. their prey. The Alabama Coushatta vs. the Anglo settlers of the Big Thicket. The Comanche from the Plains vs. my Texian ancestors over on the Brazos. The United States Department of Agriculture vs. the Others.

In nature, might makes right. But are we a part of that nature, or are we something more? And for that matter, are *they* a part of God's creation or the product of some unholy mistake of an age lost to history, a loose end, an abomination that climbed the highest mountain, rode out the Flood, then came back down and quietly hid just beyond the reach of Noah's campfire light?

Collectively, we long ago established that we have the might; but individually, *they* have the might, all of it. And they have adaptability. As long as there are a thousand contiguous acres of timberland in North America, we will never be able to exterminate them, even if we wanted to. In terms of habitat lost, they probably have outlasted the worst we had to throw at them.

Now the tide has turned, and more and more land is being set aside, more wildlife corridors created and national forests and parks designated. Yes, we have a remarkable degree of dominion over this planet. But we should be modest about that dominion. We've done our worst to pave every square inch of it, but it's still wilder and bigger than we think, even just across our own back fences.

In this age of growing sanctuaries, the Others will multiply accordingly, and then what? How does this story end? Does it end like "Dr. Miller" predicts, with a spectacular government pronouncement at the end of a twenty-year period of land set-asides? Does it end with one being hit on the highway and the driver getting the body to a scientist and a media outlet beyond the reach of shadowy G men and offers the discoverers can't refuse? I envision the finish line as the cover of *Time* magazine, headline: "Well, whaddya know." As wall-to-wall "Breaking News" coverage on TV, with panels of anthropologists and commentators and live-shots of trench coat-wearing reporters outside a cold-storage facility.

Or does it just go on like this forever, asymptotically? Dozens of sightings per year, an ever-greater body of video, audio, and track evidence, an ever-increasing body of believers and media coverage — but never the proof, never the specimen, never the body itself?

Why? Why can't I let this go? Beyond the reasons I've already stated — beyond sheer curiosity and beyond the scientific implications such a discovery would have — there is something even bigger, something more abstract at stake. There is something in all of this that feels important to me at a gut level. It feels important as a defense of objective truth.

It is quite literally the easiest thing in the world to laugh at people who believe in bigfoot. The whole subject has become a shorthand for "crackpot" and "wacko." And the more it is ridiculed, especially by those who know nothing about it but merely pile-on after the play because it's fun to jump on people, the tighter I hold onto the football and the harder I dig toward the goal line.

And it will be the easiest thing in the world to claim that you too always believed on the day *after* they are confirmed by science. "You know, I always thought they probably existed," people will crow all over social media. But there will be no glory in that, no cosmic reward, no good karma for those who played it safe, who held their cards until someone else made it safe to show them, who let others dangle in the wind of pop-culture scorn, or even denied the truth they might have known, like treacherous Edmund on his return from Narnia.

And yet with all this conviction, I sometimes awake in the night or the morning and wonder if this has all been a dream. Perhaps because the whole thing seems to obey only dream-logic, the logic of the night, and not the logic of the light of day. Did I just dream the last twenty years? I'll wonder. Is this whole thing just a fever-dream, a cheap plot device in a soap opera that will negate everything that happened this season? And when I awake for good, will I think, of course *bigfoots* are not *real!*

Then I rise from bed, go to my phone, and there, on the home screen — the photo of the footprint. And I know that either they are real or I am still dreaming.

96.44

With thirty yards left to hike, I saw the familiar dark profile of my navy extended-cab Chevy Silverado. With the end finally in literal sight, all strength left me. I plodded clumsily to the truck, dropped the tailgate with a bang, tossed my clattering bamboo poles into the bed, turned to sit on the tailgate, and let the backpack slide off my shoulders. I have tried to think of an analogy for how good that felt — something related to being lowered gently into a vat of chocolate pudding, or having goose down injected into my veins, or floating weightless across a cool desert sky at sunrise with Enya, in all her fully produced glory, singing softly in my ear — but nothing compares.

This — the end — was the part that definitely would have been better if I had opted for a marathon instead of a hike.

There were no cheering family members, no high-fives, no Gatorade baths, confetti cannons, or balloon drops. Just a family of four strangers — sister and brother running up and down the last seventy-five yards of the trail, mother and father cleaning out the SUV for the drive home.

"A hundred miles, huh?" the father asked. "That trail right there?" he pointed, incredulous.

"Yep, that one right there."

East away from the trailhead parking lot I sped toward the gravel road crossing where I had stashed my camping gear hours earlier. As before, I was astonished at the distances I had walked just that afternoon. Mile after mile the green walls that lined the blacktop blurred past — loblolly pine and yaupon and white oak and sweetgum and thorny vines of a hundred different species.

In time, I had a revelation about the forest, and it was this: Again and again I had experienced a profound change of mood going from day to night and back to day. It became crystal clear to me that my kind had evolved to occupy the day, and not the night. The same was true for the landscape I inhabited. While there might be some mammalian or even primate memory of the forest residing in a deep limbic layer of our brains, the modern human had lost this comfort level, because we completed the last stage of our evolution *not* in the forest, but on the savannah. Although one of the defining characteristics of humans is how we have made ourselves at home in every kind of biome on the planet, still, there are places we don't really belong. Above the Arctic Circle. On the open sea. In the middle of the Sahara. Space. Just because we *can* go there, and even live there, doesn't mean we were designed to, or that we should get too used to it.

I was fascinated by the forest, but at a deep, existential level, I had never been at ease there. I experienced this acutely on my first night of hammock camping here with my sons, and I continued to experience it to different degrees every single time I was in here. It was beautiful, but it also was always creepy, claustrophobia-inducing, not where we were at home.

In my own ancestral case, my family had come *through* the East Texas thicket in 1829. They did not stop here, they kept on going until they got to the open, rolling, post oak savannah, the savannah through which I drove in the fog on my way here last week. That looks much more like the east African savannah we are said to have evolved on. Open, so you can see what's coming. Enough trees to get some shade, but open. That is where humans belong.

The day belongs to us; it is what we were designed for. The oaken savannah belongs to us; it is what we were designed for. The night — the night belongs to Them; it is what They were designed for. The forest — the forest belongs to Them; it is what They were designed for.

With my gear repossessed, I hastened to Cleveland, Texas, and into a combination gas station-Arby's whereupon I devoured the largest roast beef sandwich on offer in one minute forty-five seconds, then unceremoniously chased it with curly fries, mechanically pressing them into my mouth one by one with no pause until there was naught but grease stains at the bottom of the paper carton. I sat alone in silence, slouching at the table, and soft-focus stared out at the parking lot.

In eight days I had taken 266,301 steps, including a few in a Walgreen's, a few from Ansen's car to the table of a Mexican restaurant, and a handful from Laurie's couch to her washing machine and back. With an asterisk, I had done what I set out to do. It wasn't Mount Everest. It wasn't the

Appalachian Trail. But on the other hand, I could look at a *globe* and see where I had *walked,* and to me, that was something.

I hobbled back to the truck and decided to blow off the shower at Double Lake; I could live with myself three more hours, and showering in my own bathtub would be infinitely more satisfying.

"Hey Siri!" I barked.

Bing.

"Driving directions .... Austin, Texas."

And I am gliding forward, ever forward. I am gliding ever forward.

The author at Mile 0, Trailhead No. 1

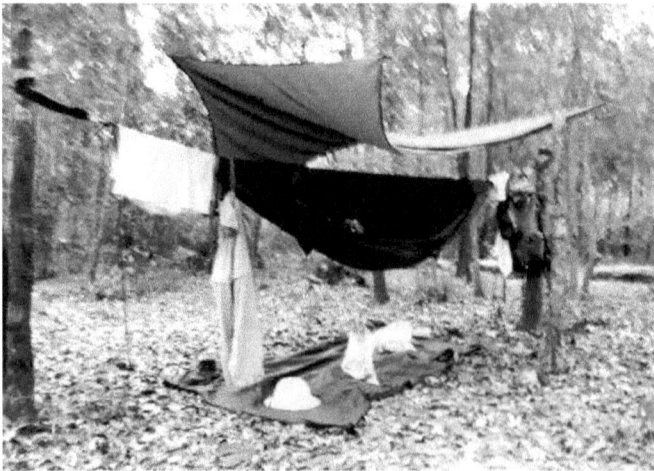

The camping setup, Night One, Mile 6

Yaupon tree bend, Mile 40; magnolia tree bend, Mile 87

"Teepee" structure (two views), Mile 80

"Magnolia Alpha Male" Print, 18 x 9 inches, Mile 67, with the author's size 10½ foot

Location of Sam Houston National Forest
within the state of Texas

The Lone Star Hiking Trail, 96.44 miles.
(Courtesy: Lone Star Hiking Trail Club,
LoneStarTrail.org)

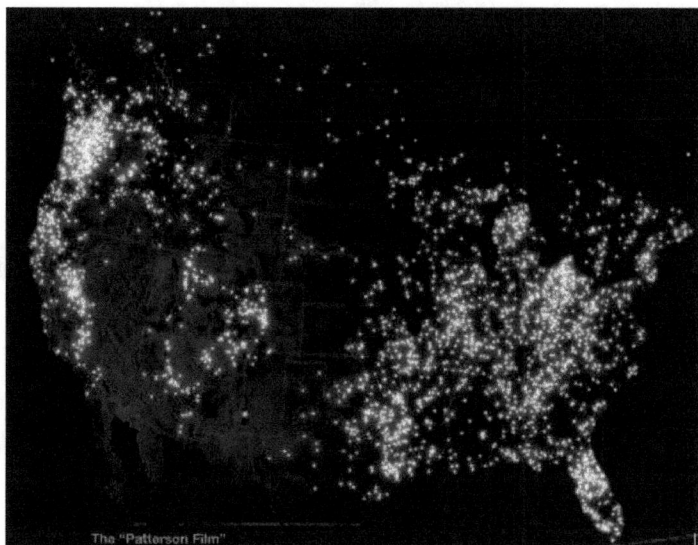

3,313 Sasquatch Sightings Over 92 Years.
(Courtesy Joshua Stevens. Data source: BFRO. Cropped.)

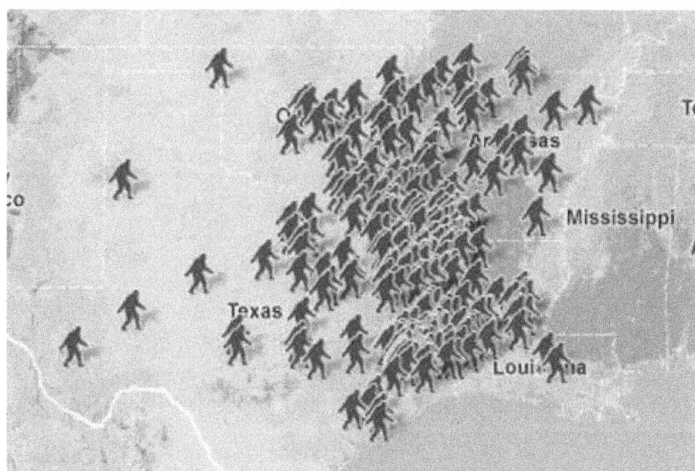

Representative Distribution of Sasquatch Sightings in
Texas, Oklahoma, Arkansas, and Louisiana
(Courtesy: North American Wood Ape Conservancy)

279

Elaborations and References

Chapter 1

How many people have not only witnessed but *reported* encountering a sasquatch? As there is no single repository, we must estimate:

The Bigfoot Field Research Organization currently hosts the largest searchable database of reports. As of this writing (July 2017), it has published 5,332 reports in the United States and Canada. An April 12, 2012, *New York Times* article stated the BFRO site contains more than 30,000 reports. An investigator familiar with the database told me that as of several years ago the site had 35,000 "submissions," but said that number included many non-reports, such as bogus reports and questions.)

Long before the digital age, journalist John Willison Green compiled a research file containing of 3,475 stories. (http://www.bigfootencounters.com/sbs/jg.htm) But as his archive is not public, we cannot determine how many of those are unique and how many might be cross-listed by the BFRO. To be conservative, I have guessed that 1,000 of them might lie outside the BFRO data, bringing our rounded total to 6,300.

Another significant source of reports has been the Animal Planet TV program *Finding Bigfoot,* which at this writing has produced 93 episodes. In nearly every episode, the cast hosts a "town hall meeting" and asks those who have had an encounter to raise their hands. My own estimate based on what is shown on screen is that on average 30 people raise their hands at these events. That would render a total of 2,790. Allowing that some small number of these witnesses might also have filed BFRO reports, I will nonetheless round that down to 2,000, which brings our estimate to 8,300.

In addition there are a number of other regional websites with reports not contained in the BFRO database, such as that of the North American Wood Ape Conservancy (which studies Texas, Louisiana, Oklahoma, and Arkansas), and innumerable social media sites, such as Facebook and the witness-based podcast *Sasquatch Chronicles,* now with more than 350 episodes. From these, I would add another 1,000 to 2,000 unique testimonies, to render my conservative estimate of more than 10,000 reports.

Again, common sense tells us that a small minority of people who actually witness a sasquatch go to the trouble and take the reputational risk of reporting them, but there is no reliable way of extrapolating reports to get the number of encounters. We could safely say that it would be at least twice 10,000, but it could easily also be twenty or thirty times greater. There is simply no way to know. It is easy to predict that the moment this species is confirmed by science, and therefore becomes safe to discuss, there could be a great flood of people coming forward with their previously unreported stories.

Carl Linnaeus' "*Homo troglodytes*" are a source of considerable curiosity. While much of his attempt to classify men and other primates simply reveals the struggle of scientists of his day to distinguish between humans who looked like themselves (Europeans), humans who did not, and primates that were being discovered at a rapid pace, especially in Africa, one passage does resonate strongly with bigfootology. In *Linnaeus: Nature and Nation*, Lisbet Koerner writes, "True, [Linnaeus] designated humankind as 'wise man' (*Homo sapiens*). But this was an arbitrary, trivial name, and not a definition. In any case, he hesitated between that binomial and 'day man' (*Homo diurnus*). In manuscripts of *Systema naturae*, he crossed out at times one, at other times the other. 'Day man' had a counterpart, the 'night man' (*Homo nocturnus*). Following the Elder Pliny, Linnaeus also termed this second human species 'troglodyte man' (*Homo troglodytes*)." p. 87.

To read the complete *McLean's* article "Hairy Giants of British Columbia":

http://www.bigfootencounters.com/legends/jwburns.htm.

To read the 1958 Jerry Crew story and learn about the emergence of "Bigfoot" as a popular name, read the 1959 article in *True* magazine "The Strange Story of America's Abominable Snowman":

http://www.bigfootencounters.com/articles/true1959.htm.

The Patterson-Gimlin Film is one of the most highly scrutinized pieces of video in the history of moving pictures. There are myriad analyses of the footage. Here is a segment on the "P-G Film" from a National Geographic Channel special, featuring Bill Munns:

https://www.youtube.com/watch?v=MKUwdHex1Zs.

I highly recommend this looping gif:

http://i.imgur.com/rFuelVu.gif, which isolates each frame from the best part of the film and overlays the creature onto a stable background. Perhaps the foremost authority on the footage is M.K. Davis. Searching YouTube with his name conjoined with "Patterson Gimlin" will yield more analysis videos than you can watch in a month of Sundays.

The Bigfoot Field Research Organization (BFRO.net), the largest and most comprehensive network of sasquatch researchers and host of the largest database of sighting reports, was founded in 1995 by Matt Moneymaker, now a member of "the team" on the aforementioned Animal Planet series *Finding Bigfoot*. Its website states: "The overall mission of the BFRO is multifaceted, but the organization essentially seeks to resolve the mystery surrounding the bigfoot phenomenon, that is, to derive conclusive documentation of the species' existence. This goal is pursued through the proactive collection of empirical data and physical evidence from the field and by means of activities designed to promote an awareness and understanding of the nature and origin of the evidence." The BFRO is a "no-kill" organization, in contrast to some other study groups.

Grover Krantz (1931-2002) was an anthropologist who authored ten books on human evolution. In 1963, he began looking into the bigfoot phenomenon and continued to research it for the remainder of his life. For much of that time, he was the only American academic willing to do actual research, and he ultimately professed his belief that the creatures existed. His book *Big Footprints* is essential reading in the field. Krantz's dying wish was that the Smithsonian Institution would display his skeleton and the skeleton of his pet Irish wolfhound. The request was granted and the bones are on display today at the end of the anthropology exhibit.

Robert Michael Pyle (b. 1947) is an expert on butterfly ecogeography and the author of the 1995 book *Where Bigfoot Walks: Crossing the Dark Divide*, the result of a Guggenheim Fellowship. At the end of this very enjoyable book, Pyle writes: "I am continually asked by those who hear I am writing about Bigfoot, 'So, tell me — do you believe?' I have never answered yes or no, and I don't intend to now. Not because I am afraid to take a stand, but because it has never been my desire to finally decide."

As I say, Jeff Meldrum (b. 1958), has essentially inherited the ecological niche once occupied by Grover Krantz, that is to say, virtually the only American academic willing to investigate the phenomenon on a sustained basis. At this writing, he is a professor of anatomy and anthropology at Idaho State University. He is an expert on bipedal locomotion and maintains a lab with a large number of purported bigfoot casts. He frequently appears on television documentaries as an expert witness on the subject of sasquatches.

John Bindernagel (b. 1941) is a Canadian wildlife biologist who, like the late Grover Krantz, has been investigating the sasquatch since 1963. He grew up in Ontario but moved to British Columbia because it was a hotter zone for bigfoot sightings. His books include *North America's Great Ape - The Sasquatch* (1998) and *The Discovery of the Sasquatch* (2010).

Christopher Noël, a Vermont resident and author of numerous books including *Our Life with Bigfoot* and *The Mind of Sasquatch*, has cultivated a number of rich and innovative lines of research, beginning with habituation sites. These are locations in which humans have experienced long-term interactions with groups of sasquatches living in adjacent areas. His research has branched into sasquatch behavior as seen through the lens of autism and seemingly "supernatural" sasquatch phenomenon as a function of their electromagnetic fields. At this writing he is leading a crowd-sourced effort to document the creatures called Project Go and See, and is writing a book called *Next of Kin Next Door: How to Find Sasquatch a Stone's Throw Away.*

The founders of Facebook Finding Bigfoot, who went by the pseudonyms Jack Barnes and Jeff Anderson, did video analyses of some 100 purported sasquatch videos. They discontinued their public activity after a hostile copyright attack on their collection, but many videos survive on YouTube. Here is a representative example of their analyses: "#18 of 62 'Sasquatch startled while watching kids shoot' bigfoot sightings" https://www.youtube.com/watch?v=Lrtj1UT-NBU

"Barnes" and "Anderson" wrote and self-published *You Are Sasquatch: How Humanity Descended from a Smarter Ape: Volume 1,* published in 2012 with byline credit shared with Jeff Caramagna and Christopher Noël.

To the question of why we have not found bones of sasquatches, first, we might reject the premise and point out that there are many claims of remains, including the 111 samples involved in the Ketchum Study. But that aside, there are several common theories for why remains are so rare, if not non-existent: The first point often made is that bones in general, no matter how common the species, are rarely found in forest environments due to the acidic nature of the soil, which breaks them down before they can fossilize, and the prevalence of scavengers. Secondly, bigfoots being highly communal (contrary to popular belief), it is probably rare that they are alone at the time of death. This means that their remains could be routinely be hidden, buried, or even eaten by fellow members of their group.

A nerdy note on writing style: Seasoned readers might notice that in general references I have adopted "bigfoots" and "sasquatches" as my preferred form. As I write in the book, one of the biggest barriers to belief stems from the fact that when people hear "bigfoot" or "sasquatch," the vast majority still envision a single creature roaming the woods. This being the case, I will always use the plural form of either word unless I am in fact talking about an individual. Further, I use lowercase to put these terms in parallel with the names of other animals: horse, not Horse; cheetah, not Cheetah, humans, not Humans, etc. In some small way, I think these stylistic changes will help lead readers away from the assumptions that put these creatures in the same category as Babe the Big Blue Ox.

Chapter 3

This baritone siren-like vocalization, known as the Ohio Howl, was recorded by BFRO founder Matt Moneymaker in 1994. https://www.youtube.com/watch?v=gew-gIOHM6g

Here is another close howl, recorded by Bob Garrett in the Big Thicket:

https://www.youtube.com/watch?v=6JvaeudtLaU

My January 2016 wood-knock report is at:

http://www.bfro.net/GDB/show_report.asp?id=50643

North American Wood Ape Conservancy report from FM 1375 bridge, January 4, 2016:

http://woodape.org/reports/report/detail/26894

Complete BFRO 9/11/01 report from FM 1375:

http://www.bfro.net/GDB/show_report.asp?id=4206

Chapter 4

Kenneth Kramm's YouTube channel:

https://www.youtube.com/user/KennethKramm

The excellent memoir about rowing around the eastern United States is *On the Water: Discovering America in a Row Boat*, by Nathaniel Stone.

Chapter 5

The Torn-Up Camp video (23:22) can be seen at https://www.youtube.com/watch?v=lUvA_SB47_M.

The *Sasquatch Chronicles* podcast debuted in 2013 and is hosted by Wes Germer and occasionally his brother, Woody Germer, and other associates in Washington state. Germer offers guests a compassionate ear and gently coaxes their stories out of them like a friendly therapist. The vast majority of his interviews paint a picture of sasquatches as extremely dangerous. At this writing, Germer and company have produced more than 350 episodes. For the purposes of this book, I direct you only to those episodes in which Big Thicket researcher Bob Garrett was his guest:

Episode 34: "Charged by a Sasquatch" https://sasquatchchronicles.com/sc-ep34-charged-by-a-sasquatch/. Points of interest are at 31:00, 46:00, 49:00. Unless he has deliberately misdirected the audience, as is sometimes done in the research community to protect areas of activity, these comments almost certainly refer to Stubblefield Campground at the head of Lake Conroe. At 1:00:00 he begins discussing population movement.

Episode 35: "Scary Night on the Lone Star Trail": https://sasquatchchronicles.com/sc-ep35-scary-night-on-the-lone-star-trail/. At about 1:22:00, he talks about Sam Houston National Forest in general.

Episode 86: "East Texas Trip Overview" https://sasquatchchronicles.com/sc-ep86-east-texas-trip-overview/

Episode 132, "A Gold Miner's Encounter, Part I" https://sasquatchchronicles.com/sc-ep132-a-gold-miners-encounter/

Episode 169: "A Gold Miner's Encounter, Part II"
https://sasquatchchronicles.com/sc-ep-169-a-gold-miners-encounter-part-two-replay/
Episode 200, Part I
https://sasquatchchronicles.com/sc-ep200-the-200th-show-part-one/. Garrett describes his first encounter as a teenager with what his community then called "the Booger." He comes on at about 30:00, and that story comes at about 56:00.
Episode 243: "The Big Thicket Saga"
https://sasquatchchronicles.com/scep243-the-big-thicket-saga/
Other *Sasquatch Chronicles* episodes relating to East Texas:
Episode 88: Jurassic Park, with "Mo"
https://sasquatchchronicles.com/sc-ep88-jurassic-park/
Episode 98: The Big Thicket Monster (Tim Sermons)
https://sasquatchchronicles.com/sc-ep98-the-big-thicket-monster/
Episode 193: Primal Fear of Being Hunted
https://sasquatchchronicles.com/sc-ep193-primal-fear-of-being-hunted/

Chapter 6

The "Miller Document" can be read in its entirety in numerous places, but this is the blog on which it first appeared: http://bigfootposts.blogspot.com/

Chapter 7

The Ouachita Project monograph is a lengthy research paper published by members of the North American Wood Ape Conservancy. The paper can be read in its entirety here:

http://woodape.org/index.php/our-research/projects/248-opmonograph

Chapter 8

The Ketchum study, formally known as the "Sasquatch Genome Study" can be accessed at:

http://sasquatchgenomeproject.org/

The press event announcing the Sasquatch Genome Study, from October 13, 2013, in Dallas, Texas, can be watched at: https://www.youtube.com/watch?v=C3bOBi1-Zes.

Chapter 9

Albert Ostman's kidnapping story can be read at: http://www.bigfootencounters.com/classics/ostman.htm

Chapter 10

Recommended: *Coyote America: A Natural & Supernatural History,* by Dan Flores.

Chapter 11

Bob Garrett's video purporting to show a sasquatch in "stealth mode" can be found at:

https://www.youtube.com/watch?v=GA5pplK-HFo

Chapter 12

The story of capturing the Gray Walker on drone video can be heard at:

https://sasquatchchronicles.com/the-big-thicket-watch-radio-the-gray-walker/

Chapter 13

To read more about "A Plague of Pigs in Texas":
http://www.smithsonianmag.com/science-nature/a-plague-of-pigs-in-texas-73769069/

Chapter 14

Pursuant to the Magnolia Section of the trail, here is Bob Garrett's account of a point-blank encounter in this section, from *Sasquatch Chronicles*: Episode 35: "Scary Night on the Lone Star Trail"

https://sasquatchchronicles.com/sc-ep35-scary-night-on-the-lone-star-trail/

In this study, epigenetic changes in a single generation of male guinea pigs were passed on to their offspring.
https://phys.org/news/2015-12-epigenetics-wild-guinea-pigs.html

Chapter 15

Recommended: *A Field Guide to Sasquatch Structures,* by Christopher Noël.

Chapter 16

Logic was risky business in the Middle Ages. William of Ockham, near London, was kept in Avignon, France, where the Pope's summer castle was located, under a loose house arrest while the church investigated him for heresy. Finally convinced of the church's corruption, on the night of May 26, 1328, he, along with some other Franciscan Friars on trial, stole some horses and fled to the court of Louis of Bavaria. All the friars were excommunicated and hunted by the church but never captured.

Although Blaise Pascal's famous wager about God is one of his most enduring legacies, he did not avail himself of it. He was a lifelong Catholic who underwent a sort of born-again experience that was mystical in nature as opposed to underpinned by a rational argument.

As of 2015, Arby's counted 3,352 restaurants in the United States and four other nations —
Canada, Turkey, Qatar, and United Arab Emirates.

Acknowledgements

Thank you ...

To my loving and longsuffering wife, Kirstin, and to my hardy sons, Andrew, Cameron, and Ian ... for being my everything.

To my mother, Jan, for life, love, and her words of wisdom, and my late father, Carl, for modeling hard work, a creative life, and thinking big. My brothers, Ansen and Erren, for their example and encouragement. My beloved extended family ... Dörte, Luca, Fernando, Phyllis, John, Greg, Esther, Nan, Jorine, and all their roots and branches.

To those friends who have encouraged me to see this through, thank you. I give you the gift of anonymity!

And to Dennis Stacy and Patrick Huyghe of Anomalist Books.

About the Author

Avrel Seale grew up in McAllen, Texas, and now lives in Austin with his wife and three sons. He has been a newspaper reporter and columnist, magazine editor, speechwriter, and messaging architect. His eclectic blog, The Trailhead, is at avrelseale.wordpress.com.